Also by David A. Harris

Profiles in Injustice: Why Racial Profiling Cannot Work

GOOD COPS

The Case for Preventive Policing

DAVID A. HARRIS

THE NEW PRESS

NEW YORK
LONDON

Requests for permission to reproduce selections
from this book should be mailed to: Permissions Department,
The New Press, 38 Greene Street, New York, NY 10013

Published in the United States by The New Press, New York, 2005
Distributed by W. W. Norton & Company, Inc., New York

LIBRARY OF CONGRESS CATALOGING-IN-PUBLICATION DATA

Harris, David A., 1957–
    Good Cops: the case for preventive policing / David A. Harris.
        p. cm.
    Includes bibliographical references and index.
        ISBN 1-56584-923-X (hc.)
1. Police—United States. 2. Law enforcement—United States.
3. Crime prevention—United States. 4. Terrorism—United States—
Prevention. I. Title

HV8139.H37 2004
363.2'3'0973—dc22   2004053673

The New Press was established in 1990 as a not-for-profit
alternative to the large, commercial publishing houses currently
dominating the book publishing industry. The New Press operates
in the public interest rather than for private gain, and is committed
to publishing, in innovative ways, works of educational, cultural,
and community value that are often deemed insufficiently profitable.

www.thenewpress.com

Book design and composition by Hall Smyth

Printed in the United States of America

10 9 8 7 6 5 4 3 2 1

For Paul Baltz, my extraordinary teacher and friend,
and Daniel Steinbock, my friend and mentor

Contents

ACKNOWLEDGMENTS viii

PART I: THE THEORY BEHIND PREVENTIVE POLICING

1. The Struggle for the Soul of Policing 3

2. The History Behind Preventive Policing: From 2-Way
Radios to 2-Way Dialogues 18

PART II: PREVENTIVE POLICING IN ACTION

3. Building Bridges 28

4. Solving Problems 57

5. Being Accountable 81

6. Leading the Way 127

7. Bending Granite or Curving Wood?
Changing the Culture of Police Departments 154

PART III: THE FUTURE OF POLICING

8. Ashcroft Policing: The Wrong Lessons 174

9. Securing the Blessings of
Preventive Policing 222

NOTES 232

INDEX 287

Acknowledgments

I was able to write this book only because of the extraordinary cooperation I received from police chiefs, police officers, and police departments. Special thanks go to Commissioner Ray Kelly of the New York Police Department, Chief Robert McNeilly of the Pittsburgh Police Bureau, former superintendent Terry Hillard and former Deputy Superintendent Barbara McDonald of the Chicago Police Department, Chief Dean Esserman of the Providence Police Department, former Commissioner Paul Evans of the Boston Police Department, Deputy Inspector Tom King of the New York Police Department, and Deputy Chief Pat McElderry of the Colorado Springs Police Department, all of whom opened their doors to me and made it possible for me to see firsthand how things really worked.

Many others in law enforcement helped me by sharing their experiences and opinions, including Chief Gil Kerlikowske of the Seattle Police Department, Commander Linda Rosato Barone of the Pittsburgh Police Bureau, Chief Jerry Barker of the Indianapolis Police Department, Deputy Commissioner Paul Joyce and Officer Bill Baxter of the Boston Police Department, former Chief Robert Olsen of the Minneapolis Police Department, Assistant Chief Rudy Landeros of the Austin Police Department, Captain John Jackson of the Overland Park Police Department, Deputy Chief Terri Moses of the Wichita Police Department, Captain Kenneth M. Howard (Ret.) of the Alexandria (Virginia) Police Department, who helped introduce me to the Law Enforcement and Society Program at the U.S. Holocaust Memorial Museum, and Assistant Chief Jon Jeter, Officer Scott Baldwin, and Officer Tim Howard of the Stamford Police Department.

Other individual officers and civilian employees of police departments, a large number of community leaders, and numerous researchers also helped me. Many of their insights and stories appear in this book, others do not, but all of them helped me to understand policing and to write about it.

I am especially thankful to Lori Fridell of the Police Executives Research Forum and to Amy Schapiro and her colleagues in the Office of Community Oriented Policing Services in the U.S. Department of Justice for helping me to find many of the excellent programs highlighted in this book.

No one can write intelligibly about policing today without relying on the important work of the many people who have dedicated their careers to the study of law enforcement. For me, two stand out because their work makes it possible to think in terms of preventive policing: Herman Goldstein of the University of Wisconsin, the father of problem-oriented policing and one of the most important scholars of policing this country has produced, and Samuel Walker of the University of Nebraska at Omaha, whose groundbreaking work in so many areas of policing, particularly regarding accountability and early warning systems, sets the standard for everyone else. The work of many scholars of community policing, particularly Robert Trojanowicz and Bonnie Bucqueroux, formerly of the National Center for Community Policing, helped me understand the importance of the numerous efforts now ongoing across the country to reconnect police departments with their communities. Thanks also to the Vera Institute of Justice in New York City and the Police Executives Research Forum of Washington, D.C., for their many timely pieces of invaluable research.

I gratefully acknowledge the help of my colleagues at the University of Toledo College of Law, and the College of Law's support of my work through the Eugene N. Balk Professorship of Law and Values. Thanks also to Marcia Herman, without whom I couldn't have had the confidence I needed in the interviews I conducted.

I am extremely appreciative of the chance to write a second book for The New Press. Even more, I am grateful for the support, help, and superb editing skills of Diane Wachtell, executive director of The New Press. Diane is that rare editor who makes a writer better every time she works on a book. This gives me the confidence to just sit down and write, because I know that, with her help, the finished product will meet the highest standards. I consider it a great gift to have had the privilege of working with her again.

Not least, my thanks to my parents, who gave me both the curiosity and the work ethic I needed to do a project like this, and to my wife Rebecca and my children, Alicia and Sam, who supported me every step of the way.

Good Cops

Part I

THE THEORY BEHIND
PREVENTIVE POLICING

1

The Struggle for the Soul of Policing

*The mood and temper of the public with regard to the treatment
of crime and criminals is one of the most unfailing tests
of the civilisation of any country.*

—WINSTON CHURCHILL, address to the House of Commons, 1910

When U.S. Attorney General John Ashcroft and his Department
of Justice pushed Congress into enacting the sweeping USA
PATRIOT Act just weeks after September 11, 2001, they also set in
motion another set of initiatives. These changes—call them
"Ashcroft policing"—were designed to alter the role of local police
forces. Although they were among the least visible of the Ashcroft
Justice Department's antiterror efforts, they have the potential to
affect public safety and the quality of American life in important
and dramatic ways—ways that could, ironically, make safety and
security against terrorism even more difficult to achieve.

The gist of Ashcroft's approach involves transforming state
and local police agencies into an adjunct force in the federal
effort to fight the war on terror, much as the Department of
Justice did in the 1980s when it recruited state and local police
into the war on drugs. Two key features of Ashcroft policing in

particular—the involvement of local police in immigration control (formerly the almost exclusive province of the federal government) and the police questioning of "nonsuspects"— represent major departures from traditional policing.

Ashcroft policing shows a lack of understanding of the foundations of good police work. Worse yet, these practices come at a point in time when the whole field of policing is poised to move in a very different, potentially far more productive, direction. Ashcroft policing runs counter to this new, successful approach, which I will call "preventive policing." Preventive policing envisions police forces that make it a priority to stop crime before it occurs rather than simply to just respond to crime after the fact. Preventive policing incorporates innovative, forward-thinking methods of law enforcement that have been productively implemented in cities and towns across the country. Where Ashcroft policing shifts away from field-tested, community-based policing strategies, rendering the police less effective against both terrorism and garden-variety crime, preventive policing collects the best aspects of successful, progressive policing and combines them into a plan that presents real hope for reducing crime, preserving rights, and enhancing civil society in the twenty-first century.

ASHCROFT POLICING

When John Ashcroft was sworn in as attorney general of the United States, he had no direct experience in crime control. Ashcroft was a lawyer, not a police officer. In his legal career, he had never worked as a prosecutor or a defense lawyer handling cases in criminal court, never served as general counsel or legal advisor to a police department—in short, he had never spent time on the front lines of the criminal justice system. After graduating from law school, he entered public service in his home state as a staff lawyer for the Missouri attorney general, John Danforth. (Danforth later became a U.S. Senator from Missouri and ambassador to the United Nations; one of Ashcroft's fellow staff members in the Missouri attorney general's office was Clarence Thomas.) Subsequently, Ashcroft served as Missouri auditor, his first elected office. He then became state attorney general, followed by two terms as governor before being elected to the U.S. Senate. While the attorney general of Missouri might claim to have law enforcement responsibilities,[1] that role is really quite limited. A unit inside the attorney general's office handles criminal appeals, and staff lawyers may supply advice and training to law enforcement agencies. In reality, as Missouri's attorney general, governor, and senator, Ashcroft worked on criminal justice or law enforcement issues only at the most indirect level; he became U.S. attorney general without any real hands-on experience. By contrast, Attorney General Janet Reno, Ashcroft's predecessor, served as an elected county prosecutor in a large urban area for more than a decade before her nomination by President Bill Clinton.

To be fair, Reno's extensive experience is the exception rather than the rule. But Ashcroft's lack of experience in matters of criminal law and policy, as well as his lack of respect for constitutional limits on police and government investigative behavior, became absolutely critical on September 11, 2001. On that day, Ashcroft was suddenly thrust to the helm of the largest, most intensive, and most important law enforcement effort ever undertaken by the federal government. Almost immediately, a pattern emerged: disregard for what state and local police and even federal antiterrorism investigators had learned through long experience, in favor of untested, misguided approaches. Thus was Ashcroft policing born.

POLICING IMMIGRANTS

In the wake of the 9/11 attacks, many called for tougher border controls and a dramatic tightening of immigration regulations. Every one of the nineteen suicide hijackers responsible for the 9/11 attacks had come from foreign countries. Thus it just seemed to make sense to the Department of Justice and to many Americans that the country should ratchet up immigration enforcement.[2]

In April 2002, word came that the U.S. Department of Justice would begin to ask local police to enforce federal immigration law for the first time. This represented a real departure from past procedure.[3] Since the passage of the Immigration and Nationality Act in 1952, local police had only the most limited authority to enforce immigration law.[4] Control of national borders was, by practical necessity and constitutional structure, a matter for the federal government. Before 2002, the law gave state and local police officers the authority to make arrests only for a narrow category of the most serious criminal immigration violations,[5] a position that the Department of Justice had reaffirmed in 1978[6] and again as recently as 1996.[7]

Attorney General Ashcroft's Office of Legal Counsel reversed this long-standing policy in one stroke, declaring that state and local police had "inherent authority" to join the federal government in enforcing civil immigration law.[8] The department went ahead with this significant policy shift despite the fact that laws of many states actually prohibited their police from making arrests for these very infractions.

News of the change elicited strong criticism from advocates for immigrants and ethnic groups nationwide. In a letter to President Bush, the leaders of the National Immigration Forum, the Leadership Conference on Civil Rights, the American Immigration Lawyers Association, the Arab American Institute, the Mexican American Legal Defense and Education Fund, and a number of other groups warned that "expanding the purview of state and local law enforcement officers to include civil immigration law could have serious detrimental effects on community safety."[9] Raul Yzaguirre, president and chief executive officer of the National Council of La Raza, told President Bush that "extending immigration enforcement authority to local police would not make the nation safer from terrorism but, rather, would lead to the erosion of trust between communities and the police . . . ,"[10] an assertion that was echoed by immigrant groups and newspaper editorials across the country.

Surely, opposition from community activists and the press could not have surprised top officials in the Department of Justice; they might well have regarded it as nothing more than noise from "the usual suspects." But one can easily imagine the surprise in the attorney general's office at comments that quickly began to come from an unexpected source: law enforcement agencies themselves. Scores of state and local law enforcement leaders, who might have been expected to applaud a proposal to give them greater authority to arrest and detain people in the war on terror, said that they wanted no part of immigration enforcement. Most major police agencies and organizations[11] vehemently rejected the attorney general's push to involve them in these efforts.

To police officers on the beat, the idea of taking on immigration enforcement duties seemed a recipe for disaster. As these departments and their commanders pointed out, state and local police officers are neither suited nor trained for such operations. Additionally, they were already overburdened, and lacked the resources to take on these new responsibilities. But the most compelling reason to not involve them in enforcing immigration law, local police said, was that acting as surrogates of the Immigration and Naturalization Service (INS) would destroy their ability to do the critical job of building connections with immigrant communities. If police began patrolling for immigration irregularities, immigrants would quickly come to fear them, law enforcement officials argued, ruining the trust-based relationships that have long helped police fight crime on the community level. "Communication is big in inner-city neighborhoods and the underpinning of that is trust," Chief Gerry Whitman of the Denver Police Department explains. "If a victim [or witness] thinks they're going to be a suspect" for violating immigration laws, "they're not going to call us."[12] The net effect would be to make the streets safer for perpetrators. According to Tom Needham, former general counsel and chief of staff to the Chicago Police Department, the Justice Department's effort to get local police involved in immigration enforcement ignores the core mission of local police. "It would be virtually impossible [to prevent and solve crimes] effectively," he says, "if witnesses and victims, no matter what their residency status, had some reluctance to come forward for fear of being deported."[13] And Chief Jim Spreine of the Laguna Beach, California, Police Department, explains the problem in a very concrete way: "Young [Hispanic] women who are raped or Hispanic women who are beaten will not come forward and report they've been a victim for fear of being deported. To us, that's wrong. Our job is to protect life and property, all life and property, including [the lives of] those that are illegally in the country."[14]

Police advocacy and research groups joined these police departments. Chief Bob McConnell, head of the California Police Chiefs Association, expressed his organization's "strong opinion" in a letter to Attorney General Ashcroft: "In order for local and state law enforcement organizations to continue to be effective partners with their communities, it is imperative that they not be placed in the role of detaining and arresting individuals based solely on a change to their immigration status."[15] Some chiefs went further than just criticism. For example, Chief Gil Kerlikowske of Seattle issued a directive to his officers prohibiting them from checking identification of persons simply to see if they are illegal immigrants, "to make sure we're focused on our most important mission: protecting people, and that means making sure that people aren't afraid to contact us" because they think police will get them into trouble with the INS.[16]

But perhaps the most stinging criticism of the attorney general's local police immigration enforcement initiative came from two men with long experience fighting terrorism at the highest levels. In an appearance in Washington, D.C., in April

2003, Harry Brandon, former director of counterterrorism operations for the FBI, and Vince Cannistraro, former head of counterterrorism for the CIA, said unequivocally that most of the immigration changes made by the U.S. Department of Justice since September 11, 2001, would *not* have prevented the attacks. Further, they said, these changes had also done little to make the nation safer since the Department of Justice put them in place.[17] Instead of working with immigrant communities as partners, Cannistraro said, "we are using immigration enforcement as a proxy for law enforcement at a time when we need the help of those communities."[18] What might have prevented the 9/11 attacks, Cannistraro said, would have been better networks of contacts among members of law enforcement and immigrant communities, which might have resulted in the passing on of crucial information to law enforcement.[19]

POLICING "NONSUSPECTS"

Just a few months after 9/11, Ashcroft's Department of Justice announced another new role for local police: helping federal agents to identify and question large numbers of noncriminal immigrants.[20] The department did not suspect the immigrants—all young men from Middle Eastern countries—of terrorism, it said; in fact, it did not suspect them of any crime at all. Rather, given their demographic similarity to the September 11 hijackers, the department thought that the men might know something—even things they did not realize were important—that might produce leads or otherwise assist in preventing and investigating terrorism. Once again, Ashcroft policing contravened the fundamental tenets that years of law enforcement, intelligence experience, and intensive research had shown to be at the heart of effective crime prevention.

In response, local police weighed in. Officials in Portland, Oregon, and in Detroit, for example, announced that they would not participate in the interviewing process. Andrew

Kirkland, then Portland's acting chief of police, said flatly that his department could not participate because state law did not allow police questioning of persons not suspected of involvement in crime: "If the FBI has something specific about a crime they are investigating, or a potential crime that these people might commit, then we would reconsider."[21] Benny Napoleon, then Detroit's chief of police, viewed the Department of Justice's interviewing plans as unconstitutional: "We're standing with the fundamental rights of individuals under the constitution and the state constitution and our municipal law," he said, sounding more like the head of the American Civil Liberties Union (ACLU) than a police chief.[22]

But what these local police were actually most concerned about was the very real danger that interviewing thousands of nonsuspects would jeopardize their hard-won relationships with immigrant communities. For example, Greg Guibord, police chief of Dearborn, Michigan, home to the largest Arab and Muslim community in the United States (and the city with the single largest number of post–9/11 interviewees—approximately 250), tried to find a way to comply with the Justice Department order without sacrificing the Arab and Muslim community's trust. His officers, he said, would help the federal government do the interviews but only after multiple meetings with Arab and Muslim leaders to explain what was happening and why. Veteran police officers in every city understood Guibord's caution perfectly. To encourage the community to share critical information, he needed to build and maintain solid relationships with Arab and Muslim citizens and groups—relationships based on mutual trust. The interviews, of course, would destroy this trust and replace it with fear—a sure path to severed lines of communication.

Even harsher criticism of the roughly five thousand "nonsuspect" interviews came from eight prominent former federal law enforcement officers, including William Webster, former head of both the FBI and the CIA. Rather than hide behind anonymous comments, as many former officials in Washington might have, all eight felt strongly enough to speak out personally in the press against the Justice Department's mass questioning initiative.[23] The FBI had run many antiterrorism investigations in the past, they said, and had successfully headed off a significant number of planned terrorist attacks.[24] From a law enforcement point of view, the possible benefits of the interviews did not offset the massive squandering of goodwill and relationships with the community. The interviews would "inevitably force the bureau to close terrorism investigations prematurely, before agents can identify all members of a terrorist cell," these former officials said.[25] Real intelligence gains, they said, came when agents who discovered suspected terrorists or terrorist cells then discreetly and stealthily followed the trail of information left by the suspects back to the field commanders, controllers, and financiers of terrorist operations. Confronting the five thousand men in face-to-face questioning would alert any of them with actual terrorist ties that they were being watched and monitored. All activities and communication relevant to these activities—the heart and soul of what intelligence agencies want to know and observe—would cease.

Tactics similar to the Ashcroft antiterrorism initiatives had been abandoned by federal law enforcement in the late 1970s, the officials said, because they proved ineffective at preventing terrorism and led to abuses of civil liberties. Oliver "Buck" Revell, former FBI executive assistant director who helped design the FBI's antiterrorism strategy during the 1980s, said he could not understand the impetus to return to old failed ways. "[Those running the Department of Justice now] don't know their history," he said, "and they are not listening to people who do."[26]

Former FBI assistant director Kenneth P. Walton, who helped establish a joint terrorism task force in New York, memorably characterized the mass interviews as part of "the Perry Mason School of Law Enforcement, where you get them in there and they confess," he said. "Well, it just doesn't work that way. It is ridiculous. You say, 'Tell me everything you know,' and they give you the recipe to Mom's chicken soup."[27]

Yet despite this criticism—from those with years of law enforcement experience with both street-level anticrime work and federal antiterrorism operations—the Department of Justice proceeded with the mass questioning. And, despite little evidence of any substantive gains from the initial round of interviews, the department actually expanded the program; it began to interview *another* three thousand young Arab men in the spring of 2002.[28] In a gross miscalculation, the Department of Justice traded state and local law enforcement's connections to the communities they served—and the potential for intelligence-gathering those ties provided—for a hostile approach to collecting information that runs contrary to everything we know about effective policing of crime or of terrorism.

PREVENTIVE POLICING

Ashcroft policing is both unnecessary and counterproductive. Over the past two decades, new practices have emerged in policing—new tactics, new strategies, new ways of fighting crime—which, for the first time, promise a type of law enforcement that is both extremely effective against crime and criminals and respectful of the civil rights and dignity of those the police serve. These tactics focus not on responding to crime after it occurs but on addressing problems that contribute to crime before it happens—precisely the type of law enforcement needed to address potential acts of terrorism. In contrast to Ashcroft policing, "preventive policing" is not an ivory-tower theory; it is real, and it is happening in many forms every day in neighborhoods, towns, and cities of all sizes across our country:

- In Chicago, the police department's civil rights office had a long history of cultivating relationships with minority groups concerning hate crimes. In 1999, these connections became the crucial link that allowed police to obtain critical evidence identifying the killer involved in a racist multi-state killing spree.

- In metropolitan Detroit, an area-wide council, including local, state, and federal law enforcement agencies, minority community groups, and advocacy organizations, was already in place on 9/11. This council offered established channels of communication between law enforcement and the Arab and Muslim communities—channels that were largely responsible for saving relationships crucial to intelligence gathering from the potentially explosive federal investigations in the aftermath of the attacks.

- In the early 1990s, San Diego adopted a "problem-solving" approach to law enforcement, training police cadets to identify, analyze, and address recurring patterns of criminal violence, prostitution, and drug dealing rather than just answering repeated calls for police service at the same locations for the same things.

- In Pittsburgh, as part of a settlement agreement between the Police Bureau and the federal government, the city installed a computerized system to track almost twenty different varieties of police officer conduct. The system, which now represents the state of the art in police work nationwide, allows all supervising and command officers, from sergeants to the chief of police, to find out instantaneously which officers are having problems—and which are performing exceptionally well. The system has greatly reduced citizen complaints and helped the department salvage troubled officers' careers, even as it has allowed the chief to pick out high-performing individuals for important anticrime assignments.

These are only a few examples of preventive policing. It is an approach that strives to prevent wrongdoing by anticipating rather than just reacting to problems. Unlike Ashcroft policing, preventive policing does not trade our rights as citizens for safety and security. We can—and we must—make sure that our police protect and respect both public safety and civil rights. Only then do we make ourselves both safe and free.

To be sure, policing has not changed everywhere, and in many ways it has not changed enough. But change has certainly begun. The "best practices" of preventive policing highlighted in this book come from a series of conceptual, practical, and technological advances—including police-citizen collaboration, problem solving, accountability, transparency, openness, and innovation—that over the last twenty years have formed its foundation. Achieving a full implementation of preventive policing, however, will ultimately require a sea change in police culture. In some very real and concrete ways, police organizations must alter some of their most basic structures to reflect changing social realities and to ensure their organizational integrity and vitality. Departments must evolve from the simplistic view of their mission as "locking up bad guys" to one in which police departments make communities safe in collaboration with those they serve. Police departments must also change recruitment methods in order to find officers who can solve problems and connect with the community on a long-term basis. They must make openness to new ideas and transparency in their operations primary values of their organizations. Incentive structures within police departments must change to reward the type of innovation, creativity, and engagement with citizens that the new preventive policing requires.

Good Cops is a guide to preventive policing, which connects the best strategies of community policing and problem-oriented policing with other innovations in law enforcement from the past twenty to thirty years. It examines the central principles that make up the structure of preventive policing and provides numerous real-world examples of how the principles have proven effective in police departments around the country. Chapter 2 explains the basic concepts of preventive policing;

chapter 3 begins the discussion of preventive policing's strategies by examining types of collaboration between police and citizens that both address specific community problems and build structures that allow the community to meet the crises of the future. Chapter 4 highlights police problem solving and discusses how this basic change to the law enforcement mindset has literally changed the lives of both police and citizens in cities, towns, and neighborhoods all over the country. In chapter 5, the discussion moves to a central ingredient in preventive policing: systems for insuring police accountability. New strategies for police accountability—everything from citizen satisfaction measurement to early warning systems designed to detect problem officers before they do damage—hold the promise of changing the way police work has been done for fifty years. Chapter 6 highlights important new advances in police leadership and the difference they make, and chapter 7 focuses on ways that the police culture—always inward-facing, insular, and prototypically "us versus them"—can, and must, transform itself to adapt to the twenty-first century. Chapter 8 then returns to the danger posed to preventive policing by Ashcroft policing—in particular, its preference for top-down authority and for disregarding the hard-won knowledge and experience of the police officers who spend their lives making the streets of our cities safe—in the misguided pursuit of security from terrorism, when, ironically, that goal could be achieved more readily through the preventive policing that is blossoming in American police departments today.

I have spent much of the last ten years studying police officers and what they do—observing them, teaching them, writing about them, and, most of all, talking to them. In *Profiles in Injustice,* published in 2002, I wrote about the problems caused by racial profiling, and in the course of the research for that book I discovered that many police departments, or groups of officers within police departments, were doing innovative, even progressive things as they struggled to find new ways to fight crime. The more I learned about these new tactics, the more I saw that their common denominator was *preventing* crime, not just responding to it, by opening up collaborative relationships with the public and by examining their own conduct. I knew that this represented a sea change. Best of all, I could see that these new methods were succeeding in practice.

I also realized that the stories of these new approaches were virtually unknown. To the extent that the public had any awareness of successful crime-fighting strategies, it came from an oversimplified view of Rudolph Giuliani's New York—that to fight crime, the authorities must get tough and make arrests, and citizens had to be prepared to sacrifice civil rights for safety. I felt that it was vital that the stories of these other, creative ways of making the streets safe—ways that did not require the constitutional rights of anyone to be sacrificed, and that were at least as successful as the NYPD's methods in New York—be told. I began to talk to police officers and public safety officials around the country: chiefs of police, patrol officers, and the sergeants and lieutenants who ran the operations of the departments day to day. I heard firsthand that, for years, many police officers had felt frustrated with their limited roles; they knew that they couldn't really make their communities better places by responding to 911 calls over and over. I also saw that in some departments, chiefs, supervisors, and officers were beginning to find both crime-fighting success and professional fulfillment they'd not experienced for ages through one or another aspect of preventive policing. It was immensely gratifying to see, and something that every American leader, policy maker, and citizen needed to know.

Good Cops is the result of interviews, research reviews, and observations of successful programs which together tell the stories of preventive policing—both its success and its further potential. One approach will never suit all communities or police departments, but all of the stories here concern actual experiences, and could be replicated in some form in most cities or towns in the nation. All are works in progress, not static; good programs always have the capacity to grow, adapt, and change in response to new circumstances, and we should not expect them to show up in exactly the same form, to be used in the same way, or even to be used to accomplish the same goals in every city.

When we look at American police departments across the nation, we will see that many have moved in the direction of preventive policing in at least some aspect of their work and that many others could also do so if they wanted to, using the examples here as a template. It is important to note, however, that the efforts highlighted here are not without controversy; even within their own cities, many of them have strong detractors who can, at the very least, make the case for better focus or management. Other critics make the point that departments that do some things right are sometimes far off the mark in other areas. For example, the same police department that is building connections and trust with the community it serves may be oblivious to the virtues of problem solving.

Nevertheless, this is an exciting moment in law enforcement, and a time of great potential in policing. Never in the past has there been a stronger consensus concerning ways to improve what will always be a very difficult job. Preventive policing holds out considerable promise—a promise of safer, more livable communities attained through partnership, problem solving, accountability, and better leadership—even as it shows the way toward security from terrorism. And, critically, preventive policing goes hand in hand with respecting constitutional rights. It is exactly what our police departments need, and exactly what the security of our nation demands. We need not accept the false trade-off between fighting crime and terrorism, and abandoning our rights as citizens. We can, and must, have both. As citizens, it is our responsibility to demand both—even in times as difficult and dangerous as these.

2

The History Behind Preventive Policing: From 2-Way Radios to 2-Way Dialogues

New approaches to policing began to emerge in the United States only in the last twenty to thirty years. This followed almost half a century in which police officers became increasingly isolated from citizens and steadily less inclined and less able to adopt effective policing strategies of any kind. The advent of the new strategies, which emphasized partnership between the department and the community, cast a long-overdue light on a forgotten idea: that police and citizens must work together, hard and consistently, to create public safety. Only working together can make prevention of crime and disorder possible.

Paid professional police departments emerged in the United States in the latter half of the nineteenth century, modeled after the first police departments in England. But professional policing, as we now conceive it, was entirely absent from nineteenth-century American police work. Not only individual officers but whole departments were corrupt and inefficient, and political interference in police business by municipal officials was almost universal. Politicians, from mayors down to the lowliest ward hacks, treated police precincts as parts of their personal fiefdoms, available to do their bidding in any way necessary, from discouraging political opponents to breaking strikes. Positions in police departments became mere patronage plums, for sale to the highest bidder.[1]

This situation changed very little until the 1920s and 1930s, when American police departments adopted two important innovations: the automobile and the two-way radio. Reformers extolled the radio-equipped patrol car as the savior of policing—the technological change that would move police work toward efficiency and rule-based law enforcement and away from the vicissitudes of political influence and graft. Before the radio car, local law enforcement depended on the policeman walking the beat—slow, inefficient, and susceptible to endless varieties of personal or political favoritism and petty corruption. August Vollmer, one of the best-known exponents of early-twentieth-century police reform, visualized the possibilities presented by the radio car this way:

> [W]ith the advent of the radio equipped car a new era has come.
> . . . [M]any square miles . . . are now covered by the roving patrol
> car, fast, efficient, stealthy, having no regular beat to patrol, just
> as liable to be within feet as 3 miles of the crook plying his trade—
> the very enigma of this specialized fellow who is coming to real-
> ize now that a few moments may bring them down about him
> like a swarm of bees—this lightening swift "angel of death."[2]

Putting radios in police cars meant that reports of crime could be sent for rapid response directly to police roaming large districts; calls for service from the public thus began to drive what police actually did day to day and moment to moment. For the reformers, this was a great advance: at least the actions of most individual officers most of the time would move beyond the immediate control of the ward boss and the outright purchase of police services into an era in which automobiles would take police services swiftly and directly to the citizens who needed them.

In addition to heavy reliance on patrols by police vehicles, radio communication, and response to calls for service, the reformers "introduced scientific principles of policing,"[3] such as studying where calls for service came from and establishment of duty schedules and assignments based on the need for police service in a given area (as demonstrated by crime patterns and calls to police).[4] Their vision of reform featured enhanced professionalism, a shifting from officers on the beat to crime control by radio-dispatched cars, centralized administration, and deliberate professional aloofness from the community.[5]

Looking back, we know that these well-intentioned reforms also had a significant unanticipated downside: isolating police officers from the public. Officers no longer walked the street, encountering citizens in ways that would allow them to build relationships over time. Instead, police officers became fleeting presences—heads, necks, and upper torsos visible in moving cars, unknown people who occasionally emerged from vehicles in the event of emergencies. Because the radio-equipped roaming patrol car could get anywhere in the district quickly, responding to calls for service became the chief task of frontline officers. The advent of special three-digit-number call systems led to "the tyranny of 911," in which responding to calls for service absorbed most police department patrol resources. Since U.S. police forces assign approximately two-thirds of their officers to patrol duty, relatively few officers, if any, remained available to do anything other than react to crime (or other minor incidents) after the fact.

The advent of patrol cars also meant the end of the one traditional channel for communities to give police departments information and feedback: the accessible beat officer himself. Paradoxically, random patrol in radio-equipped cars actually undermined efforts to control crime because it isolated officers from the public, their best source of information. As criminologist David H. Bayley writes, "The critical ingredient in solving crimes is whether the public—victims and witnesses—provide information that helps police identify the suspect. ...On their own, police are relatively helpless, regardless of the resources they devote to criminal investigation."[6] With officers stuck in cars, members of their communities had neither opportunity nor inclination to help them. Patrol-car policing fostered an "us against them" mentality, putting both "sides" at odds in ways both subtle and overt.

Racism and racially biased law enforcement exacerbated the isolation of police from African American communities, many of which have endured a long history of police abuse and harassment dating back to the days of the slave patrols (groups of whites informally deputized to harass blacks) that were the forerunners of police departments in many Southern states.[7] Well into the twentieth century, some police departments not only in the South but nationwide flaunted a hair-trigger willingness to use force and abuse to keep blacks "in their place."[8] The riots in American cities in the mid- to late 1960s were rooted in the history of such abuses, and many of the most destructive ones began with some kind of confrontation between white police officers and black residents or drivers.[9]

By the early 1970s, instead of thinking in terms of what the police and the community could do together about crime and disorder, police and civilian leaders alike adopted the same unfortunate perspective: it was the police versus the community. Police departments judged their success by the number of vehicles they could put on the street for the most extensive random patrol possible, and by their response times to calls for help. Policing had become almost purely reactive, responding to crimes that had already been committed.[10] To the extent that anyone thought about prevention of crime at all, they assumed it came as a by-product of random patrol, though there was no empirical evidence of any preventive effect.

In 1972, Kansas City, Missouri, became the site of a meticulous study of the effectiveness of random patrol. Called the Preventive

Patrol Experiment, the study examined whether, as everyone in law enforcement assumed, random patrol by marked police vehicles really prevented crime. Researchers divided the study location into three sections; each received a different level of police patrol. In the first, police came only in response to calls for assistance and performed no preventive patrol. This meant substantially reduced police presence and visibility. In the second, or control, section, police maintained normal levels of patrol. In the third, police were proactive: they increased the visibility and use of random patrol to two to three times the normal level.

The results shocked law enforcement officials. "Analysis of the data gathered revealed that the three areas experienced no significant differences in the level of crime, citizens' attitudes toward police services, citizens' fear of crime, police response time, or citizens' satisfaction with police response time."[11] In other words, increased random patrols appeared to have no effect on crime levels or citizen attitudes. The conclusions suggested the need for a major reconsideration of police strategies and priorities at a time when many people had already begun to question the very integrity of policing.

The Preventive Patrol Study's surprising findings on the efficacy of response time spurred another test. This experiment, which also took place in Kansas City just a few years later, attempted to answer questions that the first study had raised—namely, what effect did response time have on producing "favorable crime outcomes," and what effect did response time have on citizen satisfaction with the police. The Kansas City Response Time Study came to conclusions that were just as astounding to police officials as those of the earlier study: experts' long-held assumption that combating serious crime required rapid response time appeared to be "dubious."[12] As it turned out, rapid police response had no effect on the most serious crimes. Even for those crimes that response times might influence, what mattered most was how long citizens took to report crimes to the police in the first place, a factor determined by the public's own attitudes and actions. Furthermore, citizens' satisfaction with the police depended not on the actual response time but on their perceptions and expectations of what the response time should be.

The results of both studies flew so fiercely in the face of conventional wisdom that many police officials had difficulty accepting them at all. Researchers William Spellman and Dale Brown reported that police managers were "jolted" by the findings and remained "skeptical" about their relevance to other cities.[13] But a follow-up study conducted by the Police Executives Research Forum (PERF), a respected law enforcement think tank, confirmed the findings of the second Kansas City study, concluding that strategies designed to reduce response time were misguided. The PERF report recommended that "police departments' resources, long focused toward rapid response to all crime calls" should be "reallocated to other, attainable objectives."[14]

THE COMPONENTS OF PREVENTIVE POLICING

The reaction to all of this was profound: a gradual realization that the core police strategies of the previous fifty years were basically bankrupt. The emptiness discovered at the center of modern policing pushed both police departments and criminologists into a search for new approaches and strategies. The first of these was community policing. The central idea of community policing was to reconnect police with communities, a reinvigoration of the concept that—even with the potential for petty corruption—the cop on the beat, not isolated from citizens but connected to them, could make for effective crime fighting.

There are almost as many definitions of community policing and its fundamental principles as there are police departments.[15] Some efforts to use the complete community policing philosophy have been very successful, while others have been little more than hollow public relations campaigns. But every successful community policing effort has looked at the connection to local residents as an essential pillar of its philosophy.[16] Thus it is in community policing that one initially glimpses a key strategy of preventive policing: collaboration, partnership, and trust between law enforcement and the community.

The second strategy of preventive policing, problem-oriented policing, emerged in the work of professor Herman Goldstein, who also sought to describe an alternative to random patrol and rapid response (see chapter 4 for more on Goldstein). Goldstein wanted police officers and police departments to get beyond simple responses to individual incidents, and to focus instead on solving the larger problems that cause such incidents to occur time after time in the same troubled places. Goldstein's idea represented a completely new framework for American policing, and its emphasis on moving beyond reaction to proactive anticipation of future problems is an essential part of preventive policing.

Consensus concerning another strategy of preventive policing—the use of accountability mechanisms—emerged only somewhat later, chiefly in the 1990s, as law enforcement executives and policy makers sought ways to assure that their officers carried out their duties correctly and did not become problems themselves.

New leadership committed to policing driven by preventive efforts, and taking on the tough work necessary to change police culture so that prevention can take root, have emerged as essential components of preventive policing that allow the other strategies to succeed.

HOW THE STRATEGIES OF PREVENTIVE POLICING WORK TOGETHER

Preventive policing begins with the effort to connect police and communities in relationships of mutual trust. This is the foundation for all that follows. These connections are necessary for successful communication of information, without which police departments can have no real idea of what is actually happening on the streets in their cities and towns beyond their own observations. Without connections based on trust, no intelligence comes to police from the community about the clandestine activities of those in the neighborhood who produce crime, disorder, and fear. Without connections based on trust, police and communities have no basis upon which to attack problems together—that is, to attempt the problem-solving aspects of preventive policing. Mutual trust requires sharing of responsibility for action and decision making, a change in the police point of view that is essential for the creation of the partnerships necessary to fight crime and disorder successfully over the long haul, not just to defeat it temporarily or displace it to other neighborhoods.

The second component of preventive policing, problem solving, offers a plan for actually preventing crime. If traditional, reactive policing gives law enforcement a backward focus, preventive policing adds a forward-looking point of view. The officer looks not just at what has happened in an individual incident but also at how it fits into the larger pattern of incidents. From that, he or she can move to a plan of attack against the overall problems that the pattern of incidents show. Thus problem solving is the fundamental tool for conceiving plans for preventive policing and putting it into action.

Accountability mechanisms, such as citizen review boards, early warning systems, internal complaint procedures, department auditors, and community feedback, are what keep the department and its officers functioning properly and focused on the goals of prevention. All the accountability mechanisms discussed here have slightly different roles in the complex world of policing, but all are ultimately designed to protect citizens and the department. For example, failure to assure adequate discipline within a police department puts everything the department tries to achieve at risk, but nothing more so than the trust-based connections between the police and the citizens they serve.

The remaining strategies of preventive policing—leadership and cultural change—have a different role than the first three in this vision of how to create public order, but they are no less important. Leadership that insists upon prevention and creates the opportunities for it, and basic cultural shifts within police departments that allow preventive policing to flourish, are implementation strategies. They are essential if the police-community connections are to work. If police partnership with communities, problem solving, and accountability devices are the new trees in policing's forest, leadership and cultural change are the soil, rain, and sun necessary for these new ideas to grow. One might think of them as secondary because they are prophylactic (or protective) strategies for the first three, but that would be incorrect. Only the strong leadership and cultural change described in chapters 6 and 7 will permit preventive policing to succeed on a long-term basis.

Part II

PREVENTIVE POLICING
IN ACTION

3

Building Bridges

It is probably fair to say that, other than New York City, Washington, D.C., and the rural Pennsylvania area where the fourth hijacked jet went down, no place in the country felt the impact of the September 11, 2001, attacks more strongly than metropolitan Detroit. As home to the nation's largest and oldest Arab and Muslim community, numbering in the hundreds of thousands, the region immediately became the focus of intense federal investigation. Arabs and Muslims came under suspicion both by law enforcement and by some of their fellow citizens. Some Middle Easterners became targets of harassment and even hate crimes. Fear and a sense of helplessness pervaded the area's Middle Eastern communities, which felt doubly victimized—first, like everyone in America, as targets of the 9/11 terrorists, and second, as victims of backlash-related crimes and the threatening specter of overzealous enforcement efforts. This could have been disastrous were it not for the efforts of an organization with the clunky, forgettable name of ALPACT.

DETROIT: THE POWER OF TRUST

In 1998, Daedre McGhee, one of Detroit's African American leaders, decided that the time had come for minority communities and law enforcement to find common ground on the issue of racial profiling.[1] McGhee, then the associate director of the Detroit branch of the National Conference for Community and Justice, a national nonprofit organization with a history of community building and advocating fairness in the justice system, saw an opportunity: the Detroit police department had a new chief, who had changed the leadership in many parts of the organization.[2] Though McGhee had a close relationship with those in the community who distrusted police, she was also married to a high-ranking Detroit police official. This gave her credibility with both sides of the profiling debate. With the support of her colleagues,[3] McGhee pulled together a group of four local police chiefs and the leaders of four major community organizations to begin talking about profiling.

The first meetings of Advocates and Leaders for Police and Community Trust, or ALPACT, were contentious at times. Participants disagreed about everything from how to define profiling to whether it was actually happening and whether police ought to keep statistics on their stops and searches. An issue as controversial as racial profiling would probably have stirred emotions in such a group anywhere, but it was especially divisive in Detroit. Although African Americans have made up more than 40 percent of its population since at least 1970[4] and a majority of its population since 1980,[5] Detroit has had a history of tension and sometimes deadly confrontations between its black citizens and its police department dating back to the 1940s.[6] Before the 1970s, the department was mostly white; in 1973, with the city's population almost half black, blacks made up only 17 percent of the city's police force.[7] But even after the police department became predominantly black—by 1993, when about three-quarters of the city's population was black, 57 percent of the police department was black[8]—problems between police and African Americans persisted.[9]

A similar history of tension existed between blacks and the police departments of many suburban Detroit communities.[10] Well into the 1990s, Detroit remained a racially segregated city,[11] and old grudges, occasional outbursts of anger, and deep mutual distrust between blacks and law enforcement all over the Detroit area persisted. Thus, when the national discussion about racial profiling began in the late 1990s, the issue resonated powerfully in Detroit. Highly publicized incidents—such as the stopping of then–Detroit mayor Dennis Archer's son and his passenger, an assistant prosecutor, by suburban police officers who held them at gunpoint and handcuffed them,[12] and the death of an African American man at the hands of security guards at a suburban shopping mall—stoked these tensions.[13]

Daedre McGhee wanted to bring the newly conceived profiling group together in a time of relative calm, before any boiling crisis involving the community and the police made talk impossible. In these early months, McGhee picked up a valuable ally when Saul Green, then the United States Attorney for the Eastern District of Michigan and the highest-ranking African American law enforcement official in the region, began to attend and serve as co-chair.[14] Green, like McGhee, had credibility with both sides: law enforcement considered him a leader of their team; at the same time, he had had his own unfortunate experiences with race-based policing practices, and had told these personal stories to fellow members of the law enforcement community.[15] Green also had a keen awareness that racial profiling carried potentially grave consequences for all of law enforcement: juror mistrust of police testimony in court holding prosecutors to an unrealistically high standard of proof in criminal trials, and unwillingness of witnesses to trust police enough to give them information necessary to solve crimes—in short, profiling had the potential to subvert the entire system. Green and McGhee understood that, though the police and community leaders did not agree on many of the specifics of profiling, they had to learn to trust each other. McGhee proposed a conference on the issue of racial profiling, hoping that the process of organizing such an event would itself force the group to work together and trust each other. Meanwhile, she continued to cultivate and recruit other community leaders for the group, including members of the Detroit area's large Arab and Muslim communities. She looked for leaders who were "reasonable in their approach," not "militant," because she did not want anyone to feel under attack, which might damage the delicate effort to establish trust and rapport among members. By the time of the conference, in April 2000, members had forged solid relationships of trust and had even opened channels of communication outside official meetings.

The benefits of these efforts became clear almost immediately. Heaster Wheeler, executive director of the Detroit branch of the National Association for the Advancement of Colored People (NAACP), the largest branch in the country, joined ALPACT at its inception. Wheeler says that the NAACP in Detroit receives more than 3,000 complaints of race-based discrimination each year; over a third allege police misconduct.[16] Many of these incidents threaten to spark serious crises. Wheeler says that the connections that he has forged with police leaders around the region enable him to take quick and decisive action to defuse these crises before they explode: "I have been able to get some clarity or [nip] the potential conflict directly in the bud [with] a phone call directly to the head of one of the police agencies," he notes. "There's no substitute for relationships."

But only fifteen months after the conference on racial profiling, ALPACT's real test began—with the terrorist attacks of September 11, 2001. Many of the group's law enforcement members led agencies that suddenly had new and daunting antiterrorism duties. This was especially true of the leaders of federal agencies, who received orders from Attorney General

John Ashcroft's Justice Department to use immigration law, the material witness statute, and other pretexts to corral anyone with even the most tenuous connection to terrorism. Across the nation, agents rounded up hundreds of such people, almost all of them Middle Eastern Muslim men; many of these arrests took place in the Detroit area. The government detained and eventually deported detainees, even in the absence of any connection to terrorism or Al Qaeda.

Members of ALPACT who served as leaders of the Arab and Muslim groups knew that their communities felt under siege; fear, suspicion, and distrust threatened to send the situation spiraling toward panic. At this critical juncture, ALPACT turned out to be the glue that held the law enforcement and community leadership of the city together.

By coincidence, a meeting of ALPACT had been scheduled for just a few days after September 11. Kary Moss, executive director of the American Civil Liberties Union of Michigan and then co-chair of ALPACT with U.S. Attorney Saul Green, recalls people showing up for the meeting in a state of shock.[17] But the group rallied when its law enforcement members proposed that ALPACT issue a public statement against hate crimes and backlash incidents against Muslims and Arabs. The group hammered out a statement that had the unanimous support of all of the members. "It was a really great response" to what had happened and what was going on in the community, Moss remembers—all the more so because law enforcement officials had initiated the effort. "It was a clear affirmation," Moss says, "that people from the Arab community should not be punished for what had happened." Just as important, she says, it came directly from the trust that had been built among members of ALPACT, and it reaffirmed and strengthened that trust at an absolutely critical time.

Imad Hamad, an ALPACT member and director of the Michigan office of the American-Arab Anti-Discrimination Committee, remembers this period as a very difficult time for everyone,

but he credits the unusual alliances within ALPACT with allowing the best in people to come to the fore.[18] "Everybody around
the table," he says, tried to find "our common issues rather than
the issues that pushed us away from each other." The group provided a ready-made structure that allowed the leaders of the
Arab and Muslim communities "to air our concerns freely and
directly" to those in charge in law enforcement, and at the same
time to understand issues from law enforcement's point of view.

The community and law enforcement supplied each other
with critical perspectives at a time when both information and
cultural knowledge became essential to public safety. Muslim
and Arab community leaders invited FBI and other federal
agents into the community for meetings and other exchanges
of information in an effort to calm the community and get
people facts instead of rumors. Mo Abdrabboh, an Arab American attorney and member of ALPACT, used the relationships
he had built through the group to invite federal officials to
town hall meetings and seminars, and even to help federal law
enforcement organizations recruit prospective employees in
the community.[19] He also used his ALPACT contacts to debunk
rumors floating through the community about "something
terrible" happening to an Arab or Muslim, since he could pick
up the phone and talk directly to the police chief of the jurisdiction where the incident had supposedly occurred. Thus, in
the first few weeks after September 11, ALPACT showed its
strength under the worst possible circumstances, helping the
region's leadership pull together at a time when things could
have easily, and disastrously, fallen apart. Detroit was both
unusual and very lucky to have the preexisting lines of communication and partnerships that ALPACT had built. Most
cities and towns had nothing similar to turn to when the September 11 crisis occurred; not a few large police departments
found themselves with no practical working relationships
with Arab and Muslim communities in their cities, and with
no ties to them of any value.

But another challenge quickly appeared: Attorney General Ashcroft announced that the U.S. Department of Justice wanted to interview five thousand young Arab men between the ages of eighteen and thirty-three who had entered the United States since January 2000 on nonimmigrant visas.[20] The department did not suspect the men of any involvement with terrorism; in fact, it suspected them of nothing. They would simply be interviewed—voluntarily, Ashcroft said—because they might have some knowledge that would be useful in the fight against terrorism. Federal law enforcement agencies would have to comply with the attorney general's order, while local or state law enforcement agencies might or might not decide to be part of the effort.

The announcement of the interviews sent an immediate ripple of panic through Middle Eastern communities across the nation, and nowhere was this more true than in metropolitan Detroit. With its very large and well-established Arab communities, especially in the inner-ring suburb of Dearborn, the Detroit area had the single largest concentration of people to be interviewed in the entire nation. The interviews became the most important item on ALPACT's agenda, and its members immediately understood the stakes. No one could prevent the interviews, but the group knew that if FBI agents showed up unannounced at subjects' homes, schools, or places of business, relationships between federal law enforcement and these communities, already badly strained, would sustain incalculable damage. FBI agents on the ground in Detroit also knew that the nation could not afford this, because for the foreseeable future the Middle Eastern communities were likely to be the most important source of intelligence as well as of translators and cultural education on Islam and the Middle East. This made federal law enforcement officials eager to cause the least possible fear and to minimize disruption to these crucial relationships.

ALPACT's history of collaboration paid off when members agreed on a proposal for a critical preemptive measure: the FBI would send letters to prospective interviewees.[21] The letters would explain the nature of the interviews, confirm that the interviewees were not suspects, and restate that the interviews were voluntary and could take place anywhere the interviewee wanted. At the request of Jeffrey Collins, the new U.S. Attorney in Detroit and a member of ALPACT, the U.S. Department of Justice approved the proposed procedure. Collins and other officials, as well as other ALPACT members, then announced the use of the letters to the public to increase the chances that members of the community would understand their intent and receive them well.

It appears a simple solution in retrospect, but in fact the FBI did not use advance letters anywhere outside of Detroit. The results in Detroit surpassed the expectations of everyone involved: a higher percentage of people agreed to be interviewed in the Detroit area than in any other city. Collins attributes the high level of cooperation directly to the letters, noting that "only a minuscule percentage" of those contacted declined to be interviewed. Without their well-established connection with community leaders, law enforcement officials might not have sensed the fear that the prospect of hundreds of interviews would inspire in the Arab and Muslim communities. For their part, ALPACT connections allowed Middle Eastern communities to understand the perspective of federal law enforcement agents, who were duty bound to carry out the orders of the attorney general. Almost certainly, without ALPACT these communities could not have conceived of the fact that those agents were prepared to take their concerns into account and listen to their fears, and were eager to work out a better way of handling the problem. All of this allowed community leaders to establish calm and a climate of cooperation.

In the wake of the success of the initial letters, the FBI used the tactic again in metropolitan Detroit and in a number of other jurisdictions across the country in the spring of 2002 when Attorney General Ashcroft announced three thousand additional interviews, and then again in early 2003, when the government interviewed Iraqi immigrants before the U.S. invasion of Iraq.

ALPACT began with the idea of building trust between law enforcement and the community in order to facilitate real partnership, and it clearly accomplished its goal. But seldom does this kind of effort bear such tangible fruit, and in such difficult circumstances. Little wonder, then, that the group continues to meet—and that its structure and methods have been replicated elsewhere in Michigan and in other places across the nation.

WHAT PREVENTIVE POLICING OWES
TO COMMUNITY POLICING

According to Robert Trojanowicz and Bonnie Bucqueroux, two of the foremost exponents of community policing,[22] law-abiding people in the community "deserve input into the police process, in exchange for their participation and support."[23] Given such input, community members will provide the police with the kind of information that Trojanowicz and Bucqueroux call "the lifeblood of policing. Without the facts, police officers cannot solve problems. The challenge police face in getting information is that there are two kinds of people who have information about crime—perpetrators and their associates, and the law-abiding people who consciously or unconsciously possess information that the police need." To move forward and prevent crime, police must "broaden the focus to solicit information from law-abiding people, through both formal and informal contacts."[24] These kinds of contacts bring police "more and better information from victims and witnesses because they have already established a bond of trust."[25] This concept, which lies at the heart of community policing, is also a seminal component of preventive policing, which employs it in the service of the larger goal of heading off crime and disorder before it happens.

LESSONS FROM AROUND THE NATION

Over the past several years, more and more American police departments and their communities have signed on to this "new contract between the police and the citizens,"[26] creating partnerships based on collaboration and trust. As in Detroit, many of their efforts began as ad hoc responses to a troubling issue or incident but have yielded structures capable of addressing a host of related problems.

In many cities, the inciting issue has been racial profiling. In the late 1990s, racial profiling (the use of racial or ethnic appearance, among other factors, in deciding which drivers or pedestrians police should stop and search) became an issue of national importance, prompting police departments from New Jersey to California to reexamine their practices. Community leaders contended that the practice or even the perception of racial profiling undermined the integrity and legitimacy of law enforcement, the court system, and even the law itself. Many towns and cities found that dialogue between the police and communities on the issue became the most important aspect of their efforts to address the problem, because it brought police and community members together for a common purpose. This built relationships that endured beyond the initial crisis, and converted the problem of profiling into an opportunity for collaboration.

Seattle: New Partnerships for a Changing City

Seattle has long had a diverse population. As of 1990, its populace included whites (75 percent), Asians and Pacific Islanders (about 12 percent), African Americans (10 percent), Hispanics (3.6 percent), and Native Americans (1.4 percent).[27] Responding to this diversity, the Seattle Police Department has had outreach programs in minority communities for some time, starting under former police chief Norm Stamper. By 2000, Seattle had become even more diverse, absorbing immigrant groups from across the globe—not just Asians, as in decades past, but Africans too.[28] To keep pace with these accelerating demographic changes, the police department has begun to rely upon a system of advisory councils representing racial or ethnic communities or "communities of interest," such as homeless youth, or gay, lesbian, and transgendered groups.[29] For each council, the police department appoints a liaison officer to attend its monthly meetings, to help articulate its agenda, and to convey information from the group—criminal intelligence, a request for greater police presence, or an invitation to meet with department officials, for example—back to the department. This structure minimizes the number of steps of separation between the advisory council and the highest levels of police administration: the council speaks to the liaison officer, who brings its concerns directly to an assistant chief, who can then either take action or bring the issue to the chief and other top administrators.[30]

Although their work with the advisory councils constitutes an assignment in addition to their regular work, the liaison officers say that they would not give up their liaison duties. They relish the opportunity to make their city a better place to live in ways that regular police work would never permit. For example, Detective Clem Bentson, a veteran officer, is especially proud of his role in planning an all-day workshop for Seattle's growing East African community.[31] Since many East Africans have had unusual misunderstandings with Seattle police officers during what should have been routine encounters, the workshop, attended by members of both the East African community and the police department, addressed areas of community concern through mutual education, with sessions on policing issues, on immigration, and even on becoming a city employee. The East African community, Bentson says, seemed "really hungry" for information that the police could provide; for their part, the police asked the community "to teach us about them." For example, a key source of friction turned out to be the way that some police officers dealt with the women in this mainly Muslim community. Until the workshop, officers did not know they should never touch a Muslim woman, even in a casual, friendly way, such as with a handshake or pat on the arm, and that they should address a woman's husband or other male relative before speaking to her.

Officers provided important guidance to the community, too, especially about such issues as how citizens should conduct themselves during traffic stops. Since these encounters sometimes prove dangerous and violent in the United States, American police receive training on conducting stops in very particular ways to minimize risk. Most Americans have some level of familiarity with the process: when we see or hear a police car signaling to us to pull to the side of the road, we do so; we then wait in the car until the officer walks up to the side window to speak to us. We anticipate being asked for, and then retrieving, a driver's license (from wallets in pockets or purses) and vehicle registration (usually from vehicle glove compartments). In East Africa, accepted customs in these situations vary widely from American practices in ways that could prove fatal. First, drivers in Africa always get out of their vehicles and approach the police officer; it is disrespectful to sit and wait for the officer to approach the driver. Second, many male drivers keep their money and identification in their socks. Thus, an American officer stopping an East African driver might face a man who approaches the squad car and then reaches down to his ankle area. While the driver is only trying to be polite, the officer sees a rapidly approaching man reaching for a gun hidden in an ankle holster. Add language barriers—if not an inability to speak English, then almost certainly an accent—and you have a recipe for rapidly escalating and perhaps even deadly misunderstandings. Obviously both police and community members would benefit enormously from breaking through these barriers.

Both Detective Bentson and his colleague Officer Kim Bogucki, another veteran of the Seattle police force who also serves as a liaison officer, stress the direct crime-fighting value of their efforts: an enhanced flow of information and intelligence that allows officers to solve crimes already committed and prevent others from happening. Moreover, as Bogucki points out, when the community trusts officers, those officers are safer on the street. Bogucki says that, just like most other officers, she frequently has to approach groups of people who may pose a threat. If one or two in the group know her and trust that she is there to do her job and not harass them, Bogucki says, they often explain this to the members of the group she doesn't know ("It's O.K., I know her, she's cool"), instantly defusing a potentially tense situation.[32]

Seattle police chief Gil Kerlikowske tells a story that vividly illustrates the value of collaboration-based preventive policing over Ashcroft policing. Shortly after September 11, 2001, an incident took place outside the Idris Mosque in Seattle, the oldest mosque in the northwestern United States. A man approached the mosque while worshippers were inside; he attempted to vandalize some of the vehicles in the parking lot and the mosque itself with a flammable liquid. When confronted, the man threatened people with a gun.[33] Police eventually caught him; shortly after the attack, they announced in a joint news conference with Muslim and other community leaders from the mosque that they would tolerate no backlash or hate crimes against Muslims or others from Asia or the Middle East.[34] This statement led the neighbors of the Idris Mosque—the great majority of them non-Muslims—to form a twenty-four-hour, seven-day-a-week watch patrol for the mosque, which they maintained until the immediate danger of anti-Muslim retaliation had died down.[35]

This had both practical and symbolic consequences. The presence of the watch eased the burden on the police department, which did not have to provide the number of officers to maintain security that they might have otherwise. At the same time, the city was given a powerful example of American values in action even as it was made safe from hate crimes and the work of vandals. The police department made sure not to squander this momentum. In the wake of the incident and the watch, they established a hotline for the public to use to give the police information on backlash crimes, and created a new advisory committee as a liaison between the police and the Muslim community.[36] The police also increased all of their outreach efforts to the Muslim community.

The police chief's efforts did not go unnoticed. In December 2001, the Muslim community recognized the department's sincere efforts to find common ground by inviting Chief Kerlikowske to speak at its communal Ramadan service—a chance to address thousands of Muslims gathered together at Seattle's convention center for Islam's holiest days.[37] Even now, Kerlikowske seems genuinely humbled by the gesture, an honor that he says he will not forget.

Lowell, Massachusetts, and Wichita, Kansas: Big Results in Small Cities

Making police-community partnerships work is not just a task for large cities; the experiences of two smaller, but very different, cities—Lowell, Massachusetts, and Wichita, Kansas—provide a valuable counterpart to Seattle's story.

Lowell is an old-line manufacturing center typical of the northeastern United States. While the city still has some industrial jobs, the mills that were the great engine of employment and wealth creation of the city's past now employ far fewer people than they did fifty years ago.[38] But Lowell did not shrink and wither away with these changes, as some similar towns have. During the 1980s and 1990s, Lowell's population grew; at 105,000, it is now almost 20 percent larger than it was in 1980,[39] and far more diverse. Most of Lowell's new citizens are recent immigrants to the U.S. who moved to Lowell after living first in other American cities. They have come from all over the world, including Latin America, Asia, and Africa. Residents of Lowell speak more than fifty languages,[40] but the largest single block, amounting to one-third of all of Lowell's new immigrants, is compromised of Cambodians.[41] The Cambodian community in particular presented the police department with challenges it had never before encountered. It is impossible to exaggerate the potential for distrust among Cambodians of almost anyone in a position of authority.[42] This becomes understandable when one remembers that most of them immigrated as refugees from Pol Pot's genocidal Khmer Rouge regime during the 1970s, during which those in charge of the country killed thousands upon thousands of their own citizens. While the Cambodian community had no particular complaint with police in Lowell, gaining its trust would take special effort.

The people of Lowell had little experience with either the specific ethnic groups newly established in their midst or such ethnic diversity in general. Not surprisingly, this sometimes generated tensions between police and the new residents. By 2000, the issue of racial profiling flared up in Lowell. The town's police department and its superintendent, Ed Davis, realized they needed to address immigrants' perception that police sometimes enforced the law differently against minorities. There had also been some incidents of police violence against Southeast Asians.[43] Fortunately, Chief Davis also understood the value of building trusting relationships with Lowell's diverse communities.[44] Thus, the police department began a series of facilitated discussions with a group of representatives from all the city's ethnic populations called the Lowell Race Relations Council.[45]

The council's first discussion centered on the issue of racial profiling, but the council members soon realized that they wanted to broaden their focus to address race relations in general,[46] foster greater understanding of police work by the public, and promote a more nuanced understanding on the part of the police of public perceptions.[47] The council set itself five goals: education, communication, understanding, community unification, and generation of recommendations for the police department, all of which it continues to pursue at its monthly meetings and through follow-up with police and public officials.[48] Topics the council has discussed include gangs, intergenerational differences, domestic violence, various traditions of policing, language barriers, and cultural differences.[49]

The council has also made a number of recommendations for changes in departmental policy and training. For example, it brought to the police department a number of concerns about the conduct of traffic stops. The discussion resulted in a requirement that all officers stopping drivers identify themselves and their department, explain the reason for the stop, state the action the officer plans to take (citation, warning, etc.), and answer motorists' questions.[50] Council members were also shown police training videos about making traffic stops so that they could get a sense of the safety reasons that cause officers to conduct these encounters as they do.[51] Other council recommendations included: making a video to help present new cultural perspectives to police; increasing outreach to minority communities for participation in the city's citizen police academy; developing a cable television call-in show focusing on the concerns of different ethnic communities in Lowell, done in each community's language; and reviewing the police academy's training practices.[52] The council has helped produce a video on racial profiling, as well as pamphlets on expected and appropriate behavior during traffic stops in a number of languages spoken in Lowell's minority communities.

Like Seattle's advisory councils, the Lowell council has focused on mutual education of police and public above all. One council meeting, for example, featured Fru Nkimbeng, an immigrant from Cameroon, and a police officer, who together acted out a simulated traffic stop, revealing the same causes of potentially dangerous misunderstandings (approaching the officer instead of remaining in the car when stopped, reaching for a wallet in the ankle area) that officers discovered at the advisory council workshop in Seattle.[53]

Researchers Jack McDevitt and Jack Greene of Northeastern University in Boston have evaluated Lowell's efforts and found them on par with or better than any other similar program in the nation. The U.S. Department of Justice has recognized the program's unique contributions and effectiveness, and has awarded the Lowell Police Department grants that have allowed it to train police departments from cities around the country.

The experience of the Wichita, Kansas, police department is another example of how a relatively small department (645 sworn officers)[54] in a medium-size city (population 344,000)[55] can bring police and the community together as partners, with striking results. In the late 1990s, Bob Knight, Wichita's four-term mayor, took the lead in an examination of race relations as a means to promote civic harmony and growth.[56] Knight founded a committee called Building Bridges in Wichita to facilitate better race relations through community-wide dialogue and partnership,[57] and as chair of the National League of Cities in 2000, he made improved race relations his national signature issue.[58] Knight and Norman Williams, Wichita's police chief, made the police department an active part of these efforts, and when the issue of racial profiling became nationally prominent, the mayor decided to take a proactive approach.

Using the structure of community networks and meetings already created through the Building Bridges program, the police department gathered data on racial profiling in Wichita.[59] (The state of Kansas, which later legislated a ten-city data collection pilot project, had not yet mandated any requirement that Wichita or any other city collect data; the mayor and the police chief took this initiative on their own.) Deputy Chief Terri Moses, a twenty-two-year veteran of the department, led the effort.[60] With the local chapter of the National Conference on Community and Justice[61]—part of the same national organization that had helped found ALPACT in Detroit—as her partner and facilitator, Moses brought together a group of thirty to forty people—members of many different parts of the police department (not only from the command staff but from most ranks and assignments, as well as union representatives), and members of the community who had been involved in Building Bridges. The group started, Moses says, with the goal of addressing racial profiling by conducting a study that would analyze data on police stops in Wichita, but it soon embraced a far larger ambition: "to build trust between the citizens of Wichita and the Wichita Police Department."[62]

As it did in Detroit, the process of working through the difficult questions of racial profiling cemented relationships among group members. The pieces of the puzzle were so numerous, the issues so varied, that all of the participants had to trust each other for input outside their own areas of expertise. Deputy Chief Moses recalls that the group included police officers from each of the four geographic bureaus of her city in addition to those involved in police academy training, information technology, the traffic division, and others. The community members played a crucial role because they knew their neighborhoods and the issues and peculiarities that plagued each one. Brian Withrow, a criminal justice researcher from Wichita State University, volunteered to analyze the data to ensure the independence of the study's outcome.[63]

After the completion of the data collection and analysis, Deputy Chief Moses had Withrow present a summary and preliminary conclusions to the group in a nonpublic setting, which gave community leaders and the police the chance to consider what Withrow had found.[64] Then the mayor, Moses, Withrow, and all the community leaders presented the study results to the public in a meeting in the city council chamber.[65] Public reaction varied. Withrow remembers being particularly struck by the reaction of members of the black community, who were surprised that there wasn't more of a disparity between the percentage of blacks stopped by police and Wichita's black population figures; they had thought the problem was much worse than the numbers actually indicated.[66]

The process left Wichita better off: relationships had been forged, and the leaders of minority communities and law enforcement had had many occasions to work together and to grow to trust each other. They had accomplished something significant for their community—jumping into a volatile, racially charged issue, working with people they might have been disinclined to trust, and moving without fear toward whatever the data would tell them, all without any law requiring them to do so. They learned some important facts about their city and successfully completed a thorny and difficult task—one that many other American towns and cities had done everything possible to avoid.

New challenges emerged in Wichita after September 11, 2001, particularly with regard to relations between Muslims and the police. Deputy Chief Moses says that the department suddenly realized it had no real contacts with area Muslims. A Muslim member of the racial profiling study group, Y.R. Shourbaji, a retired aviation engineer, emerged after September 11 as an important and vocal presence.[67] Shourbaji quickly became a de facto liaison for the police department to the Muslim community. According to Deputy Chief Moses, Shourbaji proved an invaluable interpreter of the police department's actions and an ambassador of its good faith to other Muslims in Wichita, at the same time helping the department understand the perspectives and fears of Muslims in the wake of the terrorist attacks. Naturally, police officials met with the heads of Muslim and Islamic community groups, but it was Deputy Chief Moses's relationship with Shourbaji that she consistently found most important, and she credits it entirely to the relationships built through the group's racial profiling work. Moses, a plainspoken person not given to overstatement, calls her post-9/11 work with Shourbaji "a shining example" of trusting personal relationships as the key to effective community policing.

Chicago: Reaching Out on Race

Even if it does not officially "win" the top spot in the category, Chicago has long been considered one of the most segregated of America's cities.[68] It is a place of neighborhoods and enclaves, most with a clear ethnic or racial character, even in the twenty-first century. Nevertheless, under the leadership of former police superintendent Terrance Hillard, the Chicago Police Department—not always known in the past for its sensitivity to minorities[69]—took steps that set it on a path to becoming one of the city's leading institutions in promoting better race relations.

The journey began in 2000. Former Deputy Superintendent Barbara McDonald recalls that Superintendent Hillard talked with her and other members of Hillard's senior staff: the department had been working hard for a number of years on its fairly successful community policing efforts; what could they do now to make decisive improvement?[70] Hillard felt that the department had accomplished much, but he was also aware that not everyone in Chicago shared his belief. As an African American, Hillard knew that this was particularly true among members of the city's minority communities.[71] Hillard asked Chuck Wexler, the executive director of the Police Executives Research Forum, the law enforcement think tank, to help him address questions of race relations between the police department and Chicago's minority communities.[72] Their brainstorming produced the idea of putting together a forum of leaders from minority groups and the police department for frank, face-to-face talk: the Superintendent's Race Relations Forum.

Wexler helped the department come up with a format for the forum. He would serve as moderator. The session would begin with one to two hours of "community speak," during which community leaders would have the chance to speak their minds.[73] Wexler would consistently ask, How are the police doing? What can they do better? No representatives of law enforcement would be allowed to speak; they could only listen. After a lunch break, a one- to two-hour "police speak" session would follow, in which police could say what was on *their* minds, while community members listened. To end the day, Wexler would lead a full-group discussion designed to elicit consensus about the issues that had emerged during the day. Hillard, the command staff, and Wexler decided that the group should not exceed thirty-two members, equally divided between police and community representatives. Hillard himself picked members of the department from all ranks to participate, and he attempted to recruit community leaders who had been both critical and supportive of the department in the past. These leaders came from minority advocacy groups, faith-based organizations, schools, and community development corporations.[74] Nearly all of the invited leaders received a letter requesting their participation, followed by a telephone call from the superintendent himself. They then received a pre-meeting survey asking questions such as, "What issues challenge the relationship between the police and the city's minority communities? If you were the police superintendent, what efforts would you undertake to improve police relations within minority communities? What role should community leaders play to improve relations between the police and minority communities?"[75]

Participants in the first forum meeting recall the session as somewhat tense, albeit frank. By the end of the day, the superintendent had come to understand that "the department needed to balance effective crime control strategies with an equal appreciation of how citizens are treated,"[76] and that "reducing crime cannot be accomplished at the expense of losing the trust and active involvement" of community partners.[77] Hillard made these two essential guidelines the watch words of the forums, and the group agreed that in order to move forward, five key issues had to be addressed:

- *Communication:* A lack of communication, especially between police and immigrant communities, created tension and stood in the way of effective relationships.
- *Respect:* Citizens, especially, in minority communities, felt keenly that officers did not respect them; for their part, officers felt that they were often unfairly stereotyped.
- *Accountability:* Members of the community felt the police disciplinary system was ineffective. Police agreed that they needed to improve the disciplinary process and better inform the community about its results.
- *Freedom from fear:* Members of the minority community, especially young men, feared encounters with the police, while police felt they would be judged too fast and too harshly if they made an honest mistake. All of this created an "us against them" attitude on both sides.
- *Trust:* Members of minority groups expressed concern that officers had neither an understanding of their communities nor any real commitment to joining forces with them.[78]

The following week, Superintendent Hillard discussed the forum results at a news conference and vowed to work with the community to meet the five new goals.[79] He followed this up with a two-day retreat for almost one hundred of his top staff members in which he gave them responsibility for examining the entire department from top to bottom and devising concrete plans for change. Addressing these concerns, he said, would be the department's number-one priority.[80]

The Superintendent's Race Relations Forum continued to meet regularly. Members received ongoing reports from the police department on what actions had been taken to address their concerns and had the opportunity to raise new concerns. For example, to address community perceptions that officers who engaged in misconduct received no discipline, the department presented data showing that more than fifty police officers had been fired for misconduct during the prior year—something that none of the community members knew. This went at least some way toward moderating the view that internal police discipline was a toothless tiger.[81] Most important, regular meetings, together with evidence of action on the department's part, encouraged commitment to the forum from all participants.[82]

Among the group's early successes was a series of nine training videos for officers on dealing with the public: subjects included courtesy and demeanor; dealing with youth; making traffic stops; and reception of the public and complaints at police stations, to name just a few. The department also produced a written policy against racial profiling. After a number of successful meetings of the Race Relations Forum, the department decided to duplicate its structure in all five of the city's geographic police divisions. These local race relations forums now meet consistently all over the city.

After September 11, 2001, Chicago, like all of the other large, ethnically diverse cities in the country, saw a spike in hate crimes and other backlash incidents aimed at the area's 400,000 Muslims, as well as those perceived to be Middle Easterners—often Sikhs, whose religiously-mandated beards and turbans led to the erroneous belief that they were Arabs.[83] The police department acted quickly. Using the same structure and format that it had used for the Race Relations Forum, the department convened the Superintendent's Multicultural Forum, a group consisting of police officers and administration (including Superintendent Hillard, Deputy Superintendent McDonald, and other top members of the command staff), and leading members of the Muslim, Asian, Sikh, Hindu, Jewish, and Baha'i faiths. One of those invited to join was Kareem Irfan, chair of the Council of Islamic Organizations of Greater Chicago, a group that represents more than forty Muslim organizations in Chicago. A lawyer and assistant general counsel for a multinational company, Irfan certainly had the requisite skills and experience; he also felt passionately that government and the community must have a symbiotic, not antagonistic, relationship. However, Irfan says, many within the Muslim community expressed skepticism. They feared that the proposed Multicultural Forum would amount to little more than "symbolic gestures." In the end, Irfan convinced his members to approve his attendance, though he wondered whether he would be damaged or appear compromised as a leader if the forum did not produce real results.

Irfan says the atmosphere at the first session of the Multicultural Forum, held just after September 11, was very tense; everyone seemed to be wondering what, if anything, could come from a meeting at such difficult a time. Eventually the participants began to trust each other. "I could see that the superintendent was committed," Irfan says, "so that meant that I could commit, too." He mentions the strong commitment shown by others in the group, too—members of the community and the police department, especially former Deputy Superintendent McDonald and Police Department general counsel Karen Rowan. Irfan also points to concrete, tangible results that began to accrue as the forum continued to meet.

First, he says, it was clear from talking to the participants from the police department that many of them had never had any real experience with the communities represented at the forum, though they had all lived and worked in one of the nation's most diverse cities for many years. For their part, most members of the police department left the first couple of meetings stunned at how little they knew about Muslims, Sikhs, and other groups they met there, says former Deputy Superintendent McDonald.

As relationships began to form over the course of the forum's meetings, Irfan could see the change in the way that members of the department related to his fellow Muslims and others. Stereotypes melted away. Irfan was able to get the police department to help accommodate the Islamic community on Friday afternoons, when Friday prayers often caused traffic congestion and parking problems near mosques. And he was able to help the police understand what some members of the public saw as suspicious behavior: the reason that observant Muslims showed up at mosques at what seemed to be absurdly early hours was not to hold planning meetings for terrorism but to attend predawn prayers. Irfan remembers that he began to receive messages from Muslims applauding police, who had suddenly started to show an interest in helping work around the community's prayer schedule instead of just ticketing cars.

Then the police department, with the close cooperation of the Islamic community, produced a special video for its officers who worked the security detail at Chicago's O'Hare and Midway airports. The airports had understandably become the focal point for much of the post–9/11 friction between police and Muslims. The video, co-written by the department and the Muslim participants in the Multicultural Forum and featuring many of them on camera, explained Muslim customs, dress, and sensitivities; it was shown to all law enforcement personnel at O'Hare and Midway. The feedback was instantaneous and enthusiastic. Police officers "told us they loved it," Irfan says. Real results came almost as quickly from the community. People called Irfan—to ask him whether he knew what manner of strange things might be happening at the airports to make such a positive change in police treatment. "They were calling and saying, 'Things are pleasant—we don't understand it but we like it,'" Irfan says. In the months since, the police department has worked with other members of the Multicultural Forum to produce three more videos, one on Sikhism, one on Islam that teaches more general lessons than the one about airport security, and one about Orthodox Judaism. Others are planned. The videos are short (averaging between twelve and fifteen minutes), professional, and never adopt a preachy or politically correct tone.

All of this goes a long way toward explaining why Kareem Irfan remains strongly committed to the Multicultural Forum, and why he feels that it has been the biggest boon to the Chicago Police Department in recent memory. Says Irfan, "We cannot survive in these times with an 'us-against-them' perspective."

PAYING DIVIDENDS
How Collaborative Partnerships Helped Corner a Murderer

The real benefit of establishing relationships and collaborative partnerships is that they create possibilities for dealing with crime well beyond simply responding to 911 calls and writing reports. Preventive policing also creates structures that will be in place when a new problem arises, whether a burgeoning difficulty (for example, the sudden appearance of a new designer drug) or an immediate peril that police must deal with on the spot. It offers the first step toward improved police service by reestablishing the connection between the police and those they serve. Preventive policing begins by adopting community policing's aim of renewed relationships, but specifically aims them toward preventing harm in the future.

As anyone reading about Detroit, Seattle, Lowell, Wichita, or Chicago can see, building partnerships based on trust is essential to public safety, to good relations with the public, and to generating the support law enforcement needs to fight crime effectively. We know for certain that the reactive, respond-and-arrest ways of the past alone do not produce safe streets and livable communities; for that, police must work in partnership with those they serve. Given that Americans face threats of a type and a magnitude undreamed of just a few years ago, working collaboratively with trusted partners is the only feasible strategy. Just ask Anthony Scalise, a sergeant who has been with the Chicago Police Department for forty years.

Sergeant Scalise comes from Bridgeport, the Chicago neighborhood that has given the city both of its mayors named Daley. Scalise has been in charge of the department's civil rights enforcement unit, which investigates hate crimes, since 1991.[84] On Friday evening, July 2, 1999, Scalise received the kind of call every police officer dreads: six people had been shot in West Rogers Park, a neighborhood on Chicago's North Side.[85] Scalise was called to investigate the incident as a possible hate crime. No one knew it yet, but the six victims, Orthodox Jews who had been walking to their neighborhood synagogue for traditional Friday night Sabbath services, were the first of what were to be fifteen shooting victims, two of whom died, in a two-day shooting-and-killing spree by a young racist and anti-Semite named Benjamin Smith.[86] Smith, an acolyte of the racist Matthew Hale and his World Church of the Creator, went from Chicago to its suburbs the first day, and then into smaller towns in Indiana and downstate Illinois during the next two days. The six victims in West Rogers Park marked the beginning of his crimes.[87] When Scalise arrived at the scene, another police officer told him that witnesses to the mass shooting had been located, but they would not talk to the police.[88] Without information from the witnesses, police would have no way to begin to look for, much less apprehend, the person responsible.

The news that victims and witnesses would not talk to police did not surprise Scalise. All he had to do was look around at the people at the scene (Orthodox Jews in distinctive dress), the location and day (outside a synagogue on Friday night, the beginning of the Jewish Sabbath), and the neighborhood (well known for having the largest population of Orthodox Jews in Chicago), and he understood: the Orthodox Jewish witnesses could not respond to questioning or go to the police station; Jewish law strictly prohibited any action that might be construed as work during the Sabbath. They would not be able to talk, Scalise knew, until the end of the Sabbath after sundown on Saturday—a full twenty-four hours later.[89] Waiting that long could disadvantage the investigation in the most important way: police might not get crucial information from witnesses until it was too late to be of any use.

Within twenty minutes of the six West Rogers Park shootings, reports came over the police radio indicating a shooting of a black man in the nearby suburb of Skokie. Just thirty minutes after that, police received reports that someone had shot at an Asian couple just a few miles farther west of Skokie, in the largely Jewish suburb of Northbrook.[90] A horrifying pattern began to take shape: a string of unprovoked shootings; a willingness to shoot at whole groups of victims; and victims who shared identifiable characteristics as members of minorities.

Scalise had long experience cultivating relationships and making connections with racial and religious minorities. Given his unit's responsibility for hate crimes, Scalise had made it a regular practice to reach out to leaders of the city's diverse religious and ethnic communities, including, of course, the Jewish community. The trusted partnerships he had built through repeated contacts had laid the groundwork for his unit and the police department to respond to moments just like this.

Scalise and the officers in Chicago's Twenty-fourth District, where the crime took place, immediately called their contacts in the Jewish community. Foremost among them was Moshe Wolf,[91] an Orthodox rabbi who had served as a Jewish chaplain to the Chicago Police Department for over a decade and who often acted as an unofficial liaison between the department and the Orthodox Jewish community.[92] Wolf came to the scene, helping to coordinate police efforts; when he left, he told the officers that, despite the fact that it was the Sabbath, he would answer his home telephone (which Orthodox Jews generally would not do) to help them deal with the crisis. Later that evening, Wolf received a call: an Orthodox Jewish witness who may have seen something crucial would not talk to the police because it was the Sabbath. There was an immediate need to obtain any information that might lead to the apprehension of a killer who, it seemed, would kill again, and perhaps soon.[93] Could Wolf help?

Wolf asked for the man's address and immediately went to his house. He reminded the man that according to *bekouach nefesh*, a principle in Jewish law, when a matter of life and death presents itself, Jews may temporarily disregard the strictures of the Sabbath against doing anything that might be construed as work or business. The matter of helping the police in

4

Solving Problems

Few phrases in the American lexicon evoke such bleak images as does *public housing*: poverty, crowding, blight, disrepair, broken families, danger, and especially crime. Most public housing in early twenty-first–century American cities is indeed plagued by crime; the large multistory high-rise complexes common in big cities have often been terrorized by gangs, drug dealing, and violence.[1] Other equally intractable social problems—teenage pregnancy, inadequate school systems, chronically high rates of unemployment, drug and alcohol addiction, and lack of investment capital[2]—make tackling crime in public housing even more difficult, perhaps impossible.

Nonetheless, Betsy Lindsay and her colleagues in Los Angeles County were not intimidated. Lindsay, who had worked as a strategic planner and strategist in law enforcement agencies for some years, remembers that when she told friends and colleagues in the early 1990s that she was going to work for the Housing Authority of the County of Los Angeles (HACOLA), most told her she was crazy.[3] The scale of HACOLA's jurisdiction and its demographics made its properties very hard to police.[4] HACOLA had 3,600 housing units, with 1,800 concentrated in four large developments: Carmelitos, Harbor Hills, Nueva Maravilla, and Ujima Village. The other 1,800 units constituted smaller developments at thirty-eight scattered sites throughout South Central Los Angeles County.[5] More than 1,300 of the approximately 6,600 HACOLA residents were elderly; racially, the population was relatively mixed, including Hispanics (43 percent), blacks (37 percent), whites (15 percent), and Asians and Pacific Islanders (3 percent).

HACOLA properties had become constant targets of violent crime. Drugs were sold and used openly, and gang violence made life almost intolerable for many residents. From 1990 to 1993, HACOLA's four large developments averaged 498 Part I crimes annually (Part I crimes are the eight most serious crimes that the FBI tallies every year: murder, forcible rape, robbery, aggravated assault, burglary, larceny-theft, motor vehicle theft, and arson).[6] Since it had become clear that traditional respond-and-arrest law enforcement had failed, Lindsay and her colleagues resolved to try problem-oriented policing.

Problem-oriented policing, with its focus on taking a holistic view of troubled situations, is central to preventive policing, and Lindsay and her colleagues put this approach to work in Los Angeles County. Instead of attacking a jumble of discrete crimes on an ad hoc basis, teams of police officers and their allies—residents, property managers, and other city service providers—would examine each housing project as a whole, seeking to eliminate entire patterns of incidents using a range of approaches in addition to arrest. Lindsay calls this approach "problem solving through partnerships."[7] Lindsay and her colleagues looked for patterns using the "crime triangle"—suspects, locations, and victims—which is especially useful in revealing repeat criminals.[8] With this information, Lindsay and her team designed what she called the "housing management model," a comprehensive, four-sided partnership among housing site management, law enforcement and security, providers of resident services, and community partners.[9]

Housing site management personnel[10] contributed by performing criminal background checks on rental applicants and enforcing lease conditions—tasks that had often been neglected in the past. They began to use housing-violation forms (a simple yet little-used device to build a record of violations necessary for future enforcement actions) and handled nonrenewals of leases and evictions for lease violations. Managers instituted exclusion policies, under which troublemaking nonresidents received written notices that police would arrest them for trespassing if they came onto the property.[11] Maintenance and modernization of apartments and facilities were also given high priority.

A well-established community policing effort by the Los Angeles County Sheriff's Office and the Long Beach Police Department already had officers in place in the HACoLA developments who knew where the problems were and had the connections to community members to attack problems comprehensively. With community safety groups helping to set priorities, police antidrug and gang task forces also began to weed out the worst offenders.[12] Officers also pursued fraud investigations of tenants who might have obtained housing or other benefits falsely.

Lindsay knew that HACoLA needed to provide comprehensive services to law-abiding residents to shore up the community in the process of cleaning it up. She stressed educational services, including literacy classes for adults and young people, English as a Second Language classes for immigrants, alternative schools, computer learning centers, and job training.[13] Under her leadership, HACoLA also provided comprehensive case management for residents in need of social services, counseling, gang-recruitment prevention programs, services for the elderly, family self-sufficiency programs, and recreational opportunities for young people.[14]

The fourth set of partners comprised public agencies—housing enforcement, streets and sanitation, and the like—together

with well-established and trusted community-based organizations and private agencies that addressed large-scale social
problems. Lindsay also made sure that HACoLA maintained
memberships on important county task forces that affected
the HACOLA properties.

After a couple of successful small-scale tests, Lindsay and
the HACoLA leadership put the program into place system-
wide in 1994.[15] As with any effort of this size, it took some time
to get all of the pieces in place and properly coordinated, but
as the months went by, things began to change at the HACoLA
properties. Particular problems were addressed: corners occupied by drug dealers; groups of scruffy, threatening gang members dominating public spaces; areas that lent themselves to
public drinking, drug use, and petty crime. Problem tenants
were removed, some immediately, some through nonrenewal
of their leases. Those failing to comply with lease conditions
were weeded out, as were ineffective property managers. The
effects were immediate and dramatic. In 1994, the first full
year of the problem-oriented approach, Part I crimes dropped
at HACoLA's four large complexes by 29 percent, from 463 in
1993 to 328 in 1994. Part I crimes have never topped 400 since
the implementation of the program; the overall trend since
1994 is unequivocally downward. By 1998, the fifth year of the
program, Part I crimes were only 51 percent of their 1993 level,
the year before the program was implemented, and they were
44 percent of what they had been in the peak year, 1992. By
2001, Part I crimes were only 36 percent of what they had been
in 1992, and still declining.[16]

HACoLA's problem-oriented policing has brought Los Angeles County's public housing less crime and less fear, nicer facilities, and better-kept grounds. Residents now have the benefit of
support services that make the lives of the poor, the elderly, and
the disadvantaged somewhat easier. Best of all, they live in a
community of people who participated in their own liberation
from a scourge that had plagued them for decades.

PROBLEM-ORIENTED POLICING
What It Is and What It Does

As the HACOLA story shows, law enforcement is much more effective when police view solving problems as a primary aspect of their job, at least as important as responding to crimes already committed. This idea will no doubt strike many as obvious, but in the context of contemporary law enforcement, it's bold. Even today, most police officers conceive of their jobs in a narrow sense: when called to a crime scene, restore calm and order, arrest perpetrators, separate combatants, summon medical attention, move obstructions out of traffic, and disperse crowds of gawkers.

To be sure, reactive policing will always remain indispensible. There are shootings to respond to, robberies to stop, fleeing burglars to apprehend. But a problem-solving approach, which looks for the *patterns* of crime that make responses to individual calls for service necessary, addresses the underlying problems that these patterns reveal.

First defined by Herman Goldstein, a law professor at the University of Wisconsin, problem-oriented policing followed the studies of the 1970s, chiefly the Kansas City Preventive Patrol Experiment[17] discussed in chapter 2. As did those who based community policing on the failure of random-patrol radio-car policing, Goldstein conceived of problem-oriented policing as an entirely new point of view and philosophy for police departments. Goldstein himself puts it this way: "The lesson drawn from the studies that questioned the value of standard procedures is that the police erred in doggedly investing so much of police resources in a limited number of practices, based, in retrospect, on some rather naïve and simplistic concepts of the police role."[18] In his influential 1979 article, "Improving Policing: A Problem-Oriented Approach,"[19] Goldstein laid out a fresh way for police officers and departments to do their work; his central insight was that "the end product of policing consists of dealing with . . . *problems.*"[20] Goldstein elaborated on his theory in his 1990 book *Problem-Oriented Policing.*[21] A variety of factors, he says, account for most of the frustrations in American policing, starting with the fact that police are too preoccupied with management and focus too little on the effectiveness of their efforts in dealing with substantive problems. In addition, Goldstein says, most police resources go to responding to calls for service from citizens, with little left over for prevention. Goldstein argued that the communities in which police operate have "enormous potential, largely untapped," to help reduce problems that police must otherwise tackle, and that police departments often squander rank-and-file officers' time and talent. Finally, Goldstein explained that prior efforts to reform policing have failed because they have taken inadequate account of the "overall dynamics and complexity" of police departments.[22] Any effort to improve policing must begin from a radically different point of view. Among the key principles that Goldstein says constitute "the core of the changes that are required in the way we think about the police job"[23] are:

- *Grouping incidents.* The "first step in problem-oriented policing is to move beyond just handling incidents." Police must look for patterns and relationships among incidents, because they "are often merely overt symptoms of covert problems."
- *A focus on substantive problems.* Police must move away from focusing on the internal management of their agencies and instead set their sights on substantive problems as defined by the community—such as criminal conduct (open drug sales, aggressive panhandling) or dangerous areas (a particular housing complex, a convenience store that attracts large groups of drunk loiterers by selling fortified wine)—rather than on bureaucratically defined goals (more officers assigned to the drug squad, more officers making more arrests).
- *Concern with effectiveness.* If police concern themselves with substantive problems revealed by the patterns of incidents that

affect the community, they will inevitably cultivate "a concern for *effectiveness* in dealing with these problems."

- *Systematic inquiry and analysis.* Problem-oriented policing must include a commitment to objective, in-depth inquiry into all the aspects of the problem and what factors contribute to it, without any preconceived assumptions. Police must ask, "Why is the community concerned? What are the social costs? Who is being harmed and to what degree?" The answers will tell police what is at stake and allow them to fashion their response to a problem accordingly.
- *Tailor-made responses.* With the information produced by their systematic inquiry and analysis, police must attempt to fashion a unique response that fits the particular problem. Just as important, they cannot limit themselves to looking for solutions only inside the criminal justice system.
- *Evaluation of results.* Once police have implemented their response, measurement and evaluation of the problem should take place at appropriate intervals. Without it and without a set of baseline measurements taken before the implementation of the response, there is no way to measure effectiveness.[24]

This problem-solving approach, Goldstein argued, will allow police departments to move beyond the respond-and-arrest model by getting ahead of problems before they occur.[25] Rarely has one set of insights into a social problem proven so accurate and so beneficial to so many people.

Boston: Back from the Brink on Juvenile Homicides

The Boston Police Department's use of a problem-solving approach to confront deadly violence among young people has been studied and written about by many and widely adapted on account of its effectiveness. Boston's story begins in the late 1980s. Like many large American cities then, Boston was struck by a wave of violence related to the sale and use of crack cocaine. Gangs' involvement in drug activity clearly had something to do with the violence, but neither the city nor the police department wanted to admit that they had a gang problem.[26] The police department responded by making lots of arrests for reported or observed criminal activity.[27] But when the killings hit an annual peak of 152 in Boston in 1990, they realized the old ways had failed.

This failure was attributable in part to the police department's strained relations with the city's racial minorities. In 1989, Carol Stuart, a young, pregnant white woman, and her husband, Charles, were shot in their car in Roxbury, a primarily African American neighborhood.[28] Charles Stuart called police and reported that a black man had shot them.[29] Carol Stuart, who had been shot in the head, died soon afterward; the baby she carried died seventeen days later. The police accepted Charles Stuart's report without skepticism, and Boston police officers inundated the mostly black housing projects in the Mission Hill section of the Roxbury neighborhood in search of the perpetrator. In two days, the police reported that they had narrowed their investigation to half a dozen suspects.[30] Reports of what Roxbury residents perceived as abusive police behavior quickly surfaced among African American men; tensions between Mission Hill residents and police increased markedly.[31] Police arrested a black suspect, William Bennett, and reported that he had confessed.[32] Only then did the evidence begin to point to Charles Stuart himself.[33] Stuart eventually killed himself, but not before police went a long way toward determining that he had killed his wife.[34] By then, however, the damage had already been done: the handling of the case created a degree of distrust of the police among Boston's African American community seldom seen anywhere.[35]

As bad as the Stuart debacle made relations between blacks and the police department, tensions worsened even further when police admitted that a separate offensive against gang-related crime that followed the Stuart case had, as the community had alleged, actually consisted of a campaign in which large numbers of black males in high-crime areas were stopped and frisked, often aggressively and indiscriminately. It is fair to say that Boston in the early 1990s was experiencing the worst of all law enforcement worlds: aggressive policing had totally alienated the community, severely exacerbated racial tension, and proven completely ineffective in reducing—let alone stopping—the wave of juvenile homicides and violence, which seemed only to be swelling.

But the lowest point was still to come. In May 1992, violence erupted at a funeral for the victim of a shooting. During the service at the Morning Star Baptist Church, gang members attacked each other; the church erupted in wild shooting, sending family members and congregants scurrying for cover.[36] One young man sustained multiple stab wounds; amazingly, the gunfire did not cause any injuries.[37] The brazenness of the attack galvanized the community, especially members of the black clergy. In response they formed the Ten-Point Coalition, an organization of some forty churches set up to confront the violence by reaching out to black and Latino youth most at risk for involvement in crime. Led by the Reverends Eugene Rivers, Ray Hammond, and Jeffrey Brown, the group began regular outreach in the streets, seeking out the gang members where they roamed.[38]

The work was difficult and not immediately rewarding in the ways the ministers hoped. Violence and shootings among young people in Boston were neither eliminated nor reduced in response to Ten-Point's street outreach efforts.[39] But, by continually coming back to the street, seeking gang members out, and showing they were committed to the struggle for the long haul, the ministers gained credibility with both the gang members and the community that served to bolster their efforts over time. They were also surprised at how often the young people asked for something the ministers were uniquely qualified to offer: spiritual counseling. Reverend Jeffrey Brown recalls that some of the most profound theological conversations he has had have occurred not at the divinity school he attended or at his church, but in the parks and on street corners with gang members.[40]

Perhaps most important, the ministers' work allowed them to forge a relationship with the antigang police officers. As both the ministers and the police officers became aware that both were out on the street consistently, working to reduce gang violence,[41] they gradually warmed to each other. Again, this produced few immediate tangible results, but it marked the beginning of a partnership crucial to later success.

In 1994, two years after the clergymen formed the Ten-Point Coalition, a small group of Boston antigang officers, now called the Youth Violence Strike Force, also came together to fight gangs and the violence they spawned. Humbled by the failures of the past and imbued with a desire to make a difference without creating further problems or exacerbating racial tensions, they were determined to find a new approach. Together with David Kennedy and his colleagues at the Kennedy School of Government at Harvard University, the officers formed the core of what became the Boston Gun Project. As time went on, more partners—the United States Attorney's Office in Massachusetts; the Bureau of Alcohol, Tobacco, and Firearms; the FBI; the county district attorney; the Boston Streetworkers (specialists in gang outreach work employed by the city of Boston in an effort to reach hard-core gang members); juvenile corrections authorities; and local parole and probation offices, among others—joined the team, which began to meet regularly in January 1995.[42] It was, David Kennedy recalls, the biggest attempt at problem-oriented policing yet seen, and in many ways it was the boldest, with its goal of stopping the widespread killing and violence that was affecting an entire city.[43]

Gun Project members from law enforcement, the probation department, and the Streetworkers group contended that juvenile homicide and violence had everything to do with gangs: both shooters and victims were usually gang members with substantial prior records as offenders and long probation histories, and the violence was largely driven by gang disputes.[44] Gun Project research proved this hypothesis correct. Just 1,300 members of sixty-one gangs bore responsibility for over 60 percent of the killings—a remarkable figure that showed how concentrated the violence was.[45] Clearly, the root of the problem lay in a small group of young people among whom there was a self-perpetuating dynamic of fear, gun acquisition, and preemptive and retributive shooting.

An initial clue about how to solve the problem came from the successful approach the Youth Violence Strike Force had used to attack a parallel but smaller-scale situation. Some months earlier in 1994, there had been a problem with one particular gang, which was then the most violent in the city. Paul Joyce, then a sergeant and the leader of the Strike Force, had created a simple but elegant approach, dubbed Operation Scrap Iron. Knowing that members of the one especially violent gang were chronic offenders, with long records and probation and parole conditions they had to meet, the Strike Force teamed up with the probation, parole, corrections, and youth services departments to systematically enforce every applicable law and regulation violated by these gang members. No offense was too small or unimportant to merit police attention: from shootings and other serious crimes, to unregistered vehicles, probation violations, and outstanding arrest warrants. Strike Force members delivered an unmistakable message to the gang members over and over, face to face: the high-pressure crackdown would stop when the violence stopped. At the same time, the Streetworkers, probation officers, and even the members of the Strike Force reached out to the gang members, offering alternatives to gang life: assistance, social services, schooling, whatever was necessary for someone who wanted to get out of the cycle of violence. The Strike Force had already had some experience with these alternative approaches: Paul Joyce and his colleagues had set up the Summer of Opportunity program in connection with the John Hancock

Life Insurance Company to provide summer internships and life-skills training to inner-city youth. They offered similar programs for children aged seven to fourteen, as well as recreational opportunities. Like the ministers in the Ten-Point Coalition, the members of the Strike Force understood that it was not enough to get people to stop behaving in a particular way; they also had to offer real alternatives. The idea of Operation Scrap Iron, Paul Joyce explains, was to move from reaction to prevention—at the very least, to add a prevention component to the work the Strike Force was doing.[46]

Beyond offering gang members an alternative to the gang life, the outreach program helped to gain back some of the community's trust. People who had seen the police department as little more than an oppressive occupying army now saw that the police clearly wanted to go beyond arrest, Joyce says.[47] The all-over-you-like-a-cheap-suit enforcement, together with the clear message that stopping the violence would stop the hyperenforcement and the offer of alternatives, achieved unprecedented success for Operation Scrap Iron. According to Harvard's David Kennedy, "The crew [gang] capitulated and even, in the end, turned in many of its firearms."[48]

By early 1996, the Gun Project decided to go forward with a citywide version of Operation Scrap Iron, called Operation Cease Fire. Instead of focusing on one gang in one area, all of Boston's gang-involved chronic offenders would get the message: the violence must stop. The word went out in May: gang by gang, group by group, the 1,300 players that the Gun Project's research and intelligence had identified were "called in" to meet with members of the Gun Project. At these meetings, help was offered to those who wanted to choose another way of life. There was also a warning: for those who would not listen, law enforcement would descend, swiftly and harshly. Cease Fire would prosecute not only state charges and violations of probation and parole but also violations of federal laws. The draconian federal sentences could put offenders in tough prisons far away, cutting them off from fellow gang members, families, wives, and girlfriends for many years.

By the fall of 1996, only months after Operation Cease Fire had begun, youth homicide rates fell by approximately 60 percent.[49] Adult homicide also fell, by about 50 percent.[50] Youth gun assaults dropped by a third.[51] In the month of November 1996, not a single person under twenty-four was killed—the first time this had happened over the course of a month since the explosion of youth violence in the late 1980s.[52] Kennedy insists that the reductions in murder and violence were both statistically real, not the chance result of existing trends in Boston or elsewhere: "Most of the decline in youth violence occurred between June and September 1996, followed by a new lower rate" from that point onward.[53] For a period of two and one-half years, not a single juvenile was killed with a handgun,[54] a level of reduction in youth violence no one would have dreamed of just a short time before.

As Operation Cease Fire gathered momentum, it quickly gained new partners, none more important than the clergymen of the Ten-Point Coalition. Although the Ten-Point Coalition had not been able to bring down violence and homicides through their own earlier efforts, they proved to be critical partners for Operation Cease Fire. The Coalition had already taken a crucial step in creating the conditions for Cease Fire's success when they had said, publicly and loudly, that black-on-black violence was not just a problem for the police or a pathology that originated outside the black community, like racial discrimination. It was, rather, a problem of and for the black community, which therefore needed to acknowledge and take responsibility for it. For David Kennedy, the Ten-Point Coalition's statements along these lines were "enormously important," because they gave Operation Cease Fire credibility: it could not be dismissed as some kind of coded permission for police to come down hard on all young black men, or to turn black neighborhoods upside down with aggressive tactics.

With their long history on the streets, the ministers of the Ten-Point Coalition were also well positioned to help distinguish between gang "wannabes," who might be reached with alternatives and offers of help, and the truly hard-core gang soldiers—those who made up the 1,300 real troublemakers. Thus, by becoming part of Operation Cease Fire, the members of the Ten-Point Coalition became important sources of intelligence for the police, enabling officers to target the right people. The black clergy also kept a keen eye on police conduct, and put all on notice that the black community would not accept anything less than proper, lawful, and respectful treatment from the police.

The clergy now saw that, in Operation Cease Fire, they were working with police officers and police leadership who wanted the problem solved "honestly and uprightly and transparently," not by the discredited methods of the late 1980s and early 1990s. Police Commissioner Paul Evans was unequivocal: the police department and its allies would defeat the violence problem, but not by mistreating people, cutting corners, or tearing up the Bill of Rights.

Christopher Winship and Jenny Berrien, authors of one of the most insightful scholarly investigations of the Boston situation, summarize Operation Cease Fire's working assumptions this way:

> [Y]outh violence needs to be dealt with as a criminal problem; some kids need to be jailed for both their own good and the good of the community; a small number of youths constitute most of the problem; the ministers will work with the police in identifying problem youth; the ministers will participate in the decisions about what happens to specific individuals; and if the police use indiscriminate and abusive methods in dealing with youths, the ministers will take the stories to the media.

After Boston went approximately two and a half years without a juvenile homicide, the press dubbed Operation Cease Fire "the Boston Miracle." It had taken hard work and an unprecedented level of partnerships—between police and social service workers and ministers, and also between state and municipal government—but the problem of juvenile homicide has remained low for an extended period. Later flare-ups of youth homicide proved to be isolated occurrences. The problem was greatly reduced, if not eliminated, along with other types of violence and killing in the city. A little-known fact tells the story: over the decade of the 1990s, the rate of homicides per capita dropped most not in New York but in Boston—75.1 percent versus 71.7 percent in New York.

By 2002, violent crime in Boston had fallen to its lowest level in thirty-one years.[55] The city now faces new challenges, particularly the enormous number of ex-offenders re-entering the city after long stints in prison, and the presence of "franchises" of stronger, more sophisticated gangs from outside the city, such as the Bloods, Crips, and Latin Kings. The Operation Cease Fire structure has not remained as active as it once was; with its dramatic success, there was simply no reason for it to remain so, and some of its central actors have moved on. Still, there is reason for hope. According to David Kennedy, initial efforts at solving these new problems seem promising. While cognizant of the difficulties they face, the major players in the effort remain confident that they will find themselves equal to the new challenges.

San Diego: The Case of the Blue Roofs

The San Diego Police Department must be near the top of any list of American police agencies that make the best and most consistent use of problem-solving approaches. Problem-solving has been a part of the organization's training and culture for so many years that it has become as natural a response for a San Diego police officer as responding to a 911 call. The case of the Blue Roofs is one of the department's exemplary successes.[56]

The case began with officers Tim Hall and Cindy Brady, who surveyed the community to which they were newly assigned to get a sense of residents' concerns. The responses showed a consistent theme: people complained about crime, including drug dealing, assaults, and drive-by shootings, at the Blue Roofs, a local apartment complex. Gang activity at the Blue Roofs made many of its neighbors too fearful to venture out even in broad daylight.

Statistics from the department's crime analysis unit showed Hall and Brady that calls for police service were, in fact, much higher at and near the Blue Roofs than elsewhere, and that many arrestees lived at the Blue Roofs. Senior staff confirmed that the Blue Roofs had been a trouble spot for twenty years. The officers learned that the Blue Roofs was owned by the same absentee owner who owned another troubled complex, the Gardens, which, like the Blue Roofs, had higher rates of 911 calls and arrests than apartments in the surrounding area. The two complexes also shared the same property manager, and both had almost 50 percent of their units subsidized by a government voucher program for low-income households called Section 8.[57]

Research at the local office of the Federal Department of Housing and Urban Development (HUD), which subsidized the Section 8 apartments at both the Blue Roofs and the Gardens, revealed that a primary problem at the complexes involved management. HUD had given the absentee owner a below-market-rate loan as an inducement to keep Blue Roofs available and open to subsidized tenants. The loan enabled the owner to take almost $17 million in cash equity out of the properties in exchange for $2 million in promised improvements. The officers studied best-property-management practices at their local housing commission and also recruited informants within the property management company so they could tell whether the company had followed through on its many commitments and promises. Everything they learned told them that management was doing a poor job of screening rental applicants, of enforcing house rules and the terms of rental agreements, was not making consistent and proper use of eviction practices and procedures, and was failing to make the improvements that they had promised HUD.

With this comprehensive analysis under their belts, and with the federal housing authorities backing them up, Hall and Brady asked the management company to replace its on-site manager, implement proper tenant screening, create house rules, clarify and enforce rental agreements, post private-property signs, track problem tenants, and document evictions. The officers also asked that the management company hire competent security after they discovered that the current guard had a criminal record and had fathered at least three children with three different residents.

The management company agreed to make these changes, but continuous monitoring of the situation by Hall and Brady showed that it did not follow through on the agreement. After instigating further meetings with HUD officials, Hall and Brady succeeded in ousting the on-site manager, but a succession of replacements proved little better. Indeed, Hall and Brady's informants reported that the management company's changes were an elaborate and deliberate stall; if enough time went by, the company figured, the officers would simply give up. Instead of giving up, Hall and Brady decided to try enforcing the state's civil nuisance laws, which gave municipal authorities the legal power to act when properties become dangerous threats to public health, safety, and welfare. The officers enlisted the police department's nuisance abatement unit to corral the owner, and his lawyer agreed to a meeting. In preparation, Hall and Brady conducted a tenant survey that yielded their most outrageous discovery yet: several female tenants claimed that maintenance men would make repairs only if the women had sex with them or bought drugs from them. This information was presented at the meeting, along with other evidence of mismanagement, a HUD audit, and statistics showing disproportionate calls for service and arrests. Since the management company had already committed to tenant screening, the officers presented the results of their own background checks on the four newest, supposedly screened, tenants. All had criminal records or histories as problem tenants that should have disqualified them, but the management company had rented to them anyway. The owner finally agreed that the management company had to go. HUD fined the owner $300,000, and gave him a list of required repairs.

After a year-long effort, Hall and Brady were finally in a position to assess their results. At long last, the owner hired a management company recommended by HUD that made more repairs in the first month than the other company had made in a year. A new on-site manager was installed—a no-nonsense type who regularly inspected the property and the grounds—and problem tenants were regularly evicted. Drug and gang activity did not disappear, but they were reduced, and the rate of 911 calls—the initial reason that Hall and Brady had focused on the Blue Roofs—dropped.

Hall and Brady followed the problem-solving model meticulously, going far beyond the typical role of police officers on the beat: they looked not at individual incidents but at the whole problem; they analyzed the situation thoroughly; and they assessed the success of their efforts. It was a difficult, long, but almost picture-perfect problem-solving effort that succeeded in improving life for tenants and their neighbors outside the properties.

Stamford, Connecticut: Preventing Juvenile Crime
During the Summer

Stamford, Connecticut's, School Resource Officer (SRO) Summer Camp looks like any other day camp. Groups of middle school kids play sports while others work with computers and video equipment or play board games. One group of thirteen- and fourteen-year-old girls learns martial arts from a parent volunteer. Each group has a supervising counselor, some of high-school age, others from colleges. But on any given day, a few of those present to supervise campers may be older and more authoritative-looking than the rest. They are police officers, the only tip-off that this is not only a summer camp but an effort to combat juvenile crime. Kids who attend the camp do not hang around downtown or at the mall in clusters, causing trouble. They are not out painting buildings with graffiti, or joining gangs. Instead, they are burning off energy in constructive ways and learning proper ways to relate to each other and to strong adult role models. They also have the promise of continued positive relationships with the camp and the staff because they are able to become counselors-in-training after eighth grade, and paid staff after that.

The story of how this camp got started begins with two dedicated, seasoned police officers, Jon Jeter[58] and Scott Baldwin,[59] Stamford's first School Resource Officers (SROs) posted to middle and high schools. Both men quickly came to love the assignment, even though some police officers denigrate it as "not real police work." Jeter and Baldwin rapidly began to appreciate that their new jobs gave them a chance proactively to prevent crime.

Near the end of his second year as a school-based officer, Jeter began to wonder: What about the summer? Both Jeter and Baldwin knew that many of the students most in need of their help attended summer school, but classes lasted only until noon, leaving them unsupervised and at risk for involvement in crime the rest of the day. The middle school kids in summer school were not eligible for traditional camps that started in the morning. They were too young for summer jobs and too old for child care. Jeter had spent his first summer as an SRO visiting traditional summer camps in Stamford to talk about gangs and other problems, so when Stamford's new police chief, Dean Esserman, met with the department's ten school-based officers to discuss their assignments for the summer months, Jeter took a chance. "Why don't we have our own camp?" he said to Esserman. Why not operate a camp in one of the schools, and begin the sessions right after summer school? The kids could be fed lunch and then participate in traditional camp activities the rest of the day. The officers would get to maintain and build on relationships started during the school year, and the kids could connect with them in a less formal setting than school. SROs would staff the camp, along with high school- and college-age kids who'd serve as paid counselors, providing them with summer jobs.

Esserman was immediately enthusiastic about the proposal and set about making Jeter's vision a reality. Consistent with his philosophy of connecting the police department with the community in every way possible, he put together a strategy that involved partnerships. He got Tony Mazzullo, the superintendent of Stamford's schools, to donate the use of one of its schools as a location for the camp and to supply buses for transportation. Mayor Dan Malloy agreed to involve the city's youth department. And Esserman got the Domus Foundation, a local philanthropic organization that had long sponsored youth programs in Stamford, to provide not just money but the administrative structure critical to running the camp smoothly and safely. Finally, Esserman took money from drug-bust forfeitures, funds usually earmarked for the department's antidrug teams, and used it for the camp instead.

Just weeks after Jeter and Baldwin proposed the idea to their chief of police, the SRO Camp was born. More than one hundred students attended the camp regularly that summer every day after summer school. Approximately fifty other young people had well-paid, resume-enhancing summer jobs as counselors. All ten of Stamford's school-based officers served as staff, maintaining continuity with the students with whom they worked during the school year. Jeter, who is now assistant chief of police, has a message for those who believe that running a summer camp is not "real" police work: such programs prevent crime in both the short and long term. Kids who attend camp aren't out committing crimes and are instead involved in activities designed to build long-term personal connections to police officers and other responsible adults.

Talking to the campers, one notices how much they like the counselors, most of whom are just five or six years older than they are. The counselors themselves seem to get almost as much out of the experience as the campers. Julie, an experienced counselor, says she's grateful for the chance to help kids in their early teens to come to terms with their problems and the issues in their lives. "Everyone deserves a second chance" at this age, she says, noting that she had also had a difficult time in her own life at the same stage. A large number of the counselors want to become professional youth workers: Cliff, a tall young man with a deep voice, wants to start and manage his own group home program, as do several others. All of the counselors have drawn from their own experiences a strong sense of how important it can be for young people, whose home lives are sometimes chaotic and difficult, to know that a kind, savvy person cares what happens to them.

Just as important, campers and counselors build upon relationships with the school-based officers and the police department, literally changing the perception of police in the community—one of the single most important things a police department must do in its struggle to make communities safe, livable places. Baldwin says that because of the SRO Camp, the kids come to trust the officers, making them more likely to come to the police when they have information useful to law enforcement or when they are trying to avoid gang recruitment. Virtually all of the campers say the same thing: they have become comfortable with police officers through the camp as well as through the SRO program at school. And this is true not just of campers, but of the counselors, too. Ralph, who has been a counselor at the camp since its inception, says that his school resource officer, Officer Maldonado, saw potential in Ralph and began to encourage him. When the camp program was first announced, Maldonado helped Ralph apply for a counselor's job. Ralph is hoping to gather the financial resources so that he can finish college and do work that helps young people. Told that he has the demeanor of a natural teacher, Ralph's face lights up and he smiles. "I've been told that," he says. "I'd like to do that." Given Ralph's deep connections to Officer Maldonado, one can also imagine him in another role: police officer.

The numbers bear out police officers' positive impressions. During Esserman's tenure and the years of the SRO Camp's full operation, crime in Stamford, including crime by youth and middle schoolers, dropped dramatically. While one could not say without more evidence that the camp *caused* this, an independent evaluation of the camp shows that it probably has a direct, positive influence on many important trends. The evaluation, prepared for the Office of Community Oriented Policing Services of the U.S. Department of Justice, found that the camp not only provides middle school children with a safe, secure, and enjoyable environment, but also significantly improves connections between police and the community in a number of important respects.[60] There was also evidence, the evaluation said, that the children who attend the camp resist gang involvement, drug use, and delinquent behavior.[61]

The summer of 2003 brought a sobering twist to the story of the SRO Camp. With the severe downturn in the U.S. economy, many of Stamford's businesses and public agencies that had contributed money and other resources to the camp in its first four years found themselves in financial trouble, and contributions from the private sector virtually dried up. Of all the parts of the local government that had contributed to the camp's success, only the police department could contribute anything at all: the time of four officers. The Domus Foundation maintained its support but at a reduced level. All at once, the camp went from over 200 campers to approximately thirty-five. Instead of every middle school student in the city being able to attend, eligibility was restricted to the children who would be attending the city's summer academy for "at-risk" youth. Far fewer counselors were hired. Thus many more kids too young for summer jobs were on the street after summer school, with nothing to do and all the time in the world to do it. Jon Hoch of the Domus Foundation, the executive director of the camp, says that its essential structure has been preserved in the hopes that funding will rebound. But there is little question that the camp's impact was vastly reduced in 2003.

Thus the summer of 2003 in Stamford amounted to an unusual unintended experiment: by scaling the SRO Camp back by almost 80 percent, the city had a chance to see just what effect there might be on crime. Early indications were not encouraging. "So far, it's been a hot summer for juvenile crime," Officer Tim Howard, one of the SRO Camp's police officers, reported in mid-July 2003. "We think, unfortunately, not having the camp for so many kids in this age group is making a difference."[62]

Statistics collected after the summer of 2003 showed that Officer Howard's early impressions had been correct: crime by juveniles had indeed increased. A comparison with juvenile crime in Stamford for the two prior years, with the camp operating at full strength, puts the point starkly.[63] From June 1 through August 31, 2001, with the camp operating at full capacity, Stamford police arrested 69 juveniles and charged them with 236 crimes.[64] Figures from June 1 through August 31, 2002, with the camp still taking all 200-plus children of middle school age in Stamford who wanted to attend, police made 57 arrests and charged them with 175 crimes[65]—a decline of 17 percent in arrests and 25 percent in crimes charged over the numbers from the summer of 2001. But from June to August 31, 2003, with the camp dramatically cut in size, police arrested 105 juveniles—an increase of 84 percent—and charged them with 414 crimes, a stunning jump of more than 230 percent.[66] While we cannot conclude from this that only the downsizing of the camp caused the jump in juvenile crime in Stamford in 2003—surely, there may have been other influences on the behavior of juveniles, too—these statistical shifts, immediately following a significant change in circumstances for those most at risk of offending in the age group (children in required summer school programs), on the heels of two years of *declining* crime in the same age group, seem too convenient to dismiss as a coincidence.

Dean Esserman, the former chief in Stamford who is now chief of police in Providence, Rhode Island, believes that the fully operating SRO Camp showed the best of what police work can do: preventing crime by connecting police officers with the communities they serve. "The best way to fight crime is to invest in our children before we need to arrest them," he says. "Any crime that we're preventing is a whole lot better than any criminal we're catching."

in any of these categories, PARS notes this with a yellow or red indicator, which alerts the officer's direct supervisor (usually a sergeant), who then investigates and makes a report and recommendation: retraining needed; monitor the officer; or no action needed, because there is an acceptable explanation for the officer's conduct. Those reports go to the district commanders, who review them and then present them to the police bureau's command staff at the quarterly meeting.

At the meeting, every person with responsibility for a police district or a similar command delivers a report on the officers he or she supervises. A district commander who is one of the first to speak[2] begins her report with group statistics: so many officers "indicated yellow" and so many "indicated red" for each of the categories of police behavior. The discussion then moves to individual officers. The commander says Officer A has indicated red for a high number of searches during the quarter. The report prepared by A's sergeant shows that this would be expected because A has been assigned to an antidrug task force that does a large number of searches, so no action is recommended; the commander says she agrees with A's sergeant. Officer B has had two traffic accidents in police cars in a relatively short period of time; consistent with B's sergeant's review and recommendation, B will be sent for some retraining and will be monitored during the next quarter. Officer C has indicated red for sick days; the commander says that the review by C's supervisor disclosed that C had had the flu for a week. No further action needed, the commander says.

The commander then reports on officers who were ordered to be monitored, retrained, or otherwise dealt with during the previous quarterly meeting—follow-up on previous recommendations. Officer D, who was put on the monitoring list the previous quarter because of a heated encounter with a fellow officer that resulted in a complaint, is reported to have had no further problems, and the commander says that monitoring will be discontinued. Officer E has successfully completed retraining in the use of pepper spray after a recommendation last quarter that followed a red indicator; no further action is needed. Officer F's attitude and verbal aggression toward the public and fellow officers often increased tensions in tough situations; the commander says close monitoring instituted last quarter will continue. Officer G, who had long-standing issues regarding cultural and ethnic diversity, would also be closely monitored.

And so it went, around the room. Each commander reported on every officer under their command who had been indicated as red or yellow during the past quarter, explained what the supervising sergeants had reported to them about the reasons for the conduct, and gave their own recommendations. In most cases, the recommendation was that no action was required; the PARS system had flagged the behavior but there was an adequate explanation and no reason to be concerned. Then came the follow-up reports from the prior quarter; in most of these cases, the recommendation that had been made—for counseling, retraining, or, most often, monitoring—had been completed and no further action was needed. In a couple of cases, however, supervisors had recommended that monitoring of an officer be discontinued based on only five random field observations by the supervisor. The district commander found this insufficient and said monitoring of the officer would have to continue for another quarter. The deputy chief agreed, and asked for the names of the supervisors who had recommended ending the monitoring based on just five field observations. "That just isn't acceptable. The chief has made clear that they have to do at least twice that many" field checks in order for the monitoring to pass muster. The deputy chief told the commander that he wanted the supervisors "talked to." Thus, rank-and-file officers weren't the only ones being held accountable through PARS; supervisors—the sergeants and lieutenants—felt it, too. The meeting continued in this same way, until every officer in every unit in the police bureau who had red or yellow next to his or her name had been discussed and dealt with in some way.

The PARS system in Pittsburgh represents a new and growing trend in police work: systems designed to build accountability into law enforcement agencies. The PARS system, with
its rapid, centralized collection of information on important elements of police officer behavior, allows an officer's supervisor to
see any trends or problems as they develop. With this system,
officers know that they are accountable for their behavior and
will therefore shape their behavior accordingly. Supervising sergeants and lieutenants know that they are accountable to their
district commanders for every officer they have who indicates
red or yellow and that they must investigate the underlying facts
and pass a comprehensive report up the chain of command in
order to carry out this responsibility. District commanders
understand that they are accountable to the senior command
staff and ultimately to Chief Robert McNeilly to show at each
quarterly meeting that they know what is happening with each
"red" or "yellow" officer in their bailiwick, and that they are ultimately responsible for what happens to every one of these
officers. This builds accountability into all levels of the department—accountability that can't be brushed off with comments
like, "Come on, he's a good officer; give the guy a break."

It is a truism among those who do police work and those
who study policing that 10 percent of the officers cause 90 percent of the problems a department has. The great power invest-
ed in our police forces, including the power to use deadly force,
make it incumbent on law enforcement agencies to identify
problem officers so that they can be counseled, retrained, monitored, and, when appropriate, disciplined or dismissed.

Accountability to the public, to the rule of law, and to the goal
of fair, effective, and constitutional law enforcement promises
the best possible chance not just to control the behavior of individual officers but to create a police culture in which officers
hold themselves and each other to a high standard of conduct
and honesty. Criminologist Samuel Walker, Isaacson Professor of
Criminal Justice at the University of Nebraska at Omaha and

one of the nation's foremost scholars on policing, asserts that police accountability "*is not a matter of a few rotten apples but of failed organizations.* . . . The challenge of police accountability is not how to 'get' a few bad officers but how to fix organizations." A single-minded focus on accountability gives us the best chance to achieve real organizational change.[3]

Accountability has always been the central concept for public institutions in a democratic society; voters in a representative democracy elect officials to represent them, as legislators, as officers of the executive branch, and in some places as judges. Periodic elections are democracy's most basic accountability device; even the least civically aware American knows that if elected officials do not perform as they should, the voters can "throw the bums out." This is accountability in its most elemental form: voters can punish substandard performance by "firing" their public officials.

Public institutions beyond those run by elected officials must also be accountable; a poorly run city department should suffer the wrath of the mayor and the city council on the public's behalf, through cuts in funding or replacement of the department's management. Those who work within these institutions must be held accountable also—to their mission, to the supervisory hierarchy of the department, and to the public itself.

While some top American police officials do run for office (primarily county sheriffs), accountability for police departments and police officers is not ensured through electoral mechanisms. But, given the scope of power afforded the police, accountability is still a critical issue; in the absence of electoral control, it must be built in by other means. The alternative is a loss of credibility and legitimacy incompatible with democracy. This is what has happened in the debate over racial profiling by police on roads and highways in the United States.[4] When a substantial number of people question whether police enforce the law fairly, they implicitly question the integrity of all police action. And if, for example, many people believe police officers enforce traffic laws in a racially biased fashion and are not held accountable, even those not personally affected will question the legitimacy of police authority, and of the law itself.

Police have a truly awesome array of powers granted to no one else in our society: they may interfere in our business, stop us, ask us questions, keep us from moving on our way. Police may deprive us of our liberty through the power of arrest, and they have the power to use force to make us comply with their lawful orders. They can even kill. Police need these powers to do the difficult job they have, but power of this magnitude without accountability is an open invitation to abuse. The point is emphatically *not* that all, or even most, police officers are bad, abusive, or rotten in some way; most are not. Rather, we simply know that police officers are people, and that the behavior of some people in any group will sometimes fall outside the bounds of what is acceptable. When those few do soil their badges, we must have ways to detect their actions and hold them accountable.

Police misconduct jeopardizes police departments themselves by destroying their reputations, demolishing public trust, and putting officers on the street in danger. In extreme instances, incidents of real or perceived misconduct may result in lawsuits costing millions of dollars in damages, and, in the worst cases, provoke riots, like those that exploded in Cincinnati in 2000 and in Benton Harbor, Michigan, in 2003. Accountability mechanisms therefore protect both citizens and police themselves and preserve the integrity and legitimacy of law enforcement from the worst impulses of a few.

Even so, most police officers and many police departments have until recently fought hard against almost all methods of insuring accountability, relying on the principle long cherished among police that they and they alone are competent to oversee law enforcement. Many officers feel that their job is so difficult, so dangerous, and so singular that no one who does not also wear the uniform can possibly understand it and

that no civilian should sit in judgment of the actions of a
police officer. As long ago as 1960, the International Association of Chiefs of Police (IACP) stated its "unequivocal and vig-
orous opposition to and rejection of" any attempt by civilians
to review complaints of police misconduct.[5] During the 1960s,
Los Angeles police chief William Parker dismissed proponents
of civilian oversight and all critics as radical antipolice agita-
tors intent on destroying the ability of the police to keep criminals in check.[6]

The most implacable opponents of accountability mechanisms have often been police unions. According to Samuel
Walker, of the University of Nebraska, the movement toward
police accountability in the 1960s galvanized officers; they
reacted to proposals for "civilian interference" by unionizing.
Only a few major cities had police unions in the early 1960s; by
the early 1970s, police unions existed in almost every city
except in the southeastern U.S.[7] The unions dismissed proponents of accountability as professional antipolice troublemakers bent on destroying society. They argued that oversight
would be a waste of resources because police departments
could handle complaints against them on their own. Police
officers, they argued, should not be overseen by "amateurs"
who had no experience "on the street." To the unions, accountability was just a cover for attempts to intimidate police
officers out of enforcing the law, for the benefit of criminals.
They admitted to no problem with police misconduct that
would warrant such civilian interference.[8]

These arguments might carry some weight if the evidence
didn't show that the police actually monitor themselves poorly, sporadically, or not at all. According to Walker, police
departments have failed by and large to establish working
complaint procedures or other mechanisms to hold their own
officers accountable. Both the Mollen Commission,[9] which
examined corruption in New York City, and the Christopher
Commission,[10] which studied the problems of the Los Angeles

Police Department in the wake of the Rodney King riots, found "not only patterns of serious misconduct by police officers, but also a consistent failure . . . to investigate allegations and discipline guilty officers."[11]

The example of Los Angeles is particularly disheartening. Even after the Rodney King riots, so little changed in the LAPD that just a few years later the department was rocked by another scandal: officers detailed to the Ramparts station were found to have handcuffed a suspect, shot him, planted drugs on him, and then arrested him for narcotics trafficking.[12] This led to the discovery of a deeply ingrained pattern of serious misconduct at Ramparts; as of mid-2000, the state had been forced to free approximately one hundred convicted criminals, and thousands of cases were under review.[13] In its own internal report on the Ramparts scandal, the LAPD said that its internal procedures for accountability, personnel evaluation, and integrity control, put in place as reforms after the Christopher Commission's report, had completely failed.[14]

Unfortunately, the "only we can police ourselves" attitude persists among some officers today. Sergeant Jim Malloy of the Pittsburgh Police Bureau, a thirty-seven-year police veteran who has also been a member and an official of the Fraternal Order of Police in Pittsburgh since at least 1974, dismisses computerized monitoring systems like PARS out of hand. The only accountability system necessary, Malloy says, is himself and his fellow sergeants.[15] "Do they think I need this computer to determine how my people work for me out here? You'd have to be a goddamned imbecile and not worth the money that's paid to you if you don't know who's working and who's screwing off. I know who's working . . . I know who's clearing cases and who's not clearing cases, and I know who's abusing authority and who's not. There is no problem."

Despite such attitudes, there has been a noticeable turn in law enforcement toward accountability. Chief McNeilly of Pittsburgh, who brought the PARS system to his department, says,

"I look at police chiefs and assistant chiefs and commanders as being CEOs and executive officers of businesses."[16] The Pittsburgh Police Bureau has a budget of roughly $70 million a year, almost 20 percent of Pittsburgh's total municipal budget; it has almost 900 sworn officers and hundreds of civilian staffers.[17] McNeilly is not suggesting that the police bureau be "run like a business," but rather that running any large institution in a virtual information vacuum concerning the behavior of the personnel seems inconceivable. "How can anyone run a [multi]-million-dollar [institution] without knowing what's going on," asks McNeilly, and without putting mechanisms in place to assure that employees do the right things? This requires accurate information on how officers perform and a system that uses the information to hold them accountable. Even if rank-and-file officers do not always agree, McNeilly's attitude squares with that of other departmental heads. Chiefs don't want direct control of the officer in the field or the supervising sergeant or lieutenant, but they do want to make sure their entire staff works according to the department's standards and mission.

Other proponents of police accountability include legal advisors and risk managers—unheard of in American policing until recently—who are charged with reducing police departments' litigation and damages costs.[18] Police departments often sustain large damage awards when officers fail to abide by departmental policies, and these awards have grown larger in the past decade and a half. The Los Angeles County Sheriff's Department paid over $15 million in damages for excessive force cases between 1989 and the middle of 1992.[19] Between 1994 and 2000, New York City *alone* paid victims of police misconduct almost *$180 million* in fines and out-of-court settlements.[20] Accountability mechanisms promise to help control such costs by heading off the behavior that leads to lawsuits.

Preventive policing entails two equally important types of accountability: internal accountability, including officer accountability to police supervisors and to the department's policies, mission, and goals; and external accountability, to constituencies outside the police department.

INTERNAL ACCOUNTABILITY

Internal accountability refers to the methods, devices, and mechanisms that departments themselves can use to guarantee that police officers and their supervisors carry out their jobs in accordance with the law and the department's rules, standards, policies, and goals. As in any organization with more than a few employees, those in charge cannot simply assume that the policies they set, the rules they make, and the goals they wish to achieve always guide the behavior of subordinates. Internal accountability supplies a way to help insure that they do.

Early Warning Systems

The PARS system in Pittsburgh represents the state of the art for early-warning systems. An outside evaluation of the Pittsburgh Police Bureau conducted by the Vera Institute of Justice in 2002 found the PARS system to be a model for police departments across the nation. The concept of early warning systems dates back at least to 1981 with the appearance of *Who Is Guarding the Guardians?*[21] the U.S. Civil Rights Commission's landmark report on police misconduct. The commission's report recommended that all police departments create early-warning systems that would identify police officers "who are frequently the subject of complaints or who demonstrate identifiable patterns of inappropriate behavior."[22] As noted earlier, the idea of such a system has its foremost scholarly champion in Samuel Walker of the University of Nebraska, who has conducted much of the groundbreaking research involving early warning systems and has helped design several pioneering versions of these systems for police departments. In research for the National Institute of Justice, Walker and his colleagues argued that what police executives had long said was in fact true: a very small percentage of any department's officers cause the lion's share of its citizen complaints.[23] In Kansas City, for instance, 2 percent of its officers caused over 50 percent of the complaints filed against the department.[24] In Boston, a 1992 report found that 11 percent of all Boston police officers were responsible for "waves of abuse."[25] In Los Angeles, the Christopher Commission found that just forty-four of the department's 8,500 officers were responsible for twelve times as many complaints as all others in the department.[26] Herman Goldstein, the father of problem-oriented policing, had observed even before 1981 that problem police officers "are well known to their supervisors, to the top administrators, to their peers, and to the residents in areas in which they work," but that generally nothing was done to change their conduct.[27]

A lack of the institutional will necessary to hold officers accountable was not the only problem. The information that would alert a supervisor or commander to a pattern of misconduct was often scattered across a number of different places within the police department. Records of discipline imposed would be recorded in personnel files; citizen complaints would appear in the files of the department's internal affairs division; records of vehicle accidents would be in the files at the department motor pool; records of sick days taken and outside employment would be found at the payroll office. This "multiple file drawer problem" made it difficult and sometimes impossible to track indicators of potential officer misconduct. But the burgeoning of information technology during the 1980s and 1990s that allowed relatively small computer systems to handle large amounts of data made it possible for a complete picture to emerge—in Walker's phrase, "a database police management tool designed to identify officers whose behavior is problematic." As of 1999, 27 percent of the police agencies serving populations of 50,000 or more that responded to a national survey had an early-warning system,

with half of these systems created since 1994 and a third created since 1996. Another 12 percent reported that they
planned to put an early-warning system in place.[28]

The evidence shows that early-warning systems can and do
reduce problems among police officers, and that they have this
effect across systems with different characteristics. Evaluations
of the effectiveness of the early-warning systems in Minneapolis, New Orleans, and Miami by Walker and his colleagues all
showed "a dramatic effect on reducing citizen complaints and
other indicators of problematic police performance among
those officers subject to intervention."[29] In Minneapolis,
officers who had gone through early-warning–based intervention experienced an average of 67 percent fewer complaints
one year after the intervention; in New Orleans, the drop was
61 percent. In Miami-Dade, only 4 percent of the early-warning
group had zero use-of-force reports before intervention; after
intervention, that number climbed to 50 percent.[30]

The impact of the system on supervisors is harder to measure but may be just as important. Anecdotal accounts from
supervising sergeants and command officers in Pittsburgh suggest that the PARS system has resulted in an increased work-
load for sergeants and even some lieutenants, as they are forced
to devote time and energy to monitoring "indicated" officers,
designing and implementing intervention strategies, and
preparing reports on the process. But these stories also validate
the educated guesses of anyone who has taken a hard look at
PARS and other early-warning systems: they force the entire
chain of command, down to the sergeants who provide the
frontline supervision in the department, to focus on indicators
of potential misconduct and to take action at an early stage. If
they do not do so, anyone in the entire command staff, not just
the sergeants, stands to suffer the less-than-delicate attention
of Chief McNeilly. Pat Sullivan, a former consultant to the Pitts-
burg police who helped design the PARS system, says, "Woe
unto the commander who gets caught not knowing something

in the [PARS] report that [Chief] McNeilly has seen and wants to know about."[31] According to Samuel Walker, the very existence of such systems "communicates to supervisors their responsibility to monitor officers who have been identified by the program."[32]

In terms of the department as a whole, Walker says, it is unlikely that one would find an effective program in a department not already committed to accountability throughout the organization; conversely, even a very good early-warning system could not create support for accountability if the department has not committed itself to the idea already. But the data that these systems generate can help spot overall patterns and issues that point to possible changes needed in policies, procedures, or training. For example, Commander Linda Barone of Pittsburgh says that data from the PARS system on "subject resistance" (what most other departments call "use of force") indicated a problem: officers seemed hesitant to use the full amount of reasonable force that the law said they could, with the result that some situations were spiraling out of control and more serious uses of force became unnecessarily common. The data were strong enough, Barone says, that the department responded with a three-day retraining session for the entire force on legal and helpful aspects of nonlethal force. Following the implementation of the training, she says, "subject resistance" reports actually dropped. Reports from incidents after the training indicated that greater willingness to use low levels of force when necessary was helping officers keep control of situations that had, in the past, become more serious.[33] Barone says the department went through a similar process when the PARS data revealed an excessive number of complaints about rudeness and poor communication by officers. The department responded with a training course in using communications skills to de-escalate tense situations.[34]

Early-warning systems are no panacea for troubled police officers or dysfunctional police departments. First, they are

"only one of many tools needed to raise standards of performance" in order to move a department toward full accountability
through better management.[35] "Early-warning systems . . . are
not mechanical devices that can be programmed to automati-
cally sound an alarm," warns Samuel Walker. Rather, they are
"extremely complex, high-maintenance administrative systems that require close and on-going human attention."

Pittsburgh's Barone says, "It still comes down to accountability." The system "does not even really identify problem officers.
It just puts the relevant information in front of supervisors,"
who combine it with their own knowledge and experience.
There is still "no substitute for judgment. You must be engaged
as a supervisor" with your officers. If you are, Barone says, you'll
be able to tell which officers with higher-than-average arrests or
searches and seizures are doing their jobs properly and which
ones are not. The system "just makes it easier to see what could
be indicators of problems" before they develop, by systematically putting potential clues in front of the supervisor and requiring the supervisor to respond.[36] Viewed this way, early intervention systems are a big net plus.[37] They implant the idea of
accountability directly into the department's internal wiring.

Departmental Policies

Departmental policies crafted *by* members of the police department *for* members of the police department have almost auto-
matic legitimacy among the rank and file who must obey them.
They are more likely to be implemented, and more likely to be
followed (even when unpopular) than pronouncements on
police behavior that come from other institutions, such as
courts or legislative bodies. That is why formal departmental
policies concerning accountability and other aspects of preventive policing are essential. Policies describe the contours of
proper conduct by setting out the general parameters of how
police officers should respond to situations they face repeatedly. The aim is not to command minutely but to guide generally.

Internal policies are also necessary for fair enforcement of standards of conduct. Without a clear policy, disciplinary authorities within the department seeking to enforce standards find themselves without a proper legal basis. Just as important, internal policies can help form a bulwark against unwarranted findings of legal liability for officer misconduct. Officers usually have immunity from lawsuits in cases of police misconduct as long as they act in good faith; police departments, however, often represent a tempting deep-pocketed target for any plaintiff. By putting policies in place in advance, a department goes a considerable way toward insulating itself from charges that it must share blame for the damage caused by police officers who fail to conduct themselves appropriately.

Though they may be met with skepticism, departmental policies can dramatically affect police behavior and culture. Policies on the use of force and on high-speed police pursuits of suspects offer good examples. Both have evolved considerably over the last ten to fifteen years, as police chiefs have made a concerted effort to respond to citizen complaints and damage awards by juries. For example, in the first decade that police departments began to use internal policies to regulate and limit the use of force by officers (from the late 1960s through the late 1970s), the number of citizens shot and killed by police dropped dramatically.[38] What is more, the large racial disparity in police shootings, with blacks much more likely than whites to die by a police officer's bullet, was cut in half.[39] On the subject of high-speed pursuits, criminologist Geoffrey Alpert of the University of South Carolina examined the effectiveness of police policies regulating them.[40] In all three jurisdictions Alpert examined, police pursuits involved minor offenses like traffic infractions more often than felonies. In Omaha, Nebraska, accidents with injuries occurred in 14 percent of the pursuits; in Aiken county, South Carolina, personal injuries occurred in 12 percent of pursuits. In the Metro-Dade (Miami) area of Florida, however, which had almost six times the number of pursuits as the other two areas combined, there were accidents with personal injuries in an astounding 41 percent of all chases. Accidents with property damage occurred in at least 20 percent of all of the chases in all three jurisdictions, and in Omaha damage occurred in 40 percent of all chases.

Both the Metro-Dade and Omaha police departments made changes in their pursuit policies: Metro-Dade's new policy sought to restrict pursuits, while Omaha's new policy gave police officers wider latitude in initiating chases. Alpert found that policy changes did indeed matter. Metro-Dade's restrictive new policy resulted in a drop in pursuits of over 80 percent. For Omaha, the more permissive new policy also made a difference: the number of police chases *increased* more than sevenfold. The new policies really did change officer behavior—for the better in the case of Metro-Dade, making citizens safer from the danger posed by these chases; for the worse in Omaha, by greatly increasing chases.

A recent example of departmental policy change on high-speed chases adds important details that show real gains in public safety from policies limiting chases. For years, the Los Angeles Police Department has had a reputation of initiating chases frequently. These high-speed pursuits, and the accidents, injuries, and deaths that they caused, had become so common that Los Angeles television stations regularly broke into their programming to show live police chases filmed from the air. By early 2003, however, concerns resulting from a series of deaths and injuries in chases led police and public officials to adopt a new policy: police could no longer initiate a chase for a simple "infraction," the least serious type of offense.[41] The policy also gave officers much more discretion to cut off chases after they began, and encouraged the use of helicopters to track fleeing suspects. By the middle of 2003, police chases had fallen 62 percent, a drop one police critic called "astounding."[42] Traffic collisions resulting from these chases have also fallen dramatically. In April through June 2003, eighteen civilian drivers or pedestrians were involved in accidents as a result of chases, compared with fifty-eight in the same period of the prior year. Injuries also dropped, to four from eighteen a year earlier.[43] While those who had opposed the policy had predicted that it would lead to fewer arrests and an increase in crime, especially auto thefts and vehicle break-ins, the opposite turned out to be true. Arrests increased 10 percent, and auto thefts and vehicle burglaries fell by over 2 percent.[44]

Setting sound police policy works. As the statistics show, there is no question that policy can change police behavior. We cannot overlook this if we wish to ensure police accountability.

Compstat: Data Gathering with an Accountability Punch

Among all of the innovations in police accountability over the last twenty years, few have become better known than the Compstat system. Conceived in 1994 for the New York City Police Department by then-commissioner of police William Bratton[45] and his deputy, Lieutenant Jack Maple,[46] Compstat was designed to ensure that the police in New York did everything possible to fight crime. Compstat is an excellent idea and an important accountability mechanism. Compstat, or something like it tailored to the particulars of individual jurisdictions, should be adopted as a component of preventive policing everywhere in the country.

Bratton, who headed the Boston Police Department and New York's Transit Police before becoming NYPD's commissioner, and who as of this writing leads the Los Angeles Police Department, says that Compstat had much to do with the NYPD's success in fighting crime in New York City in the 1990s.[47] When he went to New York, Bratton says, he found to his surprise that he could not get information on crime patterns that was less than forty-five days old. Bratton knew that the NYPD would have to respond much more quickly than that in order to turn crime around. Bratton and Maple devised a system that would allow field commanders to respond to crime almost as soon as patterns began to emerge. The process had three layers. First, information on crimes would be entered into a computerized database as soon as possible; in no event would it take more than twenty-four hours for the data to be available to command staff. Second, command staff would be held responsible for understanding the patterns that emerged from the data, and for mounting initiatives in response. The NYPD command staff, all the way from precinct commanders to borough commanders to the very top levels of the department, including Bratton, Maple, and other members of Bratton's inner circle, would all be intimately familiar with the data and what it showed, and all commanders would be held accountable for this knowledge at regular Compstat meetings, at which the data would be disseminated and discussed. Third, field commanders would make a presentation to the top staff in the Compstat meeting, discussing every bit of relevant crime data from their jurisdictions, their analysis of the data for patterns, trends, issues, and problems, and the responses they had designed and implemented.

It is fair to say that presenting crime data and crime-fighting plans at a Compstat meeting gives new meaning to the phrase "being on the hot seat." The presentations are often grueling, even bruising, affairs. One police commander who did not wish to share either his name or duty assignment characterized the process of giving a report at Compstat as a combination of close combat and third-degree interrogation. "When you look up *brutal* in the dictionary," the commander said, "there's a picture of a guy presenting his stuff at a Compstat meeting."[48] At one recent Compstat meeting,[49] the borough commander presenting crime data told the NYPD's senior officers, including Commissioner Raymond Kelly, that there had been an uptick in the number of homicides in the previous three months in his jurisdiction. Before the commander could get through the homicide data on the chart projected on the screens around the room, the senior officers pounced. "So what's the problem here?" said one. "I mean, I see the numbers, but what's the pattern you see that explains the increases?" "What is it?" another immediately chimed in, before the commander could respond to the first question. "Is it, what, like drugs or gang activity or what? Have you nailed it down?" The borough commander began to explain that he thought that it might have something to do with both. "What, you don't know? I think what we'll have to do," said a third member of Commissioner Kelly's staff, "is go through all of these killings one by one."

The commander seemed momentarily nonplussed; he stood mute for a long second, and the expression on his face showed just a hint of confusion and fear. But he recovered quickly, moving directly into an explanation of the first of the homicides. He knew many particulars of the individual cases— where the killings had happened, what they appeared to be about (a drug deal gone bad or an argument over a girlfriend, for example), whether an arrest had been made—and when he did not, he nodded to a subordinate who stepped forward and filled in the picture. There were often detailed questions from the senior staff about the cases and what had been done to follow up on them; senior staff also periodically returned their questioning to the commander, asking him what overall pattern he saw in the homicides. At every juncture, the commander and his subordinates were repeatedly and forcefully pressed: What were the details? If the case was still open, what were they doing to investigate? And how did the case fit in to overall patterns of crime in the district?

This exacting process continued for well over an hour before there was a brief break in the session. At this point, one of the senior staff members doing the questioning explained to me privately that there was indeed a strategy behind what might have seemed like the unrelenting application of command authority for its own sake. "We've been over the data," he said, referring to himself and his fellow senior officers. "We can see there's no real pattern here. There doesn't seem to be any connection between these homicides. It's just an increase, and sometimes those things just happen. We just want to see that they've turned over absolutely every rock before they're even willing to think about saying that there's no pattern. This is our way of letting him and his guys know that they're responsible for it and we're watching. What we'd really be concerned about is if they hadn't looked for a pattern."

There are severe consequences for those commanders who show themselves unable to produce information, analysis, and a description of their plans to meet the challenges of crime in their jurisdictions. Any commander unfamiliar with the data for his or her command area, or incapable of understanding the data, or who does not have a plan formulated, if not already implemented, to meet the problems shown in the analysis of the data, or who cannot produce evidence that the measures he or she has implemented have had the desired effect, does not last long in the accountability-driven Compstat environment.

Compstat's rapid collection and dissemination of data on crimes is surely important. But the data alone, no matter how well systematized, disseminated, and analyzed, would not necessarily result in crime reduction, or in any change in the department unless commanders were held accountable for addressing what the data showed. While Compstat is thought of as a computerized data-collection system (its name is short for "computerized statistics"), it is accountability, and the system created to insure it, that gives the process real traction as a crime-fighting tool.

The Compstat system requires accountability not just of the department's upper ranks who might end up presenting data at a Compstat meeting; it has pushed accountability downward, into the rank and file. A visitor to borough command and precinct facilities in one of New York City's outer boroughs sees immediately how thoroughly Compstat-based accountability permeates every corner of the department across the

city. The borough command center, a solid, utilitarian building, houses police officers performing the functions associated
with most police administrative operations. In almost all of the
overcrowded office spaces, there is a posting of Compstat numbers for the borough. Sometimes the posting is a photocopied
sheet, listing figures for various serious crimes tacked to a bulletin board; sometimes it is a large chart or an erasable white-
board. Other rooms have posters that have been written upon
and erased over and over again. All of them display numbers
on the most serious crimes: homicides, shootings, serious
assaults, rapes, auto thefts, and the like. Many of these post-
ings, especially the whiteboards, carry a weeks' worth of day-
by-day figures for each type of crime, with a number for that
same crime for the same date a year earlier. A visit to a precinct
headquarters shows the very same pattern: every room in
which significant police business takes place has some posting
of Compstat material, many of them including the "same-date-
last-year" comparison. Even to the uninitiated, the message
could not be clearer: reducing crime matters; we have the
crime numbers to track how successful we are in fulfilling this
mission; if what we're doing isn't working, it will be obvious
for all to see. We are all accountable for the results.

Arguably, the numbers one sees posted go further than is
necessary or even useful in some ways. It is unlikely that anyone gets any real insight from comparing the crime statistics
of August 26 of this year to the crime statistics of the same date
last year. Particular crime data from specific dates have little
meaning; trends over time are what really indicate whether
crime is becoming less common. But this should not obscure
the larger point that making the field commanders accountable for crime reduction, with real consequences for failure to
meet the goal, leads to better results.

The success of the Compstat process has bred imitators in
police departments across the country, and justifiably so. Looking at these other processes, one immediately sees that it is not

Compstat's well-known pressure-cooker atmosphere that makes it successful. A harsh or confrontational New York style probably would not work in other places. Like any good set of procedures based upon a well-known and successful model, other police departments have shaped their Compstat-like processes to fit their own jurisdictions. The police in Overland Park, Kansas, use a Compstat-like process to assure that their department's strategic goals are being met. Called Abstrat, the process follows the Compstat model in most important respects.[50] First, data are collected, analyzed, and disseminated with a state-of-the-art computer system. These data concern the strategic goals of the department from top to bottom—everything from fewer automobile accidents with injuries at high-accident locations to raising arrest rates for serious crime. In each category, a particular police officer is named as responsible for the attainment of the department's goals. Those goals, based on comparisons to the averages of the last three years of the same activity, are listed along with the goals and how close the department has come to attaining them. All of these goals are discussed in a periodic meeting of the department's top staff and those responsible for achieving them. Captain John Jackson of the Overland Park Police Department explains that the atmosphere in these meetings is much different from what he has heard about the Compstat meetings in New York. The meetings are not "adversarial," Jackson says. The tone is much more cooperative, even collegial. Still, he says, the differences between Abstrat and Compstat are less important than what they have in common: a core requirement of accountability. Just as in New York, commanders assigned responsibilities who are not familiar with the relevant data, who have no plan in the works or implemented to get to the strategic goal that is their responsibility, or who do not produce results, do not last. "Do it," Captain Jackson says, "or you're gone." The feel and the tone might be different in Kansas than in New York, but the bottom line is the same: you're accountable, we're measuring and analyzing the data, and if you're not

doing the job, you will not keep your responsibilities and certainly will not move up to more important ones. By Jackson's
reckoning, the Abstrat system has helped focus everyone on the
department's mission and goals and has helped it move in the
direction it needs to go better than at any other time since he
has been part of the organization.

EXTERNAL ACCOUNTABILITY

Citizens have traditionally exerted control over police departments indirectly, through elected and appointed officials.
Police departments are overseen by the mayor, who typically
hires and fires the chief. The municipal legislative body usually has authority over the department's budget, and may also
have the power to confirm or withhold approval of the mayor's
nominee for chief. Courts also hold police officers accountable
for their conduct, both through lawsuits for alleged violations
of constitutional rights and through motions to suppress evidence in criminal cases in which police have allegedly violated
the Fourth, Fifth, or Sixth amendments to the Constitution.

But over the past twenty-five years, public support for involving citizens directly in police accountability has increased. Voters
have established bodies to insure accountability through citizen
oversight in San Francisco (1982), Portland, Oregon (1982), and
San Diego County, California (1991), and a Harris poll released in
1992 showed that 80 percent of those surveyed wanted a police
review process that involved both citizens and police.[51] Exposure
to community policing and problem-solving approaches has
helped to change the attitudes of police chiefs, making them less
likely to oppose accountability and citizen oversight.[52] For
officers and commanders who use problem-oriented policing,
accountability devices seem familiar; when a citizen-oversight
board reviews police practices and policies to verify the existence
of a systemic problem, they use a prototypical problem-solving
approach. Problem-oriented policing has proven itself successful

at solving problems on the street; certainly it can also help address problems within police agencies as well. Two forms of citizen oversight, the complaint review system and independent auditors, show signs of success around the country.

Complaint Review Systems

Complaint review systems are the most familiar type of external oversight mechanisms that allow citizens to become directly involved in monitoring and supervising their local police departments. Complaint review systems usually consist of appointed boards of private citizens who collectively review complaints about the conduct of particular officers in specific incidents. If the board finds that an officer's conduct has violated a law, or a standard, rule, or policy of the police department, it typically recommends consequences to the chief of the department, who may accept, reject, or modify the recommendations.

Complaint review systems have a mixed record nationally. Some have performed well; others have failed utterly; still others have hobbled along for years without being of much use to anyone. Some have proven so ineffectual that they have eventually been abolished; others were weakened or killed by the opposition of police unions.

Assuring public confidence in the fairness of the procedures for handling complaints is one of the most important functions that external accountability devices serve. It is perhaps just as important that the resolution of complaints *appears* to be fair as it is that the process actually be fair. As police officers and administrators often point out, their departments almost always have some kind of internal investigative arm, usually called the Internal Affairs Division. Internal affairs, staffed and run by police officers, investigates citizens' complaints and also investigates complaints made by officers against each other; it also assists in corruption investigations. Internal affairs may be highly professional and respected within their departments, and their judgments may be accepted by officers. (This is not always the case; the officers in these units are sometimes hated and treated as pariahs.) Still, no matter how good a job Internal Affairs does with citizen complaints, the legitimacy of its work will always be questioned by some citizens who see their determinations as inherently suspect because of potential conflicts of interest; thus the need for some kind of outside independent review involving citizens.

In order for citizen complaint review systems to have a chance to succeed, they need particular powers. Any agency that will make decisions on citizen allegations of police misconduct must, for example, be able to collect relevant information and compel witnesses—including police officers—to testify. Thus, the power to issue subpoenas and to impose fines and jail time on those who fail to comply is essential to effective oversight. A complaint investigation system with responsibility for fact-finding "that cannot require officers to testify is doomed to ineffectuality."[53] Like citizen oversight itself, however, subpoena power has been immensely unpopular with police unions. Police unions have repeatedly challenged oversight agency subpoena power in court, even though courts have tended to uphold the subpoena power once enacted.[54] In other instances, unions have attempted to defeat the subpoena power by negotiating clauses into police contracts that allow officers to ignore citizen review agencies, or by telling their members that they cannot respond to subpoenas to testify without putting themselves in legal jeopardy.[55]

Another key issue for citizen review boards is having a reasonable standard of proof. In any case in which there will be a decision about what happened under a set of rules, the parties—here, the complaining citizen and the police officer—become adversaries. The complaining party bears the burden of proof. If the complainant rightly bears the burden of proving what he or she asserts, the question becomes, how much evidence must the complainant bring forward in order to support the complaint? The law calls this idea the *standard of proof*. If it is too high (for example, requiring proof "beyond a reasonable doubt" as is proper for criminal cases), most complaints will fail. A more appropriate standard is that typically used in civil cases: "the preponderance of the evidence" (more than 50 percent of the evidence). This requires a strong degree of proof, but not so much that few complainants will ever meet it.

Complaint review agencies must also have the responsibility, the duty, and the power to make binding determinations on the complaints that come before them. Without this, they are toothless. However, there is a crucial distinction between findings of fact and disciplinary decisions. Citizen complaint review agencies should make the final determination on the facts, but, as criminologist Samuel Walker argues, disciplinary determinations are best reserved for chiefs. Taking disciplinary authority from chiefs weakens them within their organizations and ultimately diminishes their accountability. A citizen complaint review body, as Walker says, can do much to improve accountability without disciplinary power simply by focusing public attention on the chief's responsibility to impose discipline, and by holding the chief accountable for failing to do so.

The assurance of adequate staff to carry out their responsibilities has been a constant problem for complaint review agencies. Meager budgets that cannot cover the costs involved in the oversight process can hamstring an agency. Without the resources to pay for an adequate investigation staff, agencies that have fact-finding power actually have it in name only. Despite the common focus on the subpoena power, it is actually a lack of staff resources that has most undermined the effectiveness of complaint review agencies. Cities such as Baltimore and Omaha have review boards with little ability to do anything because they have no staff; at one point, Omaha's board ceased operation.[56] Cincinnati's Office of Municipal Investigations had one staff member for a police department of 1,000 sworn officers; it was eventually replaced by another agency.[57] In Washington, D.C., the Citizen Complaint Review Board had one staff member for almost 1,200 officers; an external report concluded that for the first ten years of its existence, "it was literally impossible for the CCRB to perform delegated functions in an efficient . . . manner," and the agency was eventually abolished.[58] In Oakland, California, the Citizens' Police Review Board addressed the staffing issue in one of its annual reports with refreshing candor: "With only one investigator the goals mandated . . . for handling individual complaints are not being met and cannot possibly be met."[59]

The policing profession has developed no professional standards for investigative staffing at independent complaint review agencies, or even for departmental internal affairs units.[60] Nevertheless, at least one city has taken on the issue directly. In 1995, the voters of San Francisco passed a referendum called Proposition G, which amended the city charter[61] to require that, beginning July 1, 1996, the Office of Citizen Complaints (OCC) would have one investigator for every 150 sworn officers in the San Francisco Police Department. If the ratio of one investigator to 150 sworn officers is not met for any period of thirty days, the director of the OCC may hire, and the city comptroller must pay, a temporary investigator until the city hires as many permanent investigators as necessary to restore the 1–150 ratio. Proposition G also prohibited any reduction in the size of San Francisco's sworn police force below 1993–1994 staffing levels of 1,971 officers, so that the OCC must have no fewer than thirteen investigators on its staff. This ratio of 1 to 150 is reasonable. Most other departments with complaint review bodies have investigator-to-officer ratios far below this level, raising troubling questions about their ability to have any real effect.

The people who make up the complaint review agency, particularly the investigative staff, should themselves meet high ethical standards. They should also be, and appear to be, independent of the police department. It is easy to see why some complaint review agencies might find it attractive to hire former police officers as investigators; they are, after all, trained investigators likely to have both strong convictions about how police work should be done as well as insider connections and contacts within their former departments. However, former police officers arrive with baggage as well—namely, the suspicion in the eyes of others, fair or unfair, that a person who has once served in law enforcement will always harbor a bias in favor of police officers. San Francisco's charter explicitly prohibits the hiring of anyone as a director of the Office of Citizen Complaints who is or who has ever been "a uniformed member or employee" of the police department.[62] No staff members, whether full or part time, "shall have previously served as a uniformed member of the department."[63]

Pittsburgh's Citizen Police Review Board

During the mid- to late 1990s in Pittsburgh and its suburbs, a number of citizens, including some unarmed black men, were killed or injured at the hands of police. The circumstances of these incidents varied; they involved officers from both the Pittsburgh Police Bureau and surrounding areas. The most notorious case involved Jonny Gammage, a relative of Ray Seals, then a well-known member of the Pittsburgh Steelers football team. In October 1995, Gammage was stopped by suburban police while driving Seals's Jaguar and died from asphyxiation during a struggle with officers.[64] These and other incidents exposed the raw anger that had been building in Pittsburgh's black community against Pittsburgh's police, and citizens reacted by putting a referendum on the ballot to create a citizens' oversight panel. The Police Bureau, Pittsburgh's mayor, and the Fraternal Order of Police union local fought the proposal.[65] They argued that the police could police themselves adequately through their internal affairs unit. The public disagreed.[66] On May 20, 1997, the referendum passed;[67] to the surprise of many in Pittsburgh's police and civilian power structure, the measure received not only overwhelming support from the African American community but also from white voters.[68] The Citizen Police Review Board (CPRB) came into existence in Pittsburgh in November 1997.[69]

The CPRB has everything necessary to be a strong complaint review agency. It is independent of the police department and investigates individual citizen allegations against police with its own staff. It has subpoena power, keeps evidence confidential, and has the power to hold public hearings and to take testimony under oath. Based on its findings, it makes disciplinary recommendations. It issues yearly reports on its activity and issues other reports on particular matters as needed. It does not review internal affairs investigations undertaken by the police, or act as an appellate body when a citizen is dissatisfied with how the police handle a complaint.[70] The CPRB also "evaluates policies, procedures, training, and matters of public interest or controversy."[71] It is, in short, the complete civilian review package.

Despite its potential to be a first-class external review agency, the CPRB's brief history has not always been smooth. While some small portion of the responsibility for this lies with the CPRB itself (it had to remove its first executive director, an ugly and very public process) most of the problems have arisen because the mayor, the Police Bureau, and the Fraternal Order of Police union local have continually resisted and frustrated the CPRB's efforts.[72] Certainly one of the biggest problems Pittsburgh's CPRB has had stems from "competition" with a parallel agency inside the police department: the Office of Municipal Investigations (OMI), which continues to investigate municipal employees, including police officers. According to John Burkoff, a law professor at the University of Pittsburgh and the CPRB's former chairperson, the Office of Municipal Investigations was a poorly functioning agency in 1997; its lack of credibility largely accounts for the success of the referendum establishing the CPRB.[73]

Burkoff and others agree with Bill Valenta, a Police Bureau commander who currently heads the Office of Municipal Investigations: even though it remains under the supervision of a federal judge (the Police Bureau itself was released from supervision in September 2002), OMI is doing a better job than it was a few years ago, when it constantly operated with a huge backlog of cases.[74] Nevertheless, the continued existence of the OMI creates friction because it gives those who wish to resist the CPRB's efforts a reason to say that the OMI is the "real" or "correct" agency to monitor police misconduct.

According to Elizabeth Pittinger, the CPRB's executive director, this represents a willful misreading of recent history and an effort to undermine the democratically expressed will of the people of Pittsburgh.[75] Pittinger says that without the CPRB, police discipline will be overseen by an agency deeply connected to the police department itself—a situation that practically screams "conflict of interest."[76] Burkoff, the Pittsburgh law professor and former CPRB chair, finds the continuing opposition to the Review Board by the union, leaders in the city government, and the Police Bureau puzzling and unfortunate: "They haven't figured out that [the CPRB] is the best thing that's happened to them," he says. "[The CPRB] finds for the officers most of the time. It's not there to hurt them, and it doesn't. It's really benefited them, and the chief and the mayor, too, by defusing this whole issue. But they don't see it."

Burkoff is right. The CPRB began operating in July 1998. In its first three years of operation, it received 233 sworn complaints; it recommended action in only 18 of these cases.[77] Of its 18 recommendations, Chief Robert McNeilly declined to follow eight and modified seven others. He concurred fully with only two: one in which no action was recommended and one in which the complaint was not sustained. (One case was still pending as of the end of 2001.) Clearly, the CPRB is not "out to get" the Police Bureau or individual police officers. This might be ammunition for critics who say that it could or should have done more, but it can't possibly support an argument that the CPRB does too much or acts too aggressively. Pittinger probably sums it up best: The modest statistics show progress, not some kind of antipolice vendetta, she says. The process is working *for* the police, even as it works to address the worst incidents of misconduct in the system. "We have tried to establish a credible record," Pittinger says. "If a citizen learns something about police procedure and an officer is reminded of the humanity of citizens, and both parties are held equally accountable, then we're fulfilling the spirit of the people's mandate."[78]

Auditors

Complaint review boards such as Pittsburgh's are reactive: they go into action when a citizen complains—the equivalent of calling 911. The auditor model of citizen oversight differs fundamentally. If a complaint review board's actions are like traditional police responses to calls from citizens, auditors have much more in common with problem-solving policing. Auditors focus on overall patterns and issues. Auditors look not for individual justice concerning events in the past but for institutional improvement and long-term change going forward. A relatively new development, auditors (typically, a single appointed person with a staff of investigators, analysts, and former law enforcement officers) began to appear primarily in the western United States in the mid-1990s, often as a compromise: auditors are empowered with broad oversight of police department standards and processes, but investigation and adjudication of individual cases remain the responsibility of internal units of the police department.[79] This is a feature that causes many advocates of police reform to distrust the auditor model.[80] Auditors still exist mainly in the West: in 2003, auditors presided over police departments in Los Angeles County, San Jose, Seattle, Portland, Tucson, Boise, Omaha, and Austin, as well as Philadelphia, on the East Coast.

Because auditors focus on overall procedures, auditor systems can have a much bigger impact than systems designed to address complaints one by one,[81] and represent the best hope for addressing police misconduct by remaking police behavior.

Most auditors spend considerable time and energy engaged in outreach activities designed to help the public understand the complaint process, the police department itself and its policies, and to make sure that everyone in the community has unencumbered access to the complaint process. Auditors hold and attend community meetings for this purpose, making special effort to get information to overlooked populations: minority communities, people in very poor or unsafe neighborhoods, and non–English-speaking immigrants. For example, the auditor in Austin, Texas, has produced pamphlets in English and Spanish, such as "What to Do If the Police Knock on Your Door" and "Flashing Lights in Your Rear View Mirror: How to Respond to Traffic Stops." The auditor in San Jose, California, makes complaint forms, a youth guide called "A Student's Guide to Police Practices," and a list of frequently asked questions available in English, Spanish, and Vietnamese.[82] Along these same lines, auditors also work to make filing complaints easier.[83]

Auditors make their greatest contributions through policy review, in which they examine a police department's policies and procedures and recommend new or revised ones. The focus is preemptive, and thus is in sync with preventive policing. Policy review allows an auditor to examine an entire police unit or sector and analyze the situation comprehensively, from the perspective of proper police management. Except for special postcrisis commissions, this kind of broad view of how an entire segment of a police department functions is virtually unknown. All management practices that might contribute to a troubled situation—poor or insufficient supervision of patrol officers, insufficient experience among commanders, or the use of a precinct or station as a "dumping ground" for troubled officers, for example—can be brought to light in the context of the system problems they cause on the street. Auditors are thus able to focus on the complaint process itself.

The auditor model is an oversight mechanism ideally structured to assure that the policing system as a whole works

properly. The system promises to make the entire process of policing—for example, filing, investigating, and judging civilian complaints—work in a fairer, less biased, and more legitimate way.
Critics are right that the auditor system will do nothing about
the handling of individual misconduct cases that occurred in the
past, but it is the best hope for improving all aspects of police
conduct and complaint processing going forward. Fairness and
justice in individual cases of civilian complaints are best assured
when the system as a whole runs well.

Special Counsel, Los Angeles County Sheriff's Department
Anyone interested in the possibilities for police reform presented by the auditor system should turn first to the special
counsel to the Los Angeles County Sheriff's Department
(LASD). Los Angeles County's Board of Supervisors created the
special counsel's position in 1993 to combat rising litigation
costs: a special report issued in 1992 found that Los Angeles
County had paid $18 million between 1988 and 1992 alone
because of the misconduct of its deputies.[84] Merrick Bobb,
selected as the first special counsel, has continued in the position since the creation of the office. From the beginning, Bobb
took a broad view of his job; for him, the question was not the
misconduct of a few officers but how flawed policies, procedures, and management had contributed to patterns of mis-
deeds requiring huge damage payments. In more than a
decade of service, Bobb and his staff have published regular
reports, covering a multitude of issues facing the Sheriff's
Department: shootings and other uses of force by deputies, the
use of police dogs ("guard and bark" versus "bite and hold"
policies), civil litigation and risk management, the handling of
citizen complaints, the running of the Los Angeles County jail,
training, and a host of personnel issues that have included
recruitment, sexual harassment, diversity, sexual orientation,
and psychological services.[85] Often revisiting key issues multiple times to assess progress, these reports present an all-too-

rare balanced point of view that seeks neither to castigate nor to score points but rather to spot serious problems, explore their origins, and to find the path to systemic organizational change and improvement.

One 1998 report offers a comprehensive examination of an entire division, called the Century Station. The Century Station serves an area that has had a heavily minority population and a high poverty rate; it has also had a rate of shootings by deputies three times higher than in a comparable adjacent police district. An internal investigation by the Sheriff's Department had only looked into the individual shootings. Bobb tried to identify problems and their causes with a sweeping review of virtually all aspects of police work at Century Station, as reflected in documents, extensive interviews with officers, and ride-alongs. Bobb concluded that there were "chronic serious problems," and that these problems originated not with a handful of bad officers, but rather with a laundry list of bad management practices:

- Supervisors at Century considered their deputies "too young and inexperienced," with by far the youngest median age and almost the lowest average level of experience of any of the LASD's stations.
- Century carried the LASD's highest "training burden": as many as 31 out of 180 patrol deputies were trainees—the least experienced staff for one of the most troubled patrol areas— and there was a shortage of trainers for the trainees and strong "dissatisfaction" among community members, who felt they were saddled with a continual flow of green officers.
- Century's trainers did not have enough experience themselves, with some field trainers having only one-and-a-half years behind them.
- Because of the stigma associated with working at Century Station, deputies sought to transfer out as soon as possible, resulting in high turnover and a force of patrol deputies who were less familiar with the area than they should have been.

- There was also high turnover among sergeants, the primary supervisors for street-level police officers in any department, resulting in far less supervision for deputies than necessary.[86]

These findings were important in themselves, pointing to ways in which Century Station could be improved, but they also illuminated a connection that most police reform efforts miss. As Samuel Walker puts it, "Bobb's investigation dramatized the extent to which street-level problems . . . cannot be separated from the full range of personnel and management practices in a department."[87]

Bobb and his staff reexamined the Century Station four years later, noting: "We return to Century . . . because we are convinced that management has not consistently done enough."[88] The report says that, in the wake of the previous report, the Sheriff's Department made significant changes, including a nearly complete change of sergeants and lieutenants,[89] assigning lieutenants (instead of sergeants) to handle citizen complaints, freeing up sergeants for more time in the field; and changes in policy, such as the policy on foot pursuit that had produced large numbers of shootings.[90] These changes coincided with a drop in shootings, with only one shooting during 1999 and four in 2000, including a period of 17 straight months without one shooting by a deputy[91] (Century Station had averaged twelve shootings a year between 1994 and 1998 [92]). However, once the new management team left, through routine transfers, promotions, and the like, shootings spiked to their previous level. While the report is careful to note that the coincidence of the new management and drop in shootings does not prove that the former caused the latter, it says that many at the station who worked under the new management attribute the drop in shootings to the changes.[93] It also notes that the new management team in place at the time of the report appeared to be trying its best to institutionalize changes in management and operations, and expressed cautious optimism that this might happen.[94]

All in all, the achievements of the special counsel are impressive. They represent one of the first times ever that a police department has been subjected to careful, close, consistent monitoring of its professional work, its policies, and its results. It has made for a vastly enriched source of information upon which to base changes in policies and practices, and a way to spot those changes that need to be made in order to prevent problems. The continuity one sees in the reports, with repeated attention to the most important issues and scrutiny of progress or lack of it, remains unmatched. The special counsel shows that the auditor system can work superbly; every police department in the country, every municipal government, and every group of citizens dissatisfied with police services or the performance of an existing oversight body ought to look to it as the best possible model.

The Feedback Loop: Information from the Community

If police departments and their officers are to be held accountable, they must gather information from external sources, usually the public. It is always tempting to avoid this kind of feedback from outsiders because it will frequently be critical and not always friendly, gentle, or even well-informed. The public may not understand the nuances of the police officer's job but will nevertheless feel no hesitation about expressing harshly critical opinions. This tendency to want to avoid public criticism may be especially strong in police work, which has its own insular subculture that assumes that those not "on the job" cannot understand it.

Even if much of what police learn through this process consists of public perceptions and opinions rather than facts, for a public institution like policing, perceptions count. Police department budgets come from public funds; negative public perception makes getting adequate monies to run and improve departments tougher. Police officers on patrol deal with the public constantly; if these encounters become tinged with negative attitudes, they can become more difficult, stressful, and even dangerous. Gathering information from the public can help spot problem areas that police departments can address and allow them to respond to the public's needs and desires, which is what accountability is all about. A good flow of information from the public to the police, a feedback loop, is an invaluable means to understanding how its "customers" experience its services.

In 1999, the U.S. Justice Department's Bureau of Justice Statistics conducted the second national survey on citizen encounters with police.[95] Called the Police Public Contact Survey, this ongoing study seeks information on any encounter that the surveyed citizens may have had with the police over the previous six months.[96] The 1999 survey showed that traffic stops made up more than half of all contacts between police and citizens, a number more than twice as large as the next most frequent type of encounter. Traffic stops thus emerge as a key opportunity to shape citizen perception of police. The survey also showed that blacks, especially young black men, felt they had been stopped, often multiple times, because of racial bias—an important perception whether or not it was accurate. The survey further revealed that, contrary to what many people thought, the officers performing these allegedly biased stops were as likely to be black or Latino as white. Thus, this revealing set of statistics shows that the racial profiling problem stems not from the racism of a few bad white officers but from institutional problems. Individual police departments could gain similar important insights for themselves by replicating the existing survey form, which is available on the bureau's Web site[97] and tailoring it to fit each department's setting and mission.

Some departments have begun to survey citizens who have had particular types of encounters with the police in the same way that the private sector does customer satisfaction research. For example, in Miami, officers who have encounters with citizens are required to make a brief record of the event, including an address or phone number that would allow police to make contact with the citizen later. Follow-up interviews ask what the encounter was about, whether the officer treated the citizen with respect and courtesy, whether the officer told the citizen why he or she was stopped and explained the situation so that the citizen could understand what was happening, and whether the encounter resulted in an arrest or in a citation. Such a survey might also include general questions concerning the citizen's opinion of the police department.

Giving Information to the Public

If gathering information from the public seems revolutionary to police departments, disseminating it to the public may be even more so. Police often feel that the public does not understand their work and that information they provide may be used against them—possibly even in a lawsuit. But no matter how strong the resistance to sharing information, few ideas are more important to building accountability.[98] Citizens without information cannot hold police departments accountable, and if citizens really do not understand the police officer's job, comprehension will come only with information. Some police departments understand this and offer people the chance to attend "citizen police academies," which usually consist of day- or half-day–long seminars about what police do; they sometimes include an opportunity for citizens to ride along with a police officer on duty. These efforts educate citizens and usually make them more supportive of police in the bargain.

The more compelling reason for informing the public about police conduct is the principle of transparency. Except for the most secret and sensitive national security agencies, it is simply unacceptable for public institutions in a democratic society to function without accountability to the public, no matter how important, complex, or technical their mission. Without transparency—institutional openness to public scrutiny—real accountability cannot exist, and the lifeblood of transparency is the wide dissemination of information. A government agency that functions in the shadows, without public oversight, is an open invitation for abuse. The more crucial the agency's mission and the greater its powers, the graver the danger posed by a lack of transparency. Police departments have always resisted this idea, but what will probably most surprise those who work in policing is that disseminating information about their performance can benefit them—in very substantial ways.

An example from California illustrates the point. In the late 1990s, no issue involving police work had greater public visibility than racial profiling, and no other issue created so much friction between police and the public, particularly in black and Latino communities in which people felt that they had been subjected to biased policing for a long time. Most police officials across the country initially disputed not only the need to do anything about the problem but also its very existence. A spokesman for the National Association of Police Organizations, a nationwide umbrella group for 4,000 different policing organizations, told the *Los Angeles Times* in 1998 that there was "no pressing need or justification" to take action against racial profiling; further, he said, police officers would "resent" any action that implied that they might be enforcing the law in a racially biased fashion.[99]

Thus it was something of a surprise when Bill Lansdowne, chief of police in San Jose, became one of the first police chiefs in the nation to announce that his police department would collect racial data on traffic stops and share the results with the public.[100] Lansdowne set up a community-wide task force to help design and implement the effort and made sure to include all segments of the community in his effort to collect data—the ACLU, the NAACP, Asian Americans for Community Involvement, the San Jose Peace Officers Association, and others.[101]

Eventually, the data were brought together and analyzed, and the results were announced. At least as interesting and important as the process of the data collection was the context of the data's release.[102] Lansdowne (who became San Diego's chief in August 2003[103]) released the data to the public and posted them on the San Jose Police Department's Web site. He gave the citizens of his city all the information as well as his conclusions about it. The citizens of San Jose saw the results of the study's transparent process for themselves when they watched and read news accounts of the release of the report to the public.

Lansdowne's voice was not the only one heard in the news of the study; at the news conference announcing the study's release, he was accompanied by many of the community leaders he had included in the effort. All spoke supportively of Lansdowne and the police department, even though many of them disagreed with Lansdowne's interpretation of the data.[104] (Lansdowne felt that the data showed no evidence of racial bias in traffic stops, but some leaders thought the numbers were troubling).[105] The leaders and the organizations they represented literally stood with the chief and the police department, not necessarily agreeing with them in every respect but expressing appreciation for the effort and voicing support for a continuation of the study.

Money and Accountability: Making Damages Matter

Between 1994 and 2000, the New York Police Department was hit with damages of almost $180 million in police misconduct cases.[106] This staggering figure eclipses the entire budget of all but the very largest police departments in the nation; for example, it is about two-and-a-half times the 2004 budget for the entire Pittsburgh Police Bureau.[107] Yet there is little evidence that such damage awards have done anything to control police misconduct or to change the behavior of individual officers. The Los Angeles Police Department, like many others, has for many years blamed a small number of officers for most of its problems, complaints, and disciplinary actions. Studies indicate that supervisors within the department know who these officers are but year after year do nothing to get rid of them. And the damages just keep mounting. The question seems almost too obvious: given the huge costs, why does the department allow this misconduct to continue?

The answer is surprisingly simple: despite the huge amounts of money involved, police misconduct verdicts and out-of-court settlements generally cost police departments nothing, because neither the departments nor the officers involved foot the bill. The law gives the officers "qualified immunity"; as long as they operate in good faith within very broad legal boundaries, officers are immune from citizens' lawsuits for damages. Police departments are protected because damages (as well as costs of legal defense) are paid out of the city's general funds, not the police department's budget. Thus, damages represent what economists call an externality— a cost created by one entity but borne by another. When costs are externalized, the entity that causes them has no incentive to curtail them.[108] These costs, which should serve as warnings of patterns of misconduct or mismanagement and as incentives to have problems corrected, are almost always ignored.

To address this problem and to give the police department an incentive to pay attention to damages incurred because of police misconduct, citizens in San Francisco passed a referendum in 1996 called Proposition G. This is the same referendum referred to earlier in this chapter that created a minimum staffing ratio for San Francisco's citizen review board. The part of Proposition G relevant here required that damages for police misconduct be paid out of the police department's own budget, not the city's general funds. To keep the department from swallowing the pain quietly by cutting the number of officers so that it could stay within its budget, Proposition G also prohibited the department from reducing the number of officers below then-current levels.[109] In practice, this means that the department will have fewer dollars in its budget if it racks up large damage costs due to misconduct; since it cannot reduce police personnel costs to cover these expenses, the department will be forced to go to the city government and request more money to cover the damages. At the very least, this would make the request for extra funds to pay damages subject to specific public oversight by elected officials, which would in turn bring pressure to bear on the police to reform the practices that cause damages.[110]

The Federal Stick: The Justice Department's "Pattern-or-Practice" Authority

Up to this point, this chapter has discussed internal and external devices that police departments can use to build systems of accountability. All such systems, of course, assume a willing department. There are, however, police departments in chronic difficulty that need to move toward accountability but that cannot or will not do so. How can such a police department be moved toward accountability, whether it wants to do so or not? Until recently, unless state or local officials wished to spend the political capital to take on this task—at best an unlikely scenario— no mechanism existed for addressing it. But in 1994, Congress passed the Violent Crime Control and Law Enforcement Act,[111] part of which contained what has become known as the "pattern-or-practice" law. This law gives the U.S. Department of Justice the power to bring federal civil suits against police departments if they engage in patterns or practices of conduct that deprive citizens of constitutionally protected rights. The phrase "pattern or practice" comes directly from the law itself, which reads:

> It shall be unlawful for any government authority, or any agent thereof, or any person acting on behalf of a governmental authority, to engage in a pattern or practice of conduct by law enforcement officers . . . that deprives persons of the rights, privileges, or immunities secured by the Constitution or the laws of the United States.[112]

The pattern-or-practice law is enforced by the Department of Justice's Special Litigation Section, which investigates and litigates complaints about police misconduct. If the Special Litigation Section finds evidence that the officers in the police department under investigation regularly engage in misconduct that violates the Constitution, the Department of Justice has the authority to sue in federal court and, upon proof of misconduct, to have the court enter an injunction ordering the police department to change in significant ways and to remain under court supervision. Never, however, has the pattern-or-practice authority led to a full trial. The investigation—often an involved and expensive affair—and the prospect of facing the full legal resources of the United States government in federal court make litigating these cases very unattractive.[113] Instead, the department's Special Litigation Section presents the police department with a detailed list of the findings of misconduct uncovered by its investigation, as well as a proposal for changes in the department to help insure that the patterns of unconstitutional behavior cease. If the police department agrees to do what the Department of Justice proposes, the agreement is brought before the federal court in the form of a "consent decree"—an agreement between the parties (the government and the police department, as well as the city government and any other municipal entity or agency to which the police department reports) that has the force of law. The consent decree lasts for a predetermined period, usually five years, subject to the judge's discretion.

The pattern-or-practice law targets only certain varieties of misconduct. The statute allows the federal government to target not individual police officers but the department itself; the focus is institutional, not individual. The Justice Department does, of course, look at individual incidents, but only insofar as they might indicate an overall pattern. The pattern-or-practice law gives the department no authority to discipline, sue, or prosecute individual officers; it does not pursue damages or remedies of any kind for individuals who believe that the police department has wronged them, and only the government, not individuals, may sue under the law. Rather, the law gives the federal government the tools it needs to ask whether the police department makes a regular practice of depriving citizens of their civil rights and to do something about it by forcing the police to reform in specific ways.

Settlements in the form of consent decrees have been reached with a number of departments: the New Jersey State Police (after a long-running series of revelations involving racial profiling),[114] the Pittsburgh Police Bureau[115] (most of the Pittsburgh consent decree was lifted in September of 2002, after five years[116]), the Los Angeles Police Department (in the wake of the Ramparts scandal),[117] the Detroit Police Department (in 2003, after a long investigation),[118] and the police department in Steubenville, Ohio.[119] Other jurisdictions have resolved their police misconduct disputes with voluntary "memoranda of agreement." For example, an agreement between the Special Litigation Section and the police department, county government, and the police union local in Montgomery County, Maryland, reflects not so much Justice Department findings of misconduct but the desire of all of the parties to "provide for a cooperative effort . . . to institute management practices . . . that will promote nondiscriminatory law enforcement and community support" for the police department.[120]

The threat of federal intervention under the pattern-or-practice law is one of the most effective external accountability devices imaginable. It has served as a catalyst for change, motivating police departments to improve their practices, their internal standards, and their expectations of their officers, making them more effective institutions and more respectful of those they serve. The existence of the federal "stick" can make a real difference, especially in police departments needing change and reform but whose chiefs find themselves hamstrung by weak-kneed political leadership, repeated failure to provide resources necessary to make changes, or by the reluctance or active resistance of police unions. The pattern-or-practice law provides a tool to force the worst police departments toward change and better practices, and leverage for leaders of departments who want to move their departments in positive directions but cannot.

Pattern-or-practice authority should be preserved, protected, and indeed enhanced, which requires adequate funding and support for the Special Litigation Section both in the federal budget and within the Department of Justice itself. Limited judicious use of the law since its enactment has given police departments all over the country a concrete incentive to monitor their own practices and to improve their internal management on their own, before the Special Litigation Section begins the long and often expensive process of investigation and the threat of legal action. Chiefs of police have no desire to take on the Department of Justice and its vast legal muscle over police misconduct. On the contrary, chiefs want to do everything possible to avoid one of these difficult, headline-grabbing probes at all costs. In fact, the "frequently asked questions" on the Special Litigation Section's Web site focuses on this very issue. The list of questions and answers, the section says, includes "the question frequently asked by police executives of what they can do in their agencies to ensure that they are in compliance with the law and thereby avoid a pattern-or-practice investigation and lawsuit."[121]

Joseph Brann, a former chief of police who served as the first leader of the U.S. Department of Justice's Office of Community Oriented Policing Services, says that most chiefs not only want to avoid a pattern-or-practice investigation, they really do want to meet the pattern-or-practice standards. Brann, who now works as a consultant and monitor to police departments around the country, says that the question is how to assist and support chiefs interested in "managing their way into compliance."[122] The pattern-or-practice approach can also be bolstered by creating state laws that do the same thing. California already has such a law,[123] and the state's attorney general has used it effectively in a set of controversies involving the police department in the city of Riverside.[124]

The federal pattern-or-practice law makes an effective stick, but sticks work best when accompanied by carrots. Along with continued federal pressure toward the goal of better policing,

6

Leading the Way

Deputy Inspector Tom King of the New York Police Department comes from a family of police officers.[1] Five members of his family, including his father and a brother and sister, have worn the NYPD badge. King joined the NYPD more than twenty years ago, after stints as a teacher and an accountant. He has been a patrol officer, a supervising sergeant, and a lieutenant, and he taught in-service courses at the police academy before assuming several precinct commands in the Bronx.

In January 1998, when King (then a captain) became the commanding officer of the Forty-second Precinct in the South Bronx, the NYPD was in its fourth year of aggressive anticrime policies begun under William Bratton. Beginning in 1994, Bratton and his deputies set new policies based on the now-famous "broken windows" theory of policing of James Q. Wilson and George Kelling.[2] Bratton mandated that NYPD officers strictly enforce laws and ordinances against "quality of life" offenses like urinating in public, subway-turnstile jumping, public drinking, and vandalism. The Police Department had often overlooked these offenses in the past, preferring to concentrate on more serious crimes; under the broken windows theory, taking a "zero tolerance" attitude toward not only serious crime but also these minor crimes would signal to all New Yorkers, especially potential criminals, that no law breaking was acceptable. Making lots of arrests for low-level offending would, Bratton thought, head off more serious offenses before they happened. Departmental policy emphasized frequent use of stops and frisks to discourage the carrying of firearms, which would in turn lower the rate of shootings and homicides. Detectives would question anyone found with a gun to collect information on how the suspect had obtained the weapon, allowing the NYPD to launch direct efforts against weapons suppliers.

When King took command of the Forty-second Precinct, these strong anti-crime policies were already in place, and, as in the rest of the city, crime was falling. But the number of civilian complaints in 1998 citywide was 39 percent higher than it had been in 1993. These statistics seemed to support the idea that forcing crime down inevitably resulted in increased friction between police and citizens. But in a handful of precincts, including the Forty-second under King, this was not the case. Crime fell in the Forty-second but so did complaints.

These anomalies caught the attention of Robert Davis at the Vera Institute of Justice, an independent public policy think tank in New York.[3] Davis and his colleagues looked for explanations in rumored drops in police activity and the changing demographics of the South Bronx. But careful study of the evidence led them to conclude that the only real explanation for the drop in civilian complaints in the Forty-second Precinct lay in the leadership of Tom King.

King was very much a hands-on administrator who made it a point to get to know his officers.[4] He regularly put his authority and prestige on the line to make sure he got what he wanted out of those under his command. Although the entire NYPD was supposed to do everything possible to minimize citizen complaints, the Vera study showed that King seemed to be one of the few commanders to insist on results concerning complaints as much as he insisted on results against crime. Those officers who didn't follow his directives suffered consequences, while those who did their jobs well with few (or no) complaints were rewarded. King appeared regularly at roll calls and spoke to officers in small groups, telling them that the order had come down from headquarters that while the NYPD was to fight crime, it had to do so with respect for every citizen.

King's approach reflected NYPD policy. In 1997, the department had initiated a program intended to address the rising number of civilian complaints that followed the introduction of "broken windows" policing: it was dubbed Courtesy, Professionalism, and Respect (CPR). CPR mandated new training for police recruits and in-service training for experienced officers, and mandated monitoring for individual officers who had problems dealing with the public. CPR also required monitoring of civilian complaints on a precinct-by-precinct basis through the Compstat process. While CPR was the department's official policy on civilian complaints, many precinct commanders did not make a serious effort to apply it. But Tom King considered himself bound by this order, and he held himself and his officers responsible for following it.[5] King used CPR training at roll call. He also put his own sergeant in charge of training, to ensure that his officers received instruction in CPR policies, and lectured at training sessions himself.[6]

King gave every officer personal attention. Every day, he picked a different officer to ride with him in his radio car on regular patrol duty. King wanted to get to know all of his officers, observe their approach to police work, and learn what their ambitions were.[7] A large number wanted to become detectives or work in plainclothes units, and King made sure that they understood that their ability to advance to those desirable assignments would depend not just on how many arrests they made, but on how well they handled the public. King also made a regular practice of meeting directly with any officer who was the subject of a civilian complaint as soon as he learned of it.[8]

He approached such meetings not as an occasion to bawl the "guilty" officer out, but rather as an opportunity to hear the facts directly from the officer. King would listen to the officer's version of the story, make suggestions, and then let the complaint take its course through the system.

In the case of a complaint against a "recidivist officer"(one who had had some complaints in the past), King felt that such personal meetings were even more important, and he would use the occasion not only to sort out the facts and form a preliminary judgment, but also to emphasize to the officer that repeated complaints were unacceptable.[9] Often, King said, these officers would tell him that civilian complaints were simply part of aggressive crime fighting. King would have none of it. "You've got to make them understand that that's kind of an alibi; you're not going to accept that."[10] Since he knew the records of every officer under his command, King was always in a position to tell such officers that many of their peers were equally active and did not incur civilian complaints. As one officer in King's precinct told researchers from the Vera Institute, "You've got to watch yourself on complaints because the department takes them seriously now. You can really hurt your career."[11]

King is a veteran police officer, and his methods are not revolutionary; rather, they center on old-fashioned ideas, like working according to the right values, clarity of expectations and standards, good communication, and consistent follow-through, all applied creatively and with vigor. The Vera study of King's precinct shows just how effective his leadership was. Complaints from citizens were constantly lower during his tenure in the Forty-second Precinct than they were before he came. Unfortunately, after King was transferred from the Forty-second, complaints returned to a level close to the city's average.

LEADERSHIP IN POLICE WORK

Strong, active, committed leadership is absolutely critical to the success of preventive policing. The core concepts of preventive policing—partnership with citizens based on trust, becoming proactive problem solvers instead of responders, and establishing accountability—all represent fundamental breaks with the long-held beliefs and traditions of law enforcement going back well into the twentieth century. To make them happen, to assure ourselves that preventive policing does more than become a slogan, leaders in police departments, from sergeants and lieutenants to the precinct commanders and the chief, must insist that prevention be the watchword of the organization, and that officers act accordingly. This will not be easy in such a change-resistant culture as law enforcement (see chapter 7), but without strong leadership to insist on it, it simply cannot happen. Strong leadership is integral to the success of preventive policing.

We might imagine leadership in the policing context to be less complicated and difficult than in other areas, such as business. Police departments are organized as quasi-military institutions, with a commanding officer, the chief, and "executive vice presidents" called commanders. All sworn officers are assigned ranks; authority and power are parceled out in accordance with rank. Police departments adhere to this strict chain of command, just like the military; a request from a superior is an order, and failure to obey constitutes insubordination.

But appearances can be deceiving. In a police department, the "soldiers" do not always respond as if they are part of an army. All police officers, perhaps street patrol officers most of all, treasure their autonomy and their freedom from direct supervision. Most officers do nearly all their work unsupervised, only sporadically reporting in to their sergeants or dispatchers and only rarely encountering a supervisory officer on the street. Anything that intrudes on officer autonomy—a policy or directive from the precinct commander or headquarters, a new law, or a court decision—becomes a bone in the throat of the rank-and-file officer. A chief or precinct commander cannot affect reform simply by commanding it. Indeed, change may be less likely to happen in a police department than in other kinds of organizations because of the dominant ethic of self-determination. Beyond this, however, there are other important reasons why police departments need strong and agile leadership.

Politics, Writ Large

One thing that distinguishes the leader of a police department from business leaders is that the police leader generally serves at the pleasure of the mayor or city council. We find this arrangement almost everywhere in America: police organizations are local, rooted in and chartered by the municipalities they serve, and elected officials hire and fire the chief of the department. Most often, the mayor appoints and may fire the chief; in many cities, this appointment takes at least the official form of a nomination, which the city council has the power to approve or deny. Elected bodies then exercise oversight over the police department by holding hearings on the departmental budget, appropriating its funds and even mandating certain allocations of resources within the department, and approving the chief's own salary. The chief of police may be answerable to other bodies as well, such as citizen complaint review oversight boards or police monitors or auditors. Myriad outside constituencies, such as block watch groups and advocacy groups, also have interests at stake in police issues.

So many contending issues make for a potent political brew. It is not uncommon for a mayor to regard the police department, and the police chief personally, as being at their disposal for any task regardless of its pertinence to the department's mission or strategy and even if these tasks contradict what the department might otherwise do. This is not to say that the rawest forms of politics and patronage rule police departments as they did in the early days of the twentieth century, but politics has not disappeared at the top levels of police departments. A chief who finds herself at odds with the mayor or her budget held hostage by a hostile city council will find it difficult to maintain the status quo, let alone to improve things. A chief who ends up on the wrong side of community organizations and other activists can find his motives questioned, his progress impeded, and his energies drained off into dealing with confrontation and controversy. All high-visibility jobs in municipal or state leadership are political, but for the chief of any police department, politics is usually more complicated and difficult than for most other appointed leaders.

Politics Writ Small: Us versus Them, and Us versus the Chief
On a smaller scale, police chiefs must also contend with organizational politics, involving relations between the police and the public, and relations within the department between the chief and rank-and-file officers.

No phrase characterizes the thinking of police officers more completely than the cliché "us versus them." Policing is indeed a world apart. Police officers deal with the worst, most troubled, and least caring elements of society. They see humanity at its lowest. Much more than the rest of us, they face the likelihood of meeting or using violence every time they go to work. Most shifts may be uneventful, with nothing more than traffic tickets to write, reports to take, or disgruntled neighbors to calm, but officers are also cursed at, spat upon, yelled at, and accused of things that most of us can only imagine. It is not surprising to find that police culture is insular and suspicious of outsiders. Only a brother or sister member of the force can really "get" what a police officer has to go through; when a police officer is in trouble, it will inevitably be a fellow cop who backs him up, not a civilian.

For any chief who seeks to engage with the community through community policing or problem-oriented policing, the us-versus-them attitude is a major obstacle to reform. Both community and problem-oriented policing derive their legitimacy and their potential to accomplish things from the public. Without a strong connection to the public and a willingness to work with citizens, to share information and responsibility with them, and to build mutual trust with them, departments will have community policing in name only. Instead of breeding that important trust and connection, the us-versus-them attitude breeds the ultimate political poison: mutual suspicion. The successful police chief must be able to understand and work with the politics of suspicion even as he or she moves officers away from this way of thinking.

The internal politics of police departments, inevitable in any organization of any size, may unfortunately also involve a dynamic that pits the chief and the command staff against rank-and-file officers. For officers below command level, one concern stands out when trouble strikes, such as public criticism over a police shooting of a civilian: Does the police chief back up the rank-and-file officers, no matter what the facts say and no matter how intense the crisis becomes? In cities with powerful police unions, the situation can easily become polarized, as heated rhetoric inflames tensions between the community and those in uniform.

It is easy to imagine the pressures that chiefs face in such situations. In the end, if there has been wrongdoing by members of the force, the chief typically has the final say in disciplinary matters even though the chief's need to "support the troops" may work at cross-purposes with a dispassionate review of the facts and the imposition of appropriate discipline. On the other side, municipal politicians may feel pressure, and may themselves apply pressure to the chief to do or say things that amount, in the eyes of the rank-and-file, to prejudgment or even betrayal of the officers involved. Such political crosscurrents make it most difficult for police leaders to chart a reasonable course even in calm times; in the heat of even a minor crisis, the ship can seem likely to capsize at any moment.

The political pressures that frame the chief's job make it imperative that the chief retain the power to discipline all officers under his command. One would think that this idea would be relatively uncontroversial. After all, what chief executive of a large organization does not have the ultimate say on disciplinary matters over employees? Nevertheless, police chiefs commonly complain that their power to discipline and fire officers engaged in wrongdoing has been compromised. I have heard story after story from chiefs who fired officers for misconduct, even for crimes—only to have the officers reinstated a few months later with full back pay after a hearing, either because of civil service regulations or provisions in contracts between police unions and city government.

Removing or compromising a chief's power to impose discipline undermines the very basis for the chief's authority. If a chief cannot fire anyone and is hamstrung in efforts to introduce discipline, officers on the street know. Like Deputy Inspector Tom King of the NYPD, the leaders in the stories that follow put themselves on the line in order to make the right things happen. Such leaders give us hope for the future of American police work; they are the ones who will make preventive policing possible.

PARTNERSHIP AND THE IMPORTANCE OF BRINGING EVERYONE TO THE TABLE
Jerry Barker, Indianapolis

Real understanding of the importance of partnerships in policing and the skills to build community trust remain curiously rare among police leadership. One of the leaders who does understand is Jerry Barker, the chief of police in Indianapolis.

Barker joined the police department right after his military service in Vietnam, and has served in the department for nearly four decades.[12] He has held almost every post in the department, from patrol officer to commander of one of the city's police districts to hostage negotiator. In 1994, Barker was appointed deputy chief of the city's west district. Indianapolis's West Side, as it is known to residents, was not considered an easy posting; it had a higher-than-average crime rate (especially property crime, prostitution, domestic violence) and many poor neighborhoods, high unemployment, and urban decay. It also had a diverse population, with large numbers of blacks and Appalachian whites.[13] The new assignment represented a challenge for Barker, a white man who'd spent his whole professional life in the Indianapolis Police Department.

After Barker examined the problems that had troubled previous commanders on the West Side, he concluded that, given the tense relations between police and the community in the area, an incident such as a police shooting, a death of a civilian in police custody, or a drug sting gone wrong might cause the West Side to explode. To head off catastrophe, Barker decided "to try and reach out and build relationships."[14] For Barker, this wasn't some touchy-feely way to be politically correct or to prop up the public image of the police department; it was crime fighting. "Anybody that suggests that the police can [make communities safe] all by themselves is a fool. We just can't, and we're learning that more and more every day," Barker says.[15]

As he saw it, Barker had first to extend his hand to the official representatives of the community, to elected officials and appointed heads of departments or boards, and to leaders of long-standing neighborhood institutions, such as ministers and the heads of nonprofit organizations. Then he had to reach out to unofficial leaders: community activists, volunteers, and organizers from individual blocks and neighborhoods. "[Unofficial] community leaders hold a lot of sway, they're respected by the citizenry, and many times they're more powerful and more down-to-earth and easier to work with" than official leaders, he said.[16]

Barker took advantage of the West Side's then new Weed and Seed initiative. Weed and Seed is a national program that makes federal funds available to neighborhoods to rehabilitate themselves and reverse the slide into decay and crime. Under the program, neighborhoods organize themselves, creating steering committees to set priorities and take action. When an organized structure is established, Weed and Seed charters the organization, making it eligible for grant monies. The neighborhood is then "weeded": problems that are identified by residents, like drugs, gangs, crack houses, abandoned property, and prostitution, are removed from the neighborhood through intensive police work in conjunction with neighborhood groups. The neighborhood is then "seeded" with positive influences, from social services to park rehabilitation, educational programs to public health and health-care initiatives, to economic development projects. Each neighborhood Weed and Seed group is overseen by the national Weed and Seed authorities.[17] Indianapolis now has six Weed and Seed sites, but the one on the West Side was the first. (For more on Indianapolis's Weed and Seed efforts, see chapter 7.)

Chief Barker immediately recognized the potential for Weed and Seed to advance the goals of community policing, and began to work toward making the West Side's Weed and Seed program the structure on which to base his efforts. Barker gives credit for the positive changes on the West Side to the people running the Weed and Seed program, and says that he and his officers were gratified to be partners in the effort. Yet Barker clearly played a major role in getting the initiatives to work. His most important partner was Olgen Williams. The two men did not seem like natural allies; they didn't like each other at first. Williams was a 1960s-style rabble-rousing activist,[18] and had taken on the police department in the past. Barker saw Williams as one of the community's "unofficial leaders": he held no office, elected or appointed, but had a long history of activism on behalf of his neighborhood and clearly had the trust of the people who lived and worked there.[19] Today Williams and Barker sometimes disagree but share a deep admiration for each other as allies in the same struggle to make the West Side a better place to live.

Barker's partnership with Olgen Williams was tested one day in September 1998 when there was a shootout between police and a drug dealer who had been under surveillance. The dealer emerged from his house with an AK-47, firing at police. The officers returned fire and wounded him.[20] Crowds started showing up almost immediately, Barker recalls, looking for an "excuse for anarchy."[21] Rumors quickly spread through the crowd that white police officers had shot a young black man five times.[22] When police officers recognized Olgen Williams, who happened to have driven by and stopped when he saw the crowd, they invited him behind the police crime-scene tape so that he could get the facts.[23] Williams then crossed back over the police-tape barrier and talked directly to the people milling around, giving them real information instead of rumor and insinuation. As a result, an incident that could have turned into a major disturbance—as did the shooting of a young black man in 2001 in Cincinnati, which led to three days of rioting—was defused.

Barker and Williams are still partners, and their relationship is still paying dividends for the citizens of Indianapolis. Barker has moved from deputy chief in charge of the West Side to the chief of the department; Williams now serves as executive director of Christamore House, a family and community center. Their city has benefited from their partnership, but it is important to remember that the partnership began with Jerry Barker's creative leadership—his willingness to look for an ally in the unlikely person of Olgen Williams, activist and vocal police critic. Clearly, this move risked much for Barker and the police department. Williams might have proved a poor choice in any number of ways, and he might have become an even sharper thorn in the department's side than he had been in the past. But Barker knew that in order to lead the department to a new way of doing things, he had to move in new directions, with new partners. Barker was enough of a leader to see that intelligent risk-taking was imperative, regardless of the potential downsides for himself and his career. And he was willing to try.

PUSHING AUTHORITY AND ACCOUNTABILITY
DOWN THE CHAIN OF COMMAND
Dean Esserman, Providence, Rhode Island

When Dean Esserman was the police chief in Stamford, Connecticut, he showed a willingness to lead by taking creative risks. He was the chief who allowed school officers Jon Jeter and Scott Baldwin to start the successful SRO summer camp as a way to fight juvenile crime and build on connections between the school officers and the students (see chapter 4). If Esserman, who is now the chief in Providence, Rhode Island, is unusual among police chiefs for his willingness to try things far out of the ordinary, he has an even more unusual attitude about power. In order to lead reform in the department he now heads, Esserman has done the unthinkable: he has given his power away.[24] He has pushed aspects of his own authority down the chain of command, giving commanders of police districts the authority to run those districts themselves, making them "mini-chiefs" in those areas. In exchange, he has held them all accountable for results in their campaigns against crime, disorder, and fear in their communities.

Leadership, especially in police departments, has always been associated with strength—with consolidation of power in the hands of the chief, allowing him to bend the department ever more to his will. This goes along with the quasi-military structure of police departments, with authority dependent on rank and a strict chain of command making its presence felt in every aspect of the department's work. Seen against this, Esserman's effort literally to give away the authority of his office to his subordinates shows a leader willing to take risks of the most counterintuitive type, when the stakes are as high as they get: his own power. But Esserman knows that doing this will

enable him to empower his subordinates to do their jobs, and
it will allow him to hold them accountable for the results. They
are best positioned to know the ins and outs of the city they've
served for years; they certainly know it better than Esserman,
who came from outside the department. Esserman thus takes
a risk, but it is a shrewd one—one that only the best leaders
would feel comfortable enough to try.

When Esserman became Providence's chief in January 2003,
he faced a difficult situation. He came into a department that
had become completely demoralized. The long-serving mayor of
Providence, Vincent "Buddy" Cianci, had been convicted in a federal corruption probe and sent to prison; Cianci had treated the
police department as his own personal fiefdom, to do with as his
political whims or needs dictated. Police officers in Providence
"lived [through] over twenty years of domination by a tyrant
mayor," Esserman says. "He ripped the hearts out of these people."[25] At Cianci's trial the former police chief had testified that
the hiring and promotion process within the department had
been corrupted with money and by special help on exams.[26] One
witness, the mother of a potential police recruit, testified that
she had paid $5,000 to get her son into the academy.[27]

Because of the taint of years of this corruption, Esserman
asked the entire top command staff to retire when he became
chief.[28] He also had to confront a class of new recruits who
might have been selected for the police force in a corrupt way,
and he had to deal with the lawsuit that arose as a result.[29] As
if that were not enough, after just weeks on the job, Esserman
discovered that a sophisticated eavesdropping system had been
built into the telephone equipment at the new $50 million
police headquarters building. The system was capable of wire-
tapping every line in the building. Esserman had the system
removed and had those responsible fired.[30]

When Esserman arrived in Providence, there were four patrol
districts and twenty-nine patrol posts. No one in the department
had any idea why. Esserman started from scratch: he gave

selected lieutenants and sergeants the job of figuring out where the districts and stations should be.[31] "I have the lieutenants and the sergeants sitting around the table for the first time in their careers reengineering" the department, he says. He gave them "one marching order: build it around the neighborhoods of the city."[32] Once the new districts were set, he drew their commanders from among the lieutenants who had drawn them up; they would have the authority to run the districts autonomously and would be fully accountable for the results. The reaction to this shift in paradigm? "They're having the time of their lives," Esserman says. "For the first time, you walk around headquarters (and) they're talking about the job again. Cops are coming in having scratched out plans" at home on their kitchen tables.[33] They were reengaged with the job, with the department, and with the city, some for the first time in a very long time. There was a palpable sense of excitement in the air.

By May 2003, just four months into the job, Esserman had plans from his lieutenants and sergeants and announced the creation of nine new neighborhood districts and the nine lieutenants who would have responsibility for each.[34] All nine districts would have their own substations and group of assigned officers, with the district's commanding lieutenant functioning as the district's "chief." One of the new district commander's first tasks, Esserman said, would be to get together with the community to decide on the location for the new substation.[35] As the new substations opened within the next few months, the reaction from community residents, businesses, and institutions, many of whom had been asking for an increased police presence for years, was overwhelmingly positive. The downtown district substation opened in office space donated by a local property company; a local college's criminal justice department set up a practice program with the substation in which sophomore students intern in the substation, staffing it for nine hours of school credit. And when the substation in South Providence opened, residents were ecstatic.[36]

The decentralization of the police department remains one of the cornerstones of Esserman's leadership. It was a bold, gutsy move, sure to upset the settled workings of the department in a way that few other changes could. Esserman led by literally creating an entirely new power structure—both physically, with the new substations strategically located in neighborhoods and built around them, and in terms of personnel, with his new "mini-chiefs"—the lieutenants in charge of each of the new districts. Giving away power instead of accumulating it was incredibly unusual behavior to see from a police chief, but if anything, it has succeeded beyond anyone's expectations—even as it has added to, not detracted from, Esserman's own stature in his adopted town. Esserman says that the decentralization of the department will produce gains against crime and disorder, since his police officers will be deployed in ways that make more sense vis-à-vis the neighborhood and its issues than they used to.

He also knows that, with officers more connected to the neighborhoods and the people in them, policing will become more service-oriented and respectful toward citizens. When people know each other, they are that much less likely to treat each other badly. Beyond this, it will bring the police and the community together as partners in producing public safety. On this point at least, the evidence is already clear. Both officers and residents of Providence love the new regime. The residents are glad to have the police in their neighborhoods working with them, and the police officers have begun to rediscover why they wanted to get into policing in the first place. One officer quoted in a newspaper article spoke for many in the department: "He's given me my career back," said Lt. George Stamatakos, who says he prefers Esserman's accountability-based system requiring officers to produce results on the street to the patronage and office work of prior days. "Now you're going to have as much success as you put into it. What more can you ask for?"37

BUILDING TRUST AND THE FOUNDATION
FOR COLLABORATION
Paul Evans, Boston Police Department

On March 25, 1994, not long into Paul Evans's tenure as Boston's police commissioner, a routine police operation went horribly wrong. Boston police officers executed a warrant obtained in a drug case, forcibly entering a house and holding the occupant at gunpoint. But the police officers, heavily armed and wearing the SWAT gear that is customary for such "entries," had burst into the wrong house. The man they found in the apartment was not a drug dealer, but Accelyne Williams, a seventy-five-year-old retired United Methodist minister with a heart condition.[38] Reverend Williams died of a heart attack on the spot; some said he was literally scared to death.[39] By any account, Reverend Williams's death was a tragedy. The police faced humiliation, a lawsuit, and the prospect of having the real culprit escape.

Naturally, Evans ordered an investigation and a review of policies to see whether any systemic failure had taken place; after the completion of the investigation, he suspended the lieutenant in charge of the raid.[40]

But just as important was what Evans did just one day after the raid: he publicly apologized on behalf of the department, calling Reverend Williams's death a grave, tragic mistake, and expressed sympathy to his family. To some, this may seem unremarkable, but Evans's statement was unusual in its candor, its clear expression of remorse, and its unequivocal acceptance of responsibility. In similar circumstances, police departments rarely issue apologies. In the context of Boston's history of racial antagonism between police and African Americans, Evans's statement was seen as a watershed event. An incident that might have inflamed tensions between the police and black citizens instead, according to one writer, "symbolized the city's progress."[41]

For a sense of how his simple apology distinguished Evans from other public officials involved in law enforcement, we need only look at the shooting of Patrick Dorismond several years later in New York City. Dorismond, who was working as a security guard outside a New York City club, was approached by an undercover police officer who wanted Dorismond to sell him some marijuana. When Dorismond refused, the undercover officer persisted. Dorismond became angry, and a fight ensued in which Dorismond died from a police gunshot wound. Dorismond was blameless; he was not a drug dealer, he had no marijuana, he had refused to sell anything to the undercover officer, and he had told the officer to get lost. He had not initiated any contact with the police or engaged in any criminal activity; for his trouble, he was killed. Yet not only was there no official apology, but Mayor Giuliani himself quickly began a public campaign to blame Dorismond for what had happened. Someone in the mayor's office, the police department, or the city government managed to dig up juvenile arrest records on Dorismond that were supposed to be confidential, and Giuliani used them to try to destroy Dorismond's reputation, making the victim out as a criminal who somehow deserved what he got.[42] None of the juvenile records had even the remotest connection with the incident in which Dorismond was killed. Giuliani's actions represent an extreme reaction to a police mistake: not just failure to acknowledge the deadly error but a despicable effort to assassinate the character of the victim. Giuliani's actions showed leadership of the worst kind.

By contrast, Evans's apology revealed him as a wholly different kind of leader from Giuliani. He understood that the trust of the community was at stake, and that he should do what he could, without prejudging the case, at least to admit the mistake. Reverend Jeffrey Brown of Boston's Ten-Point Coalition, one of the influential black ministers in the city who had started working the streets and had joined forces with the police in their efforts to control youth violence, looks back at Evans's apology for the death of Reverend Williams as a critical juncture, a moment at which the then-blossoming efforts at cooperation and partnership hung in the balance.[43] In the eyes of the community, Evans passed his first real test.

Evans's next test came only eighteen months later: with the killing of Paul McLaughlin. McLaughlin was a Boston prosecutor, part of a unit that handled Boston's toughest gang crime and violence cases. More than once, this had brought McLaughlin face to face with a violent sociopath named Jeffrey Bly, a young black man who was one of the leaders of a gang in the city's dangerous Mattapan neighborhood.[44] Bly had become involved in gang activities at age fourteen; by the time he was twenty, he had accumulated a substantial record of violent crime and had become known in his neighborhood as a remorseless thug who killed both friends and enemies and shot at passing cars from his front porch for fun.[45] In 1993, Bly shot his onetime friend Lee Simmons, who had had the temerity to tell Bly that he wanted Bly to return his bike.[46]

In 1995, McLaughlin tried Bly twice in court: once for a drive-by shooting, and once for selling drugs near a school.[47] Bly was acquitted on both charges, but McLaughlin intended to try him a third time, for assault with intent to commit murder and carjacking. On September 25, 1995, with his trial about to begin, Bly ambushed McLaughlin with a .38-caliber handgun during McLaughlin's commute home from work, killing him with a bullet in the head.[48]

The case sent shockwaves through the city. This was not just another gang killing but the calculated murder of a high-ranking government official in a blatant attempt to subvert justice. The message, if indeed any was intended, was clear: the criminal justice system was powerless to stop thugs like Bly. The murder was an expression of utter contempt not just for Paul McLaughlin himself, who Bly certainly perceived as his enemy, but for civil society and the rule of law. Several years later, the prosecutor at Bly's trial for the murder said bluntly that McLaughlin had been assassinated. "It was a planned execution. Paul McLaughlin was executed for doing his job."[49]

The murder presented Commissioner Evans and the BPD with a number of complicating factors. There were witnesses at the busy train stop and parking lot where McLaughlin was murdered, but the description they gave police was vague: a black man, probably young, wearing an oversize black hooded sweatshirt, with a bandana covering part of his face. This description fit too many young black men to identify anyone. Moreover, the black assailant had committed his crime in West Roxbury, a predominantly white, middle-class area, and the victim was a white government official charged with confronting violent crime. Reverend Jeffrey Brown and many others in the community recognized the combustible mix with which they were dealing: black-on-white murder, possible gang connections, and a direct assault against the criminal justice system. All of this led Brown and others to fear that police might react by pouring into minority neighborhoods, stopping, searching, questioning, and maltreating young black men matching the ambiguous description of McLaughlin's assailant—that is to say, almost every young black man.[50]

Brown and his colleagues contacted their trusted partner: Commissioner Evans. Brown, Evans, and others had a series of conversations throughout the day following McLaughlin's murder, and everyone agreed that a police response like the one in the Stuart case served no one's interest. When Commissioner Evans made a public statement about the McLaughlin case, he said that there would be an intense, complete, thorough, and speedy investigation. The police would find the killer, but they would do so using proper procedures, lawful tactics, and strategies that respected citizens and neighborhoods. Evans's tone, even when faced with the assassination of a senior law enforcement official, showed just how much the Boston Police Department had changed. According to David Kennedy of Harvard, one of the main architects of Boston's new approach to public safety in the mid-1990s (see chapter 4), Evans and his top leadership "made it very clear to the public and to their people that this was a problem that was going to be solved, that it was going to be solved honestly and uprightly and transparently, that Boston was not a place where black kids were going to be turned upside down on the street."

According to Reverend Brown, Evans and the department were true to his word: no street sweeps, no mass arrests, no arrests of questionable suspects who had to be released later. Evans's partners in the community, Reverend Brown and other members of the Ten-Point Coalition, followed the commissioner's press conference with their own. The black community, they said, stood united with the police, the prosecutors, and the entire criminal justice system in condemning the killing of McLaughlin and in calling for the community to be vigilant so that they could give the police department every possible assistance in apprehending McLaughlin's murderer. There was no equivocating, no hint of justification for "misunderstood" or "disadvantaged" or "misguided" youth.

Bly was eventually caught, tried, and convicted for McLaughlin's murder. The successful solution of the case proved to everyone that Evans's leadership was paying tangible dividends. It had helped the city avoid another race-driven investigation debacle. During the next six years of Evans's leadership, the Boston Police Department's incredible turnaround not just on crime generally but on solving the seemingly intractable problem of juvenile homicide (see chapter 4) made Boston's police one of the most lauded and studied in the country. Evans himself was often given credit for this, but he always gave it to the men and women in the department. However, it is surely fair to say that Evans's willingness to engage and work with the public set the tone and made possible much of what his subordinates accomplished.

Despite this consistent long-term success, unparalleled in most other cities, another dramatic test awaited Evans's leadership. In 2002, there were four fatal shootings by Boston police in the year's first eight months and ten days; three of those involved officers shooting at moving vehicles. In nearly one hundred shooting incidents by Boston Police between 1990 and 2002, forty included shots fired at moving vehicles.[51] In May 2002 alone, there were two incidents of police shooting at moving vehicles. In one, an unarmed man died when police officers shot him after he rammed a stolen car into their police car.[52] In the other, an officer shot and wounded a man driving a fleeing car near Copley Square; one of the bullets the officer fired went through a large party tent filled with prominent citizens attending a black-tie benefit for the Boston Public Library. No one in the tent was injured.[53]

These and other police shootings prompted Commissioner Evans to convene a high-level internal review board. Its mandate was to examine the patterns in the incidents in order to see if changes in policy, training, or supervision might be warranted[54]—a classic problem-oriented policing response. This investigation of police policy about shooting at vehicles was well underway on September 8, 2002, when, in the early morning hours, police officers in Boston attempted to halt a car that had failed to stop for a red light. The driver sped away, and soon came to a street where two other Boston police officers were involved in another unrelated incident. The driver struck one of the officers, who had tried to step in front of the driver's car. The officer rolled off the hood of the car; when the driver kept going, the other officer shot at the back of the fleeing vehicle several times. The bullets crashed through the rear window of the car, killing twenty-five-year-old Eveline Barros-Cepeda, a rear-seat passenger.[55]

In the immediate aftermath, there was an anguished outcry and a demand for action. Even the commissioner's allies within the black clergy did not hold back. Reverend Ray Hammond, then chairman of the Ten-Point Coalition, criticized both police training and policy. "This is not just an unmitigated tragedy; it demands an immediate response in policy and training and to the needs of the family," Hammond said. "I think we need to hear very quickly what the department is going to do to change procedures to ensure we don't have any more situations like this."[56] The car in which Barros-Cepeda was riding had already passed the police officers; the police gunshots had hit her through the back window. "You don't try to stop a driver from the rear," Hammond said, "especially when the car might be occupied."[57]

The next move was Evans's, and everyone knew it; the city looked to him for leadership on what could only become an even more volatile issue if it was mishandled. Evans did not flinch. Since the review board had been considering policy changes on the issue of shooting at moving cars for several months, he was ready to announce a new approach. From this point forward, Evans said, police department policy would prohibit shooting at any moving vehicle when the vehicle is the only force that a suspect has used, even if the vehicle is being used as a weapon against an officer.[58] His public statements were unequivocal: the new policy "prohibits firing at motor vehicles, period," Evans said. The department simply did not accept "the ability of a bullet to stop a car."[59] In a letter to the unions representing Boston police officers explaining the new policy, Evans elaborated. Shooting at a moving vehicle rarely stopped it and would inevitably lead to serious injuries and deaths, and such dangerous, ineffective tactics threatened to undo the department's relationship-building successes: "In order to police this city, we must have the support, trust, and respect of the public we serve. We must acknowledge that the use of deadly force, regardless of whether force is justified, has the potential to destroy the relationships that we have so diligently maintained over the past years."[60]

Equally unequivocal was the reaction of Boston's police unions, which ranged from outrage to apoplexy. "If a moving car is putting [an officer] in danger, [Evans is] encouraging the person to die or to allow people to be killed," said Thomas Drescher, a lawyer representing the Boston Police Patrolmen's Association (BPPA), the union for the department's rank-and-file members.[61] Drescher called the policy changes a "panicked response" to the death of Ms. Barros-Cepeda, despite the fact that the policy review had been under way for months. Thomas Nee, president of the BPPA, took an even harsher view. Commissioner Evans had prejudged the case and jumped to conclusions before the investigation had been concluded. Worse still, he had failed to back his officers. "Officers are out there risking their lives, and Evans is second-guessing them," Nee said.[62]

A little over a week after the shooting and the announcement of the policy change on shooting at moving vehicles, Evans "found himself at war with a union membership who felt betrayed," according to one Boston writer.[63] The union did not hesitate to wheel out its biggest weapon: the membership passed a unanimous vote of no-confidence and called for Evans's resignation. The commissioner, the BPPA said, should resign immediately; it was the police officers on the beat, not Evans, who had turned crime around in Boston.[64] Just a day later, another police union, the Superior Officers' Federation (SOF), announced that its members also disapproved of Evans's newly announced policy.[65] The SOF had "serious concerns" about the policy, it said, though it stopped short of either calling for Evans's resignation or taking a no-confidence vote. The SOF's president warned, however, that the union's position could change, and that it might yet decide to join the BPPA.[66] A third bargaining unit, the detective's union, withheld judgment pending a review of the policy, but it did not defend Evans either, although it, unlike the other unions, had had generally cordial relations with Evans in the past.[67] That is where Evans found himself days after the tragic shooting: on the wrong side of the unions representing most of his officers, who felt betrayed because he had tacitly condemned the officer who fired the fatal shots when he announced his new policy.

While Evans continued to take a public beating from within his own department, his nonpolice partners rose to his defense. Marlena Richardson, president of the Garrison Trotter

Neighborhood Association, was one of many representatives of neighborhood groups who came out strongly in support of Evans and his policy against shooting at moving vehicles.[68] While not all of the support for the commissioner came from citizen groups or organizations based in minority neighborhoods (the Boston Chamber of Commerce also issued a statement supporting him),[69] by far the most important support Evans got came from his closest allies in the community: the members of black clergy groups such as the Ten-Point Coalition, with whom Evans had painstakingly worked to address crime and violence in Boston and to whom Evans had continually proved himself—with his apology for the death of Reverend Accelyne Williams, with his strong but principled and restrained approach to the murder of prosecutor Paul McLaughlin, and in a thousand other ways.

These leaders knew what they had in their partnership with Evans, and they were not about to see it slip away in an internecine battle among the police ranks over who was "more blue." Reverend Ray Hammond of the Ten-Point Coalition said at a press conference that "we really do appreciate the difficulty of the job police officers do every day. But we also want to be sure that innocent bystanders and civilians aren't hurt, and that we don't undermine the trust that's been built up over the years between the police and the community."[70] Reverend Eugene Rivers, one of the founders of the Ten-Point Coalition and often a vociferous critic of the police, said that he wholeheartedly supported Evans, under whom the Boston Police Department had become "the most progressive police force in the United States."[71] He also said that the police were not responsible for the uptick in police-involved shooting in recent months; it was due to a small contingent of misbehaving youth and young adults in the black community itself [72]— surely a sentiment rarely heard at news conferences called to address issues involving tension between the police and the community. In discussions across the community, Reverend

Jeffrey Brown and other black leaders came to an immediate consensus. "We said, 'This man has been open and forthcoming and has been sensitive to what we're doing. Have we always agreed? No, but we've got a relationship here.'"[73] Brown says that they were ready and willing to take on the unions. "For the unions to take advantage of this, as a way to get rid of [Evans], we said, 'No way.'"[74]

Within a few days, Boston's mayor and Evans's boss, Thomas Menino, announced that he "continued to back the commissioner one hundred percent." Besides the fact that Evans had done a good job, Menino focused specifically on the support Evans had received in the community: "I think the community has confidence in him."[75] The state's attorney general threw his support behind Evans too, saying, "This department has come so far, and Paul Evans and his officers both deserve credit for that."[76]

Paul Evans did not resign; he served another year as Boston's police commissioner, eventually leaving to take a position advising police executives in Great Britain. His survival in the job despite an overwhelming show of no confidence from his officers was no accident. It happened not only because Evans had achieved results in the fight against crime, but because of his exemplary style of leadership. Paul Evans had not been "rewarded" with community support at the crucial hour; he had earned it.

The leaders in all of these examples have different personalities and personal styles. Their law enforcement agencies struggle against different background problems: corruption in Providence, for example, and the racial cast of past enforcement efforts in Boston. What the agencies have in common is leadership willing to work creatively, to take risks, to insist on results— even to give away the leader's own authority as a way of producing results. For preventive policing, this type of leadership could not be more important. Preventive policing—police work focused on getting ahead of problems before they produce social damage, on seeking long-term solutions that prevent crime rather than react to it after the damage is done, as traditional law enforcement does—represents a sea change in what police do and how they understand the job. Bringing law enforcement into this new era will take strong, independent, even iconoclastic leaders like Tom King, Dean Esserman, Jerry Barker, and Paul Evans. Police departments tend to be very traditional, even hidebound, organizations. Without the kind of leadership these chiefs have shown, preventive policing will remain an idea. But with their leadership, it can be the future.

7

Bending Granite or Curving Wood? Changing the Culture of Police Departments

In 1979, Dorothy Guyot published an influential piece of scholarship on police called "Bending Granite: Attempts to Change the Rank Structure of Police Departments."[1] Guyot voiced the frustration many felt when faced with the resistance of police organizations to change. Guyot said that rank structure in police departments led to lack of management flexibility, built-in impediments to free-flowing communications, and lack of incentives for police officers. Others have since borrowed Guyot's metaphor. In 1987, James F. Gilsinan and James R. Valentine turned the idea around, focusing on those who studied the police rather than on the police themselves. In "Bending Granite: Attempts to Change the Management Perspective of American Criminologists and Police Reformers,"[2] the authors argued that their data, gathered through the observation of a major police department's research and planning unit, showed that criminologists and reformers had overestimated the possibilities for change in police agencies. The data, they said, "indicate a rather limited potential for" any such reforms,[3] given the granitelike qualities of the "occupational culture" of policing.[4]

Whether the resistance comes from policing's quasi-military rank structure or from something else, most agree that police departments strongly resist change. Yet the distinguished scholar of policing Samuel Walker of the University of Nebraska insists that reform always requires changing the organization as a whole. The challenge, Walker says, is "how to change the organizational culture of police departments."[5] Real reform in police departments entails addressing every aspect of the culture that allows corruption to flourish and brutality to exist unpunished, and that condones breaking the law to enforce the law.

All successful cultural changes in police departments, from Boston to San Diego, have certain common features:

- Reconceptualizing and changing the mission of policing
- Measuring what matters in police departments, so that police departments do what matters
- Addressing the recruiting puzzle, because who becomes a cop has a lot to do with what kind of police department citizens get
- Changing the training that police receive to include an emphasis on human rights equal to the emphasis on crime-fighting strategy and tactics
- Changing incentive and reward structures, so that prevention and service-oriented police behavior are encouraged at least as much as arrests and emergency response

Through all of this, there must be leadership committed to changing the norms and values of the department to emphasize prevention and service, and a commitment to stay the course over the long period needed for true change. Real, deep change in police culture will take root only after "a generation" of police officers has been trained in and "raised" in the new, prevention-based, problem-oriented culture, to the point that "problem solving becomes the standard" and special rewards and recognition are no longer necessary.[6] The task of cultural change in police departments is not the impossible toil of bending granite but the process of curving wood: a slow, careful, and consistent pressure toward a new shape over time.

THE MISSIONS OF POLICE DEPARTMENTS
Rethinking What Police Do and Why They Do It

In 2001, Captain Ron Davis, a twenty-year veteran of the Oakland, California, Police Department, led an in-service training session on racial profiling at the Performance Institute in Washington, D.C.[7] Davis began by asking the assembled officers a simple question: "What is your job?" Silence and puzzled looks prompted Davis to explain further. "What I want to know," he asked, "is, what is your mission, and the mission of your department? To what are you dedicating your time, day after day?"

The replies were predictable. Most of the answers were variations on "fighting crime": "Catching bad guys"; "Getting criminals off the street"; "Keeping the streets safe from predators"; "Chasing crooks"; "Taking down the guys that need to be taken down"; "Responding to nine-one-one emergencies"; "Helping the department achieve its goals"; "Carrying out the chief's orders."

Davis told his audience that their answers were typical of those he heard everywhere. Then he asked, "What does your oath say? When you graduated from the academy and became a cop, you all raised your hand and took an oath. What did you swear to do?" Again, puzzled silence. Davis prodded the officers by asking, "Did anyone take an oath to fight crime? Who took an oath to catch bad guys? Raise your hands if you took an oath to respond to calls. Who took an oath to the chief, or to the department?" Silence. Finally, Davis repeated his initial question: "Does anyone remember what you took an oath to do?"

Eventually, an officer gave Davis the answer he sought: "We swear to uphold the law and the Constitution." Another officer spoke up. "Well, sure, that's the oath," he said, "but everyone knows what this job is really about. And if you don't figure it out in the academy, you learn it real fast after you hit the street. We go out, we patrol, we answer calls, and most of all we're supposed to catch the bad guys and lock them up. It's that simple."

"I agree that's what we think our mission is, that's how we see the job," Davis responded. "But that's the problem. The way we see the mission has got to change. Fighting crime is one thing we do, and it's very important, but it is just part of the job, not the whole thing. When we see ourselves that narrowly, the ways we respond to the situations we face and the range of people we encounter will be narrow. And we just can't keep doing that. We've got to broaden the way we think about our mission and what we do."

It is not wrong for police to enforce the law and fight crime, or to consider that task part of their mission. But to view their mission as confined to crime fighting cuts off the police officer from the public and neglects some of the most important reasons for having police. Any organization must start with a mission. If a police department does not inculcate its mission in its officers from the very start of their careers, they will come up with a mission for themselves, which may not be the mission the public or the department wants.[8] Law enforcement, Davis says, "is a tool, not a strategy or the mission" of a police department[9]; the primary goal of any police agency must be "effective, efficient, and ethical *service*" for the public.[10] Police departments that focus on enforcement can lose the public's goodwill in a single bad incident. Unless they have built up a reservoir of public trust by cultivating connections with the community, they will have nothing to fall back on.[11]

The mission of a police department, as adopted and promulgated by the chief, should set the tone of the department and give it direction that informs and guides everything the department does, from recruitment, to training, to the focus of officers' efforts in the field. Moving police toward an overall mission focused on service will necessarily bring them into

harmony with the core principles of preventive policing: building trust and partnership with the community, problem solving, and accountability. An agency focused narrowly on
enforcement will, by nature, encourage accountability only for
crime fighting, and even if successful, it will have little regard
for citizen input or the possible abuses of power that result in
citizen complaints and lawsuits, and little patience for the
"interference" of outsiders. Issues such as a given officer's willingness to use force, stop minority or female drivers at disproportionate rates, or treat the public rudely will also be of small
concern. Under a mission of service, by contrast, police act
according to and are judged by a far broader range of goals:
how they treat citizens, their building of relationships and
partnerships with them, and their ability to solve problems.

MEASUREMENT AND HOW IT CAN
TRANSFORM POLICE CULTURE
The Pass Model, Colorado Springs, Colorado

For some years, the Colorado Springs Police Department has had
a well-deserved reputation as an innovative, forward-thinking
organization.[12] During the 1970s, for example, the department
was one of the first in the country to hire its own crime analysts,
and it was among the earliest departments to encourage officers
to become closer to their communities and to engage in problem
solving.[13] By the late 1990s, the Police Department had reorgan-
ized its precinct structure to reflect the growing city's neighborhoods and adopted problem-oriented policing as the tactical
means to implement a community policing strategy.[14]

Two veterans of the Colorado Springs police team, Deputy
Chief Pat McElderry[15] and civilian employee Mora Fiedler,[16]
began developing a program in 1999 that would consolidate
these reforms and improve the department's entire culture. They
sought to engage the community in an accountability process
that would set goals and measure results. The new system they

devised is based on standards for police service generated jointly by the department and the community; they called it the Police Accountability and Service Standards, or PASS, Model.[17]

Fiedler and McElderry knew that many of the measurements that police agencies used to evaluate their effectiveness (arrest statistics, crime rates, the FBI's Uniform Crime Reports, amounts of drugs seized) do not in fact demonstrate effectiveness but merely record police activity. The PASS Model gives the Colorado Springs police the ability to measure accountability for police services.[18] It brings together the core concepts of preventive policing in a uniquely usable and beneficial form. The model provides the Colorado Springs police with a way to evaluate its organization, its supervisors, and its police officers from the community's perspective in order to match "police service outcomes" with the expectations of its citizens.[19] PASS identifies the public's expectations of police service as well as its emerging concerns and provides feedback that enables the department to modify its performance and service to meet changing needs and expectations.[20] The PASS Model unites police and the community around a joint set of expectations about the priorities set for, and the delivery of, police services, and in so doing, reforms and directs the police department and its culture in ways that citizens want.

The process of designing the PASS standards began with an effort by a small working group from within the department to formulate service standards. The working group brought its draft service standards to ten diverse citizen focus groups to help refine them into a tentative program. Working with citizens helped the department get a high degree of public buy-in for the standards that eventually emerged.[21] The city council approved the final standards, and they were incorporated into the long-range plan for the city and the police department.

As they emerged from the process, the Colorado Springs department's seven categories of service standards are:

- Response time
- Officer deployment
- Traffic issues
- Clearance rates
- Drug and vice activity
- Neighborhood policing
- Citizen satisfaction with police services

Each one of the service standards has outcome measures. For example, under response time, the service standard states that "the first police unit to respond to emergency calls for service will arrive within 8 minutes 90 percent of the time."[22] For traffic accidents without injuries: "The police response to non injury traffic crashes will occur within 20 minutes 90 percent of the time."[23] For telephone calls for police service: "The Public Safety Communications Center will answer incoming calls on the E-922 telephone lines within 10 seconds 90 percent of the time."[24]

Deputy Chief McElderry says that, for police officials, emergency response time might well be a lower priority, given the research showing that it is less important than most people think in solving crimes and public safety, but clearly response time is important to public perception of safety, so the police department must make it a priority. According to the surveys and focus groups, McElderry says, "what [members of the public] want to know is that if they really need you, you are deployed and ready to be there rapidly."[25] Supervisors and managers within the department can be held accountable, because the percentage of times that they meet each standard can be measured without ambiguity.[26] Citizen satisfaction with police services is then measured by regular citizen satisfaction surveys.[27] The results are used to establish a "baseline" of citizen satisfaction with police and the perception of public safety—a "satisfaction rate," we might say—that the department, all its managers, and all its officers seek to meet or surpass in the succeeding year.[28]

The police department's service standards reflect the priorities and concerns of the citizens and police officers of Colorado Springs; another city's service standards might be different. The incidence of serious crime in Colorado Springs is, fortunately, fairly moderate; citizens tell the police department that the crime rate is not as important to them as the handling of traffic issues and the way that individual police officers deal with citizens.[29] Of course, citizens' priorities may change in the future, but the PASS Model's service standards are not static; continual, periodic surveys and focus groups guarantee a responsive system.

PASS provides the Colorado Springs city council with clear criteria for evaluating the validity of requests for budget increases or new equipment. Every year, the city council asks, How well is the department doing in attaining its goals under the service standards? For example, in the most recent measurement period, the department met its service standard goal of responding to emergencies within eight minutes, not 90 percent, but only 58 percent of the time.[30] In order to achieve the goal, which the community helped to formulate, the department would need approximately X dollars for more officers and patrol cars. The council might or might not choose to supply these funds, but under PASS, all parties to the budget process have a clear idea of a definite goal and what resources it would take to attain it. The feedback mechanism built into the PASS Model demands that the department measure itself against citizen expectations, and citizens begin to expect involvement in the formulation of departmental priorities. The police and the community become connected; the communication that flows back and forth, Deputy Chief McElderry says, transforms the culture and values of the entire organization: "The input we have gotten from the community actually changes the way we do business."[31]

IF POLICE DEPARTMENTS ARE WHO THEY HIRE,
HOW DO THEY HIRE FOR CHANGE?
Police Recruitment and Hiring in St. Paul and Indianapolis

The people who graduate from a city's police academy determine the style of its police department. Hence, no city can change its policing culture without reexamining its recruiting and hiring policies. Hiring begins with recruitment, which offers police departments the first opportunities to express their mission and vision to potential applicants. Captain Ron Davis of Oakland recalls a slick recruiting commercial for a large police department he once saw on television. A thumping rock 'n' roll soundtrack blasted as young men and women took action, rappelling down the sides of tall buildings on ropes, charging forward in a group with assault weapons at the ready, wearing helmets and other military gear. They were the very picture of action-oriented, grab-the-situation-by-the-throat heroes. Davis thought that the ad was a commercial for military recruitment until he saw the graphic at the end, which asked those interested to call the police department's recruiting hotline.[32] Though the commercial may very well draw those who want to become crime-fighting action heroes, such an ad is unlikely to attract candidates with a service outlook toward policing. Not a single image of a citizen appeared in the entire advertisement. While physical courage, camaraderie, weapons, and heroism all play a role in police work, most day-to-day policing demands an entirely different set of skills: the communication-oriented approaches of building partnerships, solving problems, and providing leadership. More and more police departments emphasize working with the public and rendering service. If this kind of preventive policing is the future of law enforcement, we need to figure out how to attract more officers who will have the skills, desire, and values to do it.

Police departments in most cities typically get many more applicants for each police academy class than they can hire. The department winnows this applicant pool down to those who match their recruitment criteria; often just 10 or 20 percent of applicants are permitted to enroll at the academy with the hope of becoming a new (usually probationary) officer. The department attempts to weed out the obvious problem cases, such as those with criminal records or gang affiliations. Almost all departments also do psychological testing of one type or another to eliminate unsuitable candidates. Some use a more recently designed approach, called an assessment center, that focuses more closely on finding the right skills for the job.

The stories that follow from St. Paul and Indianapolis illustrate how two police departments succeeded in grappling with the difficulties of recruitment. Both involve race, but in neither story was race the factor that determined what the department ultimately did. Both departments are now poised for major breakthroughs in who, and how, they recruit. These reforms are as likely to change the cultures of their police departments as anything else they do.

As a member of the St. Paul, Minnesota, Police Department, Sergeant Dennis Conroy was one of those responsible for coming to grips with a department-wide recruiting problem.[33] Conroy, who served with the St. Paul Police Department for more than thirty years before retiring, had a background that made him uniquely suited to understand questions of the psychological makeup of his colleagues. He had served "just about everywhere" in the department, and had earned a Ph.D. in clinical psychology during his tenure. For the last ten or so years of his police career, he served as director of the employee assistance program, which counseled officers with alcohol and substance-abuse problems. Having been both on the street and "in the suite," he knew that some number of officers who became his counseling clients seemed both ill-suited to, and dissatisfied with, police work. He also knew that some significant number of the department's top-level leaders and training officers felt disappointed with the quality of the department's new recruits.[34]

Conroy's reexamination of the department's hiring and recruiting practices was provoked by the issue of racial profiling—or as Conroy calls it, racially biased policing. As in many cities in the United States, minority communities in St. Paul felt that police did not treat them equally. When those inside the department looking at the racial profiling issue asked Conroy what he thought they should do to eliminate it, he gave them a simple answer: hire people who don't do it.[35] Easier said than done, Conroy knew, but ultimately the St. Paul police realized that Conroy was on to something important. The department decided to rethink and restructure its whole hiring process from the ground up in order to make Conroy's straightforward advice a reality, and Conroy was given the job of spearheading the task.

While some might first have consulted the academic literature on employee screening or police recruiting in particular, or talked to experts in human resource management, Conroy took the unusual step of going to the community, especially to the minority community.[36] This approach made sense, Conroy thought, because these were the people most directly affected by racially biased policing. Conroy met with individuals, community groups, block groups, leaders of nonprofit organizations, and many others in order to answer a crucial question: What did these constituencies want in their police officers?

Despite meeting with much initial skepticism from both the minority community, who suspected Conroy merely wanted to polish the department's image,[37] and from the psychologists and other experts he consulted who dismissed the validity of community input out of hand, Conroy persisted.[38] Perhaps surprisingly, Conroy met little resistance from police officers and managers themselves, who took a pragmatic view: they simply wanted the best officers hired, and if the community could help them do that, they welcomed the assistance.

Conroy's surveys of citizen groups yielded surprising results. He had anticipated that respondents would focus on categories of race and sex that they believed to be underrepresented on the force (black men, women, and so on).[39] Instead, they detailed the personal characteristics that would make a good police officer. The traits they wanted most were:

Enthusiasm
Self-motivation
Good judgment
Creativity
Respect
Self-confidence
Courage
Tenacity
Tolerance and compassion
Honesty and responsibility
Loyalty
Good communication skills
Commitment to the community

The way people defined these traits in the context of policing also surprised Conroy. When citizens said that they wanted police officers to have courage, they meant more than physical courage to chase down a crook: "The courage to get out of their squad cars and walk over and talk to a group of kids hanging out on the corner. . . . The courage to admit that they've made a mistake."[40] When people said they wanted "commitment to the community," they didn't necessarily mean living in the community but an attitude of active commitment.[41]

Conroy and his colleagues concluded from the data they had gathered that the academy had not sought the right aptitudes in the past. Often they had looked for law enforcement experience, such as previous work as a police officer in another community, or as a military policeman. Conroy now realized that the guiding question should be not What have you done in law enforcement or some closely related field? but What kind of person are you?[42] In order to facilitate recruiting along these lines, the police department took these results to an industrial psychology firm, which helped them design guidelines for managers and recruitment specialists, as well as testing to identify crucial traits. They also put together protocols for the preemployment psychological screening interviews to enable them to do a better job of identifying potential recruits. Experience still counts, Conroy says, but a different kind of experience. Now a recruit will be asked not just (or not primarily) about experience related to law enforcement. There will be other questions: Have you done volunteer work in your community? Have you served on the boards of community nonprofit organizations? Do you coach Little League baseball or soccer or other sports? What kinds of things have you done, and what will you do, to connect with the community? Conroy says it's a complete shift in perspective: it's "hiring based on who someone is rather than what they've done."[43]

The St. Paul Police Department is now prepared to head in an entirely new direction on hiring, to begin the process of changing the culture of the department. This will be due in no small part to the efforts of Conroy and everyone who worked with him—both in the police department and in the community—to change the department's hiring process in a subtle but highly significant way. Conroy himself puts it in a nutshell: "It's easier and better," he says, "to hire good people and teach them to be cops, than to hire cops and teach them to be good people."[44]

The Indianapolis Police Department, whose chief, Jerry Barker, was introduced in chapter 6, has come up with a fresh approach to a recurring problem in police departments all over the country: recruiting minority police officers. As the nation becomes more diverse, especially with burgeoning Hispanic and Asian populations in areas that previously had few of either, police agencies have realized that they badly need officers from diverse backgrounds. Even in recent years, it has proved difficult for many cities to recruit, train, and field a force that "looks like" their cities. For many African Americans and Hispanics, law enforcement is not a top career choice, chiefly because of the long history of strained relations between police departments and minority communities. Yet it is vital that police departments recruit a growing number of minority group members if they are to build bridges with these communities and create partnerships based on trust. White officers are, of course, perfectly capable of doing this, but communities of color will remain distrustful of an all-white police department. When the problems that divide police and communities also include language and culture, as is often the case with Hispanic or Asian communities, there is simply no substitute for officers who speak the languages well and claim the culture as their own.

In Indianapolis, the police department attempted to increase the number of minority officers within its ranks by using Indianapolis's Weed and Seed organizations (see chapter 6) to get the word out to neighborhood residents on the police recruitment effort, and to actively recruit minority officer candidates through them.[45] Given the department's strong relationship to Weed and Seed, this was a logical, targeted way to enlarge the department's applicant pool among minority populations. At the same time, the department designed a brand new marketing effort to bring in not only more minority candidates, but a different kind of candidate altogether. The theme of Indianapolis's recruiting campaign was "Everyday Heroes"; the department wanted regular folks who could also be heroes in law enforcement. The campaign, with ads featuring the ordinary faces of real Indianapolis police officers, ran on television and appeared in local newspapers and on city buses.[46] Anyone living in Marion County, where Indianapolis sits, was encouraged to apply. Liz Allison, the department's grants administrator and one of the program's leaders, says that the department specifically wanted its recruits "homegrown" so they'd start out with a good feel for the community.[47]

Along with the Weed and Seed connections and the ad campaign, the police department set up what Allison calls a "virtual academy."[48] Anyone applying to be part of the class could come to a daylong simulation of the police training experi-

ence. The applicants received two hours of classroom instruction, took weapons training, drove a patrol car on a road
course, and spent four hours on shift with an actual officer.
The virtual academy proved very popular.

The next steps in the recruiting process were written and oral
exams and an agility test. The first two of these steps had proved
to be major stumbling blocks for minority applicants in the
past, Liz Allison says, largely because of their lack of experience
with test-taking situations and with the expectations of those
conducting the oral exam.[49] So Allison and her colleagues decided that they would offer tutoring in test-taking skills. Beat
officers and academy instructors taught an eight-week class in
exam-taking strategies to a group of candidates, ninety-eight of
whom came from minority groups; seventy-six of the minority
candidates stayed through the length of the course and took the
test. Seventy-three percent of these candidates passed, a marked
improvement from the 50 percent of minority candidates who
had passed in previous years and nearly the same as the 75 percent pass rate for white male candidates.[50] Liz Allison and her
colleagues then offered a two-week tutoring class on taking the
oral exam and interview, a phase of the process that had often
proved difficult for candidates with little formal job interview
experience. For the agility test, a phase of the process that had
knocked out many black female candidates in the past, the
department designed an eight-week training course.

The results were impressive. Indianapolis trains two police
academy classes a year. In the year *before* the new recruiting program, the city had nine black men in its two recruiting classes
combined, the highest figure ever but still much lower than the
department wanted. (For the five prior years, the city had averaged four black men in both of each year's two recruiting classes
combined.) The first class *after* implementing the new recruiting
program included eight black men in just one recruiting class—
fully one-third of the whole group. "We know we aren't there
yet," Liz Allison says, "but we are certainly off to a great start."

TRAINING TO CHANGE POLICE CULTURE
What's Human Rights Got to Do with Law Enforcement?

In America, nearly every law enforcement job with a public agency requires the successful completion of a substantial number of weeks of formal training, followed by some period of field training in which the recruit rides with an experienced officer. Candidates learn everything from the substance of the law they'll enforce, to the limits that the U.S. Constitution puts on investigative practices, to the radio codes they'll use to call the dispatcher or each other. They will have training on the use of lethal and nonlethal weapons, conducting investigations, making arrests, interviewing witnesses, crowd and riot control, and how to fill out reports properly. Most also receive instruction on how to patrol an area in a squad car, how to chase a suspect in a squad car, the use of the car's siren and lights, and the way that the car must be taken out and returned after a shift. There will almost certainly be training on the finer points of the chain of command, the proper way to wear the uniform, and the way that a police officer should conduct him or herself in public.

But it is unlikely that most police officer trainees will receive any training in civil or human rights, the flashpoint for so many of the struggles in our society between police officers and the public, particularly minority groups. Those departments that do cover these topics in their training typically spend little time on them. Moreover, whatever training recruits get in civil rights or constitutional law is usually taught not to help officers understand how to protect these important American values, but as part of a section on "avoiding liability"—how to steer clear of lawsuits for violating the rights of the public. Little effort is made in such classes to show how a genuine regard for human and civil rights properly sets the standards for law enforcement and police conduct.

A few organizations concerned with human rights have recently begun to offer training sessions in human rights to both new recruits and veteran police officers. Among the most original and powerful versions of this new type of training for police is conducted by the U.S. Holocaust Museum in Washington, D.C. The museum is well known for the power of its exhibits and its emphasis on public education and outreach. Within the larger Holocaust story, some of the museum's photos and artifacts tell an important story-within-a-story: it's the tale of how the pre–World War II police of Germany—by all accounts, a professional, nonpolitical arm of government under the Weimar Republic—were gradually co-opted by the Nazi regime in the service of its racist ideology and eventually became a tool that facilitated the legal persecution of Jews and other minorities. The museum makes clear that the co-opting of the German police played a key role in the Nazi's ability to bring about the Holocaust.

Ken Howard, a retired police captain with thirty years of service in the Washington, D.C., area who now works for the U.S. Department of Justice's Office of Community Oriented Policing Services, has worked as a volunteer facilitator of the human rights training for police at the museum during the last several years. In all the time that Howard worked the street as a police officer, supervised patrol officers, and even taught them in the police academy, the subject of human rights or civil rights came up only in the context of what officers should do in order to avoid legal trouble.[51] At the museum, Howard and the other trainers work with officers to elicit relevant lessons from the full exhibit, focusing on what the history of the police in 1930s Germany reveals about a proper conception of the police officer's role in a civil society. "The role of a police officer is to protect everyone in society, not just some people," Howard says. "When we look back in history to 1930s Germany, we see when the police began the slide [toward] not being independent professionals, not protecting everyone, and what happened as a result. And we see how that comes into play when someone above them decides who gets protection and who doesn't." From there, the discussions continue with an emphasis on how the lessons of history connect with issues contemporary law enforcement faces, including race relations and racial profiling.

There is, Ken Howard says, some occasional resistance to the training. He rarely sees this in new recruits, who come to the training as part of their academy curricula, but he does see it sometimes among veteran officers who come for in-service training. They think that the program is about something Jewish and therefore not of interest to them, or that having to go through the program somehow implies that they are Nazis. But the overwhelming response is positive. Howard reads the anonymous evaluations the officers fill out before leaving, and he says most of the officers really "get it."[52]

Until now, the training at the Holocaust Museum has been available only to officers in or near the Washington, D.C., area, for practical and geographic reasons. But the U.S. Department of Justice's Office of Community Oriented Policing Services began an effort in 2003 to take the Holocaust-based training national. Howard says that the lessons of his work are very clear to police officers in post–9/11 America. These officers are, of course, the first responders to any emergency. They're the ones who will be there, on the ground, if there is another terrorist attack. "And we have to be aware that because someone has dark skin, or wears a turban, or has a beard, that we cannot single those folks out. We can't take shortcuts across the Constitution. Law enforcement gets a lot of pressure from the community to take those shortcuts," Howard says. "And it's the chiefs and the sheriffs that have to stand up and say, *No, no, no, no!*" Howard says that police leaders are increasingly willing to assert "that a lot of the things we're getting pressure to do are inconsistent with our relations with the community and our charge to the Constitution of this country."[53]

Part III

THE FUTURE OF POLICING

8

Ashcroft Policing: The Wrong Lessons

You should inquire whether the individual . . .
has ever had any personal involvement in [advocating, planning,
supporting, or committing terrorist activities.][1]

—One of the questions John Ashcroft's Justice Department
instructed FBI agents to ask post–9/11 interview subjects

I doubt they got anything to fight terrorism. To ask whether you
advocate terrorism? What kind of jackass would say yes?[2]

—MO ABDRABBOH, attorney who represented
numerous interview subjects

The following is a transcript of an actual post–9/11 interview
conducted by the FBI following Attorney General John
Ashcroft's order. It was recorded by the interviewee's attorney.

FBI AGENT: Do you have any knowledge regarding the cause
of the events on September 11? [3]
INTERVIEWEE: No, sir.

AGENT: Okay. Are you aware of any person, that his reaction to the events of September 11, made it seem as though they weren't surprised?
INTERVIEWEE: No.

AGENT: Maybe had some advance knowledge or they thought that this was going to happen?
INTERVIEWEE: No.

AGENT: Do you know of anybody who has any knowledge or involvement in advocating, planning, supporting, or committing terrorist acts?
INTERVIEWEE: No.

AGENT: Anybody you've ever come across?
INTERVIEWEE: No.

AGENT: Do you know anybody that you would determine would be capable or willing to carry out acts of terrorism?
INTERVIEWEE: No.

AGENT: Are you aware of any plans or discussions about the commission of terrorists acts? Obviously not.
INTERVIEWEE: No.

AGENT: Do you have any ideas about how future terrorism could be prevented? Maybe anything you've ever heard of in your travels—you would have a better idea than I or Agent [another agent's name] because you have actually traveled in this country from a foreign nation. Was there something that you saw as you were coming in that you said, "Boy, you know, that's probably—"
INTERVIEWEE: No.

AGENT: Nothing like that?
INTERVIEWEE: No.

AGENT: Have you ever heard of anything in the course of—you know, where you've heard people say, "This is how you could do this," or, "If you wanted to get to the United States and you don't have a visa, you could do this"; you've never heard any—
INTERVIEWEE: No.

AGENT: Would you recognize the names of any of the suspects of September 11?
INTERVIEWEE: No.

AGENT: 'Course not. I don't think there were any [citizens from interviewee's country of origin] who were associated—
INTERVIEWEE: No. I think they were all [inaudible].

AGENT: Yes. Are you aware of anyone raising money for terrorist activities? Either here or back home? I'm trying to think that, in your country, there's a faction, is it Hamas, or Hezbollah?
INTERVIEWEE: Hezbollah.

AGENT: No knowledge of anyone here who's doing fund-raising or financing?
INTERVIEWEE: No.

AGENT: Have you personally ever contributed to an entity which you know or suspected, where you think, well, you're donating money to a cause which maybe you heard that money is being funneled off somewhere else?
INTERVIEWEE: No.

AGENT: A terrorism fund?
INTERVIEWEE: No.

AGENT: You're not aware of anyone who's raising any money through drug trafficking or fraud schemes?
INTERVIEWEE: No.

AGENT: Are you aware of anybody receiving training at military camps or other facilities?
INTERVIEWEE: No.

AGENT: Okay. Have you ever know anyone who has taken flight lessons? To fly airplanes or—
INTERVIEWEE: No.

AGENT: Are you aware of anybody who may have sympathies for the September 11 hijackers or other terrorists?
INTERVIEWEE: No, never.

AGENT: No? Right. Are you aware of anyone receiving training in the use of weapons?
INTERVIEWEE: No.

AGENT: Bombs, chemicals, something like that?
INTERVIEWEE: No.

AGENT: Have you ever heard of anybody here in the United States or abroad recruiting individuals for the purpose of engaging in violent acts against the United States government?
INTERVIEWEE: No.

AGENT: Do you know of anyone who is preaching violent jihad or urging others to overthrow or attack the United States?
INTERVIEWEE: No.

AGENT: No. Do you have access to guns, explosives, or harmful chemicals? Even if you haven't, do you hunt? I don't know, people hunt; do you target shoot?
INTERVIEWEE: No.

AGENT: No harm in that.
INTERVIEWEE: I didn't even know you could . . .

AGENT: Now, do you know of anybody who possesses or who has tried to purchase firearms or explosives or chemicals?
INTERVIEWEE: No.

AGENT: No? Okay. Do you know of anybody who would have a background maybe in biochemistry or something who would be capable of fashioning some kind of biological or chemical weapon?
INTERVIEWEE: No.

AGENT: Yeah, I just want to say to you that there are certain things that we don't expect people to have any knowledge of, and there are certain things that I know are prevalent in the community that we don't have a complete understanding of how it works. Now, I know one thing that particularly in [interviewee's town] we discovered is that there's an underground market for identification. I'm sure you've seen some of the things on television about commercial driver's licenses. Things such as that. I mean, are you aware of anybody who possesses, or could be involved in the selling or supplying other people with false identification, or fraudulent documents that would be used in support of supplying for the false identification?
INTERVIEWEE: This is first time I hear.

AGENT: You never heard of anything like this before?
INTERVIEWEE: No. First time.

AGENT: That's good. Yeah. And it's something that [inaudible] recorded yet. Some people we talked to, they do have some knowledge, and we talked to people and they say, "Oh yeah," and it seems to be prevalent, and that's why we're hoping that we can maybe tie it up so [inaudible] . . . Were you aware of any person or groups in your homeland who might be planning or advocating terrorist acts against the United States?
INTERVIEWEE: No.

AGENT: Okay. Do you know of anybody who could help the U.S. in its fight against terrorism?
INTERVIEWEE: [Inaudible].

AGENT: Okay. Where you're living on [interviewee's street], are you aware of any suspicious activity in the neighborhood, or community, or circle of acquaintances that might suggest—
INTERVIEWEE: No. My neighbor is an old lady.

AGENT: [Inaudible] or anyone you go to school with or—
INTERVIEWEE: No.

AGENT: Is it a younger neighborhood, or an older neighborhood, or—
INTERVIEWEE: My neighbor, she is old.

AGENT: Yeah?
INTERVIEWEE: Yeah.

AGENT: Okay. Do you know of anybody else that might have some information on the topics we discussed? Someone who may know something about obtaining false documents, someone who may know something about—
INTERVIEWEE: No.

AGENT: No? Okay. Are you aware of any criminal activity whatsoever? Regardless of whether it's terrorism or not, anything that might be of interest to the United States government?
INTERVIEWEE: No.

At this point, the agent winds the interview up by asking for the interviewee's help.

AGENT: Would you do me a favor? If I left you a business card, your attorney already has one, if you do think of anything, or

if something does come up, even if you think it could be totally unrelated, or you think it's not important, but it's kind of a
little bit suspicious, if you could just call me with it? Would
you be willing to do that?
INTERVIEWEE: No problem.

AGENT: Would you be interested, which it obviously has, and
I don't know to what degree it's going to continue, we've had a
tremendous [inaudible], we need translators, we need tran-
scribers, people who could read Middle Eastern, or Arabic, languages or writing. Would you be interested or does your
schedule permit that?
INTERVIEWEE: I don't know, you know, I am doing my mas-
ter's, and I—

AGENT: But if time permitted—
INTERVIEWEE: If I have time.

AGENT: Do you have any questions for me? You've been a
tremendous help, if there's anything I can do to help, explain
what it is we're doing, any questions I can answer for you?
INTERVIEWEE: No.

AGENT: No?
INTERVIEWEE: No.

AGENT: Well, nice talking to you.

*   *   *

The interviewee's attorney says that given his experience and
that of the other attorneys he knows who have represented many
interviewees, this interview is strongly representative of the interviews the government conducted. Perhaps not surprisingly, the

Department of Justice never shared any of the specifics of what it learned through these interviews; Attorney General Ashcroft simply assured the public that the Department gained valuable information. Yet a General Accounting Office study found that there was no evidence of anything productive emerging from the interviews, calling the results of the interviews "difficult to measure"; it also noted that as of April 2003, the Justice Department had not analyzed either all the data obtained in the interviews or how effectively it had implemented the interview project.[4]

Robert Olson, former chief of police in Minneapolis and former national president of the Police Executive Research Forum, a widely respected organization that does in-depth research for police leadership around the country, remembers that as chief in Minneapolis he examined the list of questions the Department of Justice wanted police to ask before the questioning began.[5] Olson was appalled. "I said, 'This is an interrogation, it's not an interview.'"[6] He told the federal authorities in his city that if he sent his officers to interview those on the Minneapolis list, who were mainly Somali, he foresaw the destruction of the relationships his department had worked hard to build with the Somali community, whose members reacted with fear and suspicion to police because of the history of violent and corrupt police and government officials in their home country. Olson said the Justice Department was "nuts," and he didn't want his officers participating in "this blanket thing."[7] "I said, 'I go there and it's just going to drive a wedge between us [and the Somali community] and they're going to tie us directly to the federal government, INS, the whole schmear.' And so I just quietly said [to the federal authorities], 'I don't want to do that.'"[8] And ultimately, the Minneapolis police did not participate.

This questioning of "nonsuspects" is emblematic of the Department of Justice's approach to antiterrorism investigation and of Ashcroft policing in general. It is a shotgun approach, sprayed over huge numbers of remote possibilities. It ignores the hard-won knowledge of on-the-street law enforcement officers and even its own veteran FBI agents who have long experience in antiterrorism work. It threatens to swamp the rights and civil liberties of those it puts in its crosshairs, often by going to the very edge of what is legally permissible and sometimes beyond. Just as important, Ashcroft policing completely ignores the important and growing opportunities for, and lessons taught by, preventive policing. By ignoring these lessons, the Department of Justice threatens to destroy preventive policing just as it has begun to take root and succeed, and in so doing, Ashcroft policing blithely ignores an opportunity that only preventive policing provides: the greatest possible chance to prevent another terrorist attack.

ASHCROFT'S WAR ON IMMIGRANTS

In the months following the September 11 attacks, one of the main strategies of John Ashcroft's Department of Justice emerged: using violations of immigration law, even the most technical ones, as a pretext to arrest, detain, and investigate people as potential terrorists. This approach quickly gained steam, showing up in a number of Department of Justice initiatives, despite objections by police that it would be disastrously counterproductive because it would destroy the trust of immigrant communities in law enforcement. But the effect of the "war on immigrants" strategy actually reverberated far more widely than just these government initiatives. In a bid to gain traction on the larger issue of illegal immigration, anti-immigration groups quickly seized on the Justice Department's line of attack to further their own agendas by labeling immigration policies that they did not consider sufficiently tough as harmful to the war on terror and national security.

The war against immigrants began in the aftermath of the September 11 attacks as a direct response by the Department of Justice to the threat posed by the terrorists of Al Qaeda. All of the nineteen suicide hijackers were young Muslim men from the Arab world; enforcement would therefore focus on people from the same groups who were in the United States. This would include not just young Muslims from the Middle East in the country temporarily on visas, but immigrants from Muslim countries generally. The legal problem raised by this thinking was that only the tiniest number of those in this large population had even the weakest imaginable links to terrorism. And only a very small number of them had actually committed any crimes for which police could take them into custody. Even if police did find evidence of criminal activity for which to arrest and jail them, the government would then have had to follow the normal protocols of due process: charging them relatively quickly, giving them lawyers, and the possibility that they might be granted bail. So immigration law, which required none of these legal protections, became one of the chief tools the department adopted for use in the war on terror to target and detain those it suspected but against whom it had no evidence of terrorist activity.[9]

Beginning right after the September 11 attacks, hundreds of Arabs and Muslims were taken into custody by the F B I.[10] Virtually all were detained; while 3 percent were detained for three weeks or less, the government kept the average detainee in jail for eighty days, and a quarter were confined for over three months.[11] The department held the detainees incommunicado, refusing to release any information on their identities even to their families.[12] Inverting the usual presumption of innocence, Ashcroft's policy on the detainees was "hold until cleared," regardless of the lack of evidence that any detainee had involvement in the crimes of September 11 or any other aspect of terrorism.[13] Since immigration cases are almost always civil and not criminal matters, the Justice Department claimed that the presumption of innocence did not apply because the detainees were in the country illegally[14]—even though, by any fair definition of the word, the detainees were imprisoned. Even once cleared, most of the detainees—those whose immigration status was the least bit out of order—were deported; others were released as harmless or held for petty crimes.[15] Not one was involved in terrorist actions.[16]

On the heels of these detentions came the announcement of the "voluntary" interviews of the five thousand young "non-suspects" from Arab and Muslim countries in the Middle East. This was followed by other actions targeting Muslim immigrants, like the institution of the National Security Entry-Exit Registration System, or N-SEERS, which required all visitors from certain foreign countries to be photographed, finger-printed, and interviewed—to provide a variety of detailed personal information every time they entered the country—and then periodically to reregister. N-SEERS began by requiring registration for visitors from five countries (Syria, Libya, Iraq, Iran, and Sudan) and was then quickly expanded to twenty-five countries—all Muslim nations, except North Korea.

A great deal of controversy greeted the N-SEERS program, and its implementation was a confusing mess from the beginning. Compounding the disarray, Ashcroft announced that individuals who violated N-SEERS—including those who failed to leave the country by the time of the expiration of a visa (a civil law violation)—would have their names and identifying information entered into the National Crime Information Center (NCIC) database. This is the database that receives queries from police officers every time they make a traffic stop or an arrest; it tells them whether the person is wanted on warrants for anything, anywhere, and gives them information on criminal history. Putting immigration violations into the database meant that violators of immigration law would show up in the system as wanted, and police would arrest them. In practical terms, this meant that local police would virtually have to enforce immigration law. (Ashcroft later expanded this policy by directing the federal government to enter more immigration information, including information on those who had violated immigration orders to leave the country, into the NCIC database.)[17] Officials also announced their intention to enter information on foreign students into the crime database; any time a person on a student visa did not maintain a sufficient number of credits or a high enough grade point average, they would show up in the database. In a routine encounter with police, this would result in an arrest.[18]

According to professor Michael Wishnie of New York University Law School, putting this information into the NCIC database is illegal. "Congress carefully delineated the categories of information that may be entered into this very powerful database" in order to assure its accuracy, since law enforcement officials use NCIC data millions of times every day, Wishnie says.[19] Neither NCIC data nor its use have ever had anything to do with immigration.[20] Immigration records are also notoriously inaccurate and out of date. Thus, in its zeal to have local police enforce immigration law whether they want to or not, the Ashcroft Justice Department is willing not only to exceed what the law allows but to risk corrupting NCIC with inaccurate data.

The Ashcroft Justice Department began pressing local police directly into the business of enforcing immigration law in April 2002,[21] changing a long-standing official policy to the contrary.[22] Ashcroft did this despite laws in many states prohibiting the police from making arrests for these very immigration infractions. He wanted police departments to enforce not just serious criminal violations of immigration law but relatively trivial civil immigration violations as well—the most common and least serious infractions. Republican members of Congress attempted to force this obligation onto state and local police by introducing the Clear Law Enforcement for Criminal Alien Removal (CLEAR) Act of 2003,[23] which affirmed the Department of Justice's desire to get local police involved in immigration enforcement. The act and its companion bill in the Senate[24] faced immediate and significant opposition. Some objected to yet another unfunded federal mandate; others, such as Grover Norquist of the strongly conservative Americans for Tax Reform and David Keene of the American Conservative Union, told President Bush that the CLEAR Act would set a dangerous precedent by giving local officials the power to enforce many federal laws.[25] But the loudest outcry came from state and local police officers themselves, who recognized the huge threat to public safety that local immigration enforcement by state and local police would create, because it would alienate local police and immigrant communities from each other. The police on America's streets knew implicitly that if immigrants, legal or not, thought that local police were working with immigration agents, they would not report crime for fear that they or members of their households might be detained or deported. Police would stop receiving information and intelligence on crime in these neighborhoods, and witnesses would hesitate to come forward. Victims would not receive the help they needed; predators would remain on the street to victimize others. Unfortunately, the Department of Justice and its allies on Capitol Hill seemed willing to ignore the hard lessons local police had learned about this in the past, in places like Chandler, Arizona.

The Chandler Fiasco

For a case study in why local law enforcement agencies should not be involved in immigration enforcement, the Department of Justice and members of Congress need look no further than Chandler, Arizona. By the mid-1990s, Chandler had become one of the fastest growing cities in the United States, with a population of over 100,000, about 20 percent of it Hispanic.[26] Just 150 miles from the Mexican border, Chandler had long attracted its share of immigrants, both legal and illegal. As it began to grow in the early 1990s, new jobs became available, especially in construction, and undocumented workers from Mexico often filled the jobs and built the homes, schools, and commercial structures that the community needed. But the increasing population of undocumented workers also caused some residents to complain, and in 1997, the Chandler Police Department joined the INS and U.S. Border Patrol to do something about it.

From July 27 through July 31, 1997, the Chandler police and INS/Border Patrol conducted a joint operation to ferret out and capture illegal immigrants. Over this five-day period, 432 undocumented persons, all of them Hispanic, were arrested and deported.[27] The operation was highly visible and attracted considerable media attention. The police and INS trumpeted their success and commended one another on their cooperation.[28] But in the days and weeks that followed, Hispanic residents vented their outrage at how they and many others had been treated in the course of the operation. Many described incidents in which they were humiliated, harassed, and made to produce citizenship or residency papers, despite having been born in Arizona and having family roots in the United States for many generations. The media coverage, initially favorable, quickly turned negative as the Hispanic community's reaction took center stage. The law enforcement officials involved defended their actions. Chandler police chief Bobby Joe Harris told the local newspaper that police had had full legal probable cause for every contact they made with anyone during the operation. If officers had gone to a home, Harris said, it was because someone had told officers that there were illegal aliens in it: "We didn't just randomly go to these places."[29] Frank Mendoza, a spokesman for the Chandler police, told the newspaper that officers were not "hanging around schools, harassing children or busting down doors in search of illegal immigrants."[30]

When complaints began to mount, however, Arizona attorney general Grant Wood began a formal investigation, and his findings directly contradicted the police department's statements.[31] The operation had been mounted on the basis of an informal working relationship between the Chandler police and the INS, without either the written agreement required by

INS regulations[32] or any training or education for police officers
in immigration law.[33] Though their own regulations specifically
prohibited it (their role was strictly "limited to providing security to immigration officers" in such an operation),[34] Chandler
officers often took the lead, stopping and detaining American
citizens, legal residents, and illegal workers without any
INS/Border Patrol presence, just to inquire about citizenship
and immigration status.[35] Often, police records showed that
officers and agents did not explain the reasons for stops or
record them anywhere. Rather, people were stopped on a mere
pretext for the purpose of investigating their immigration status "for no other apparent reason than their skin color or Mexican appearance or use of the Spanish language."[36] From a
legal point of view, they were often stopped without probable
cause or even reasonable suspicion (a lower standard) that they
might be illegal aliens.[37] Homes were entered without warrants, sometimes because of tips that were completely
unverified.[38] American citizens were ridiculed and humiliated
while under detention, children were interrogated, and
schools and businesses were targeted. Scores of people were
put through the wringer in a city where some had lived their
entire lives. Some children were so traumatized either by their
own encounters with police or by witnessing the questioning
of parents and grandparents that they remain fearful whenev-
er they see police or hear a knock on the door.

   If these abuses were both illegal (Attorney General Wood
found that the Chandler police and the INS violated both the
Fourth and Fourteenth Amendments to the U.S. Constitution)[39]
and personally harmful to those who endured them, the worst
damage may have been done to the Chandler Police Department
itself. The operation virtually destroyed its relationship with the
Hispanic community. Just a week after the end of the operation,
more than one hundred citizens attended a special neighborhood meeting at which public officials heard an outpouring of
complaints and anger from city residents.[40] A week after that,

several hundred people attended a city council meeting on the operation. Many residents testified at the meeting about their experiences during the police action, all of them expressing anguish and outrage.[41] Chandler police also held two other meetings of their own with angry residents.[42]

Incredibly, police and INS officials continued to wonder what the fuss was about. Chief Harris welcomed Wood's announcement of an investigation, stating that the Chandler police "have nothing to hide."[43] Rob Daniels, a spokesman for the INS, said that the criticism frustrated INS agents. "What I have found in my dealings with Hispanic activists is that they're no different from any other extremist group," he said. "They're going to exaggerate to make their point."[44] The damage to the relationship between the Chandler police and the public, Wood said, was profound:

> The joint operation created an atmosphere of fear and uncertainty. . . . [It] has damaged the relationship between a local law enforcement agency and the public it serves. . . . Community policing efforts. . . . are predicated upon the belief that enhancing relationships between "beat" officers and neighborhood residents will lead to mutual trust and respect. It is this mutual trust and respect that will in turn enhance the ability of local police to obtain from willing citizens the information and support necessary to carry out their mission to protect and serve. [The operation] greatly harmed the trust relationship between the Chandler Police and many of the City's residents.[45]

Immigration Opponents Along for the Ride: Latinos in the Crosshairs

The war on immigrants in the aftermath of September 11, 2001, began as a war against Middle Eastern immigrants, but it has become a war against all immigrants. This is not only because of government initiatives (though legislative proposals like the CLEAR Act would focus local law enforcement on all immigrants, regardless of their countries of origin). Rather, a number of nongovernmental organizations that have long argued for immigration crackdowns have latched on to the post–9/11 interest in securing our borders against terrorists, using it as an opportunity to pursue their own agendas: namely, tougher government action against immigration from Mexico. In so doing, they have shown themselves willing to make the most cynical use of the need for border security for their own ends by claiming that illegal immigration of Latinos presents a grave threat of terrorism—despite the lack of any credible evidence implicating Mexico in cross-border terrorism or even as an Al Qaeda staging ground or transit point. And if they have their way, these anti-immigration groups will push the government to abandon one of the most successful preventive policing initiatives of recent years.

By most estimates, there are roughly 8 million illegal immigrants in the United States, mostly from Mexico.[46] With a growing population of young people of working age, Mexico has chronically high unemployment. The United States has many employers who will hire undocumented workers because they can typically pay them much less than they would pay U.S. citizens. Those who cross the border illegally risk being caught and deported and even dying in harsh desert conditions, yet thousands upon thousands of Mexicans find it worth their while to try. The labor of illegal undocumented workers from Mexico is likely to remain part of our economy for years to come; it is fully integrated into the American way of life.[47]

The presence of illegal workers in the United States creates a unique crime problem, separate and apart from their immigration status. Because these millions of workers cannot obtain any official documentation of their identities, such as a Social Security number, they cannot open bank accounts. Since they often live in transient circumstances with groups of relative strangers, they must keep the cash they earn with them at all times, at least until they are able to send it home to Mexico, typically via expensive wire transfers. This makes them enticing victims for robbers: the predators know they carry lots of money and that they are extremely unlikely to call the police for help, given their immigration status. To see how preventive policing solved this problem, we have to leave the cloistered confines of the Department of Justice and Washington's airy think-tank debates and get down to the streets of Austin, Texas, where Rudy Landeros makes his living.

Landeros has been with the police force in Austin throughout his entire career, and now holds the rank of assistant chief.[48] In 2000, Austin police realized that while 28 percent of the population was Latino, Latinos made up *47 percent* of all reported robbery victims. Landeros and his colleagues knew, moreover, that hundreds of other robberies of Spanish-speaking immigrants went unreported, simply because the victims were afraid that the police might report them to INS.[49] Their reluctance to report crimes made these Latinos uniquely vulnerable. In 2000, Austin saw four violent robbery-homicides; all the victims were immigrants, three from Mexico, one from Nicaragua.[50] Landeros gathered a working group, including representatives of the police department, the Catholic Diocese, two members of the city council, the Texas secretary of state, the Texas Association Against Sexual Assault, and the Hispanic Chamber of Commerce to work on the problem. They launched a Spanish-language outreach campaign to encourage undocumented immigrants to come to the police when they were victims, witnesses, or when they had information on who in the community was committing crimes. According to Landeros, the message was unambiguous: "Trust us. We are not immigration, we are not going to arrest you, and we are not going to deport you."[51]

The outreach program helped; reports of armed robberies in Austin climbed 20 percent almost immediately as a direct result of the appeal to illegal immigrants to report crimes to the police.[52] But Landeros knew that to make real headway, he

had to try to prevent crimes before they happened by addressing the root of the problem: illegal immigrants who could not
put their money into banks because of the lack of acceptable
identification to open accounts. Landeros and the working
group approached Wells Fargo Bank, which agreed to allow
immigrants to use a piece of identification called the *matricula
consular* to open bank accounts. The *matricula consular*, a document issued by Mexican consulates to its citizens abroad, was
not new; it had been in use for decades, though only sparingly.
But Wells Fargo saw an opportunity to serve the large market
of Mexican workers in the U.S. by accepting the card as a form
of identification to open bank accounts. In the bargain, these
people became safer from opportunistic predators who wanted
to steal the money they carried.

Landeros remembers the almost instant enthusiasm for the
matricula consular bank account proposal in the community as
word spread. Landeros and his officers began attending community meetings along with a Wells Fargo representative. Up
to 1,500 people attended in some places. At one meeting, Landeros was seated next to an immigrant, a laborer with cal-
loused hands. When the man heard that he could get a bank
account, he turned to Landeros. "He said, 'I want to join now, I
want to open a bank account right now.' He took out his wallet, and he showed it to me. He had $7,000 in his wallet. I asked
him why he carried so much money with him, and he said, 'I
can't leave it at home and there's no place else to put it.'"[53] The
man was, of course, a perfect robbery target.

The program was successful immediately. Immigrants
signed up with Wells Fargo by the thousands. Other large
banks jumped in, among them Bank of America, Bank One, JP
Morgan Chase, and CitiBank. Mexican president Vicente Fox
ordered all Mexican consulates in the United States to work
with local police departments and banks to duplicate the success of Austin's efforts. While a relatively small number of the
cards were issued for over a century, Mexican consulates in the

United States suddenly began issuing an increasing number, with more than 1 million issued before 2002 and a million more in 2002 alone.[54] Austin saw an immediate reduction in robberies and violent crimes. Between March 2001 and March 2002, the number of Hispanic victims reporting robberies jumped dramatically due to the outreach campaign. Even better, between March 2001 and March 2003, the Austin Police Department arrested 154 people who were committing these crimes on a serial basis. By August 2003, not only many banks, but many governmental institutions—more than one hundred cities, 900 police departments, and thirteen states—were accepting the *matricula consular* as identification. Of course, it cannot be used to attain citizenship, to vote, or to get a Social Security number or a work permit. But it does help the undocumented population come out of the shadows enough to prevent a significant number of major violent crimes.

Yet despite the *matricula consular*'s place as the linchpin of a hugely successful crime prevention program, immigration opponents have pulled out all the stops to turn the acceptance of the *matricula consular* back, by attempting to jump on the antiterrorism bandwagon. Marti Dinerstein of the Center for Immigration Studies, a Washington think tank that has long advocated much tougher immigration enforcement, says that the *matricula consular* is the main weapon of an "audacious political maneuver" by the Mexican government to "achieve at least quasi-legal status for its undocumented population in the U.S."[55] She calls the card fraud-prone and a tool for criminals and terrorists. While she concedes that "the vast majority of illegal Mexican immigrants are not terrorists," she says that many undocumented Mexicans are criminals "who routinely commit other crimes."[56] The *matricula*, she says, has "become a shield that hides any past criminal activity."[57]

Why, then, would police applaud and encourage its use? Dinerstein answers with a slanderous slap in the face of law enforcement: police are deluded and lazy. Police departments want to accept the *matricula* card, she says, because "some ID is better than no ID" and they have decided they don't want to be bothered making immigration arrests.[58] Congressman Tom Tancredo of Colorado, who has consistently taken antiimmigrant positions during his tenure in Congress, sees the acceptance of the *matricula* as nothing less than an "attack on the whole concept of citizenship" that allows Mexico to get money sent home from Mexican workers in America even as the nation is diminished.[59] Mark Krikorian, executive director of the Center for Immigration Studies, calls the use of the *matricula consular* "a challenge by Mexico to American sovereignty."[60] Congressman Tancredo displayed a three-foot-long version of a *matricula consular* card at a news conference. The card featured a large photograph of Mexican president Vicente Fox, an "excess" that drew strong protests from the Mexican ambassador to the United States.[61]

With the U.S. Treasury Department prepared in 2003 to issue formal regulations giving banks the option of accepting the *matricula*, Tancredo and other opponents in Congress, including Rep. F. James Sensenbrenner, chair of the House Judiciary Committee, persuaded the Treasury Department to take the highly unusual step of reconsidering the new regulations, which by then were essentially finished. After reconsideration, the Treasury Department still elected to allow banks to accept the *matricula*. According to a spokesman for Treasury, "This was a decision on whether the rules were adequate to deal with the security concerns"[62] raised by Tancredo, Sensenbrenner, and others that the *matricula* was susceptible to fraud and therefore endangered national security and the struggle against terror.[63] According to Treasury officials, the numerous security measures already in place "provide an ample mechanism to address any security concerns."[64] Nevertheless, Representative Sensenbrenner and others said that the Treasury's regulations would not be the final word on the *matricula*, and Sensenbrenner said he was considering legislation to reverse the regulations.[65]

Tellingly, the statements of Representatives Sensenbrenner and Tancredo make no mention of the drastic improvements in public safety that the *matricula* has meant in places like Austin, where Assistant Chief Landeros works. Opponents of the *matricula* continue to call it a threat to national security, even though the Bush administration's own Treasury Department has twice found that existing procedures adequately address any possible threat. David Aufhauser, the well-respected former Treasury official in charge of stopping the flow of money to terrorist organizations after September 11, strongly agrees. "The idea that the *matricula* cards pose, currently, a threat to national security, is comic," says Aufhauser. "I cannot remember a single time when a counterfeit *matricula* card was used by a Mexican immigrant in a terrorist plot in the United States."[66] Yet immigration opponents continue to bash away at the use of the *matricula consular* in the most extreme terms. For example, Mark Krikorian of the Center for Immigration Studies calls acceptance of the *matricula* "a de facto creeping amnesty to take place without the White House having to sign its name to it."[67] If this sentiment prevails, police will be set back, and Ashcroft policing will once more have triumphed over sensible preventive policing tactics.

PROFILING INSTEAD OF PROBLEM SOLVING

Prior to the terrorist attacks of September 11, 2001, almost 60 percent of all Americans—not just African Americans and Latinos, who had long complained about the practice, but all Americans—said that racial profiling was a widely used police tactic; more than 80 percent said they disapproved of racial profiling and wanted it rooted out of law enforcement.[68] But within days of the attack, poll takers spotted a dramatic shift in opinion on the issue. In the post–9/11 world, almost 60 percent of all Americans, including African Americans and Latinos and others who had experienced it, now approved of profiling—as long as those scrutinized were Arabs and Muslims.[69]

Many members of the organizations in charge of law enforcement and airport security shared these views. In a cover story in *Time* magazine on airport safety, officials in charge of security complained of being forced to abandon profiling because of political correctness, despite its obvious usefulness in the situation. One airport security officer at Denver International Airport told *Time* that for him, "profiling is the only way to be conscientious in doing the job. I make decisions based on who I wouldn't like to be seated next to on an airplane." According to the officer, appearance was all-important, despite the possibility of stereotyping or prejudice. "If someone is unkempt and nervous or it they look like they belong on a bus instead of a plane, if they wear a baseball cap backwards, and, without question, if they look to be foreign or of Middle Eastern descent," that person would be stopped and searched.[70] Bruce Baumgartner, the manager of aviation at Denver International, was one of a number of officials at the airport who told the magazine that "more profiling needs to be done, not less."[71]

These sentiments are not hard to understand. In the minds of the public, it may seem obvious that we should focus our law enforcement and antiterror efforts on members of the same ethnic group from which the nineteen suicide hijackers came. Accordingly, the Department of Justice has made profiling of Arabs and other Middle Easterners a basic component of Ashcroft policing, despite protestations to the contrary. But what may be an understandable aspect of public opinion turns into a grave mistake when the Justice Department makes it into public policy and law enforcement strategy, because, whatever else one can say about racial or ethnic profiling, one fact stands out: it doesn't work. Using it now, as Ashcroft policing does, as a key antiterror tactic will not make us more safe; it will make us *less* safe. By any measure, it fails to qualify as preventive policing.

To get a sense of why racial profiling cannot work as a law enforcement or antiterrorism tool, we need to look at the new research on the topic, done in the two or three years preceding

September 11, 2001.[72] That research revealed, for the first time, that when police do not have a particular suspect's description, using race or ethnic appearance as a clue to decide who to stop, question, and search is *not* an effective way to target law enforcement efforts. On the contrary, making race or ethnicity a factor in a profile results in a significant *drop* in the accuracy and efficiency of police work.[73] Police are less likely to catch crooks when they use race than when they don't, because race takes their eyes off what is important—keen observation of suspicious behavior—and puts them on a factor that doesn't predict criminality: skin color. Profiling is, in short, an attempt to gain an advantage for the police that actually decreases law enforcement's accuracy.[74]

For example, a study conducted by two well-respected Columbia University researchers in 1999 at the request of New York State's attorney general[75] revealed that police in New York were, in fact, targeting individuals for stops and frisks based on race,[76] and that using race this way did not help the NYPD catch more criminals. In fact, the police were *less* successful catching bad guys when they used race than when they did not use it.[77] When police stopped and frisked whites, without using racial cues, they succeed in finding a criminal about 20 percent more often than when they used race as a factor in deciding to search blacks.[78]

Another example is even more eye-catching because it illustrates how the problem can be overcome. In the late 1990s, the U.S. Customs Service admitted that it actively profiled black women passengers on overseas flights and investigated them with strip searches and body cavity examinations.[79] Since it did not analyze its own data, the Customs Service did not know that its targeting policies were actually hindering its efforts: searches using race were actually less successful than searches not using race.[80] Once the media uncovered these practices, the Customs Service's then-new commissioner, Ray Kelly, who is now the commissioner of the New York Police Department, promised to change things. Among the many modifications Kelly made in Customs procedure were to (1) require a supervisor's permission for any kind of body search; (2) require that any line customs officer be able to articulate a factual basis for suspicion, and (3) require that all suspicion be based on behavior, not appearance. He also instituted training to make sure these changes "took."[81] The results were dramatic. In just two years, searches dropped to one-third of their former level. Hit rates—the rates at which Customs searches found criminal activity—rose from the range of 5 to 6 percent to approximately 13 to 14 percent, a stunning 250 percent increase. And the hit rates across racial groups evened out, with all demographic groups coming out at roughly the same rate.[82]

The smart move right now for law enforcement groups most intimately involved in the fight against terrorism would be to turn away from racial profiling to one of the primary tools of preventive policing: problem solving. And some in law enforcement seemed to get this right away. Just days after the 9/11 terrorist attacks, five high-ranking members of the American intelligence and law enforcement services disseminated a memorandum to officials throughout the government. As reported in the *Boston Globe*, the five antiterrorism specialists identified the primary tool for those interested in defeating terrorism: close observation of suspicious behavior that might precede another attack.[83] The memorandum cautioned American law enforcement worldwide against using profiles based on race, nationality, or other physical characteristics, and counseled that only looking at behavior, not appearance, would solve the problem. Investigators should look at "what a person has done and plans to do, rather than who that person is," in order to prevent terrorism.[84] Even though the September 11 hijackings were carried out by Arab Muslims, "looking for a person who fits a profile of a terrorist is not as useful as looking for behavior" that indicates participation in an attack,[85] one of the intelligence specialists who wrote the memorandum said, "It's only human to say these people are different. But fundamentally, believing that you can achieve safety by looking at characteristics instead of behaviors is silly. If your goal is preventing attacks . . . you want your eyes and ears looking for pre-attack behaviors, not characteristics."[86]

These experts acknowledged that the behavior-not-characteristics approach would seem counterintuitive to many people who believed that they knew that profiling Arabs and Middle Easterners was the obvious, commonsense solution. More troubling, though, was that the Department of Justice so clearly and decisively rejected their counsel, even though it came from years of experience and knowledge gained in the trenches of counterterrorism work.

In the first days following September 11, the administration did at least "talk the talk" against profiling. Both President Bush, in one of his first presidential speeches,[87] and Attorney General Ashcroft, in the hearings on his own nomination,[88] had taken the position that racial profiling was wrong and would end under their watch. Ashcroft was unequivocal: racial profiling, he said, "is wrong and unconstitutional no matter what the context."[89] And, after the attacks, President Bush and the Department of Justice delivered the same message. Bush visited a Washington, D.C., mosque and condemned those who had targeted Arab Americans for abuse, harassment, or hate crimes. All people, he said, should be treated as individuals and not tainted by group guilt.[90] Attorney General Ashcroft's statement, just two days after the terrorist attacks, condemned such ethnic targeting as worthy of Al Qaeda, not the United States. "We must not descend to the level of those who perpetrated Tuesday's violence by targeting individuals based on their race, religion, or their national origin."[91] One of Ashcroft's chief deputies, Michael Chertoff, then head of the Department of Justice's Criminal Division, told senators that the department and the administration "emphatically rejected ethnic profiling."[92]

But when we look at the actions of federal law enforcement after September 11, a very different picture emerges, and ethnic profiling of Arabs, Muslims, and Middle Easterners is its central feature. As discussed earlier in this chapter, in the first weeks and months after September 11, the Department of Justice detained hundreds of men, the overwhelming majority of them Arabs, Muslims, and others of Middle Eastern and South Asian descent. Almost all of these men were detained for immigration violations; a few were jailed for petty criminal activity.[93] Almost all were deported; not a single one had any links to Al Qaeda, the September 11 attacks, or terrorism in any form.[94] Despite Attorney General Ashcroft's words, these actions showed an undeniable pattern: the government equated "Arab or Middle Eastern Muslim male" with "potential terrorism suspect." And this pattern continued, with the "voluntary" questioning of the thousands of Middle Eastern "nonsuspects."

Ashcroft's Department of Justice targeted Arabs and Muslims again in January of 2002, when he announced the "Absconder Apprehension Initiative."[95] Under this program, the INS, which was part of the Department of Justice,[96] would make it a priority to apprehend and deport six thousand absconders—foreigners who had been ordered deported but who had somehow remained in the country.[97] Clearly the department was not wrong to try to catch them and deport them; they had previously been ordered deported. What made the "absconder initiative" suspect, though, was the fact that of over three hundred thousand absconders at large in the United States, most were from Latin America, while the six thousand the Department of Justice would pursue on a high priority basis were all from Arab or Muslim countries.[98]

The pattern of profiling by the Ashcroft Justice Department has continued in the time since. On September 11, 2002, the one-year anniversary of the attacks, the Justice Department launched the N-SEERS program, which, as discussed earlier, required foreigners from particular countries (again, almost all of them in the Arab or Muslim world) to go through a registration process when entering the country. The process included photographing and fingerprinting, and the individuals processed had to reregister thirty days after entry, then after a year, and then as they left the country. Failure to register was made a crime. Fifteen months into the program, over 80,000 immigrants had registered, and the federal government was preparing to deport approximately 13,000 of them.[99] And the pattern continued into 2003, as reports began to circulate that the FBI had directed its field offices to make a census of mosques in their territories. This would be used to construct a demographic profile that the agency would use to assess whether each office had conducted a sufficient number of terrorism investigations and wiretaps. A senior official of the FBI told *Newsweek* magazine that the bureau needed the mosque census because of "concern about undetected 'sleeper cells' and troublesome evidence that mosques may be serving as cover for terrorist activity."[100] When the program became public knowledge, the FBI tried to spin it as an effort not to target Muslims but to protect them. Mosques were being counted, FBI officials explained, because "in the past they had been targeted for violence."[101]

Federal instructors also began to train state and local officers in the use of traffic stops as a pretext to spot potential terrorists, just as they once did for the purpose of catching drug couriers. The methods these instructors have imparted to their police officer "students" have been far from subtle. Just as the officers in the 1990s were trained to look for drug indicators—things like air fresheners and fast-food wrappers—today the federal government is training these officers to look for indicators of, for lack of a better term, "Muslimness." Among the items police are taught to look for besides phony passports or fake or stolen driver's licenses," *USA Today* reported, are "prayer rugs and copies of the Koran, Islam's holy book."[102]

There did come a point at which Attorney General Ashcroft and the president had a chance to make clear, once and for all, whether their words about racial profiling were anything more than rhetoric. In June 2003, Ashcroft announced that the Justice Department would issue "policy guidance" to fulfill President Bush's promise to end racial profiling in America. The department announced that the policy guidance "bars federal law enforcement officials from engaging in racial profiling" when making "routine law enforcement decisions—such as deciding which motorists to stop for traffic infractions."[103] In a "fact sheet," the department clarified just what it meant. First, when federal law enforcement agents engaged in routine activities, such as "traffic or foot patrols," that did not involve ongoing criminal investigation of specific criminal activity with a description of a particular suspect, the prevention of catastrophic events, or national security, "these general responsibilities should be carried out without *any* consideration of race or ethnicity."[104] The fact sheet also said explicitly that "stereotyping certain races as having a greater propensity to commit crimes is absolutely prohibited" and "reliance upon generalized stereotypes continues to be absolutely forbidden."[105]

But the "policy guidance" applied only to federal agencies, not to state and local departments, which do the great bulk of law enforcement work that might involve profiling. Neither the Justice Department nor Congress could regulate racial or ethnic profiling by state or local agencies directly, but there have been proposals in Congress that would make the receipt of federal funds by state and local police departments contingent upon taking actions against profiling, such as the End Racial Profiling Act.[106] As of the middle of 2004, however, the Ashcroft Justice Department had never supported the End Racial Profiling Act or any comparable effort. Even more telling, however, is what the Department of Justice wrote into its policy: an exception that allows the use of race or ethnicity "to prevent threats to national security . . . or in enforcing laws protecting the integrity of the nation's borders."[107] Federal law enforcement can make use of race, ethnic appearance, or alien

Top priority will go to the prevention of terrorist attacks and the apprehension of terror suspects before they can do their terrible damage.[109] Thus the FBI is, in every sense, the top law enforcement agency on the terrorism beat in the country. While local and state police departments also have many tasks related to homeland security, the FBI has the primary job of ferreting out terrorists in the United States and stopping their plans for mass casualty attacks. If we are to be protected from terrorist actions in America, nothing is more important than assuring that the FBI's culture is appropriate to this all-important job.

The FBI and its leaders know this, and they realize that they need help, particularly from agents and employees who speak Arabic and understand Arab culture. FBI director Mueller understood this well enough that just days after the 9/11 attacks, he pleaded for Americans with foreign language skills to sign up as government linguists.[110] The bureau's need for translators had become particularly acute by late 2003. Only 21 of its more than 11,000 agents spoke Arabic, and it had managed to hire just a fraction of the number of translators it needed to comb through the ever-increasing numbers of recordings made through a rapidly growing network of FBI wiretaps and bugs. Despite a heavy recruiting campaign, the FBI had just over 200 Arabic linguists by the end of 2003, still nothing close to the number it needed. Instead of the twelve-hour turnaround for translation of critical documents that Mueller has mandated, recordings still languish in secure storage lockers, waiting, sometimes for months, to be translated. Asked by *Newsweek* if the FBI was meeting Mueller's twelve-hour goal, a senior FBI official's reaction said it all: he just laughed.[111] Surely the laughter signified not something funny, but something sad: agents at every level of the FBI know that if something is left untranslated too long there could be potentially catastrophic results. According to *Newsweek*, before September 11, "millions of hours of talk by suspected terrorists" captured on tape were not translated until after the attacks.[112] Since the need for agents and translators and others who understand the language, culture, and nuances that will allow the FBI to gather intelligence is so desperate, one would probably assume that Director Mueller and his top people would do everything in their power to transform the FBI into an organization that would welcome the people who could help it with its mammoth task.

Not so. While many agents in the field seem to understand what kinds of cultural changes it may take to attract and keep people from the Middle Eastern community as agents and translators, many others clearly do not. This has an impact both inside and outside the bureau that we can ill afford. The FBI's alleged treatment of two of its own agents is a telling example. Both had had extensive counterterrorism experience and were well regarded for years within the FBI. But after September 11, at a time when the FBI seemed to need them the most, both found their careers damaged—one fired, and one sidetracked.

Gamel Abdel-Hafiz, an Egyptian-born American, seemed to be just the type of person the FBI needed in the post–9/11 era. He'd been with the bureau for a decade, first as a translator and then as an agent. He was a Muslim and fluent in Arabic.[113] He had served as the FBI deputy legal attaché in Saudi Arabia, gathering crucial confessions in the case against an alleged terror cell in Lackawanna, New York, and in the suicide bombing of the USS *Cole* in 2000.[114] He had also worked on the terrorist bombings of two U.S. embassies in East Africa in 1998, and led an investigation of charities tied to terrorist organizations.[115]

Despite his unique skills and key work in antiterror investigations, some members of the FBI began to raise doubts about Abdel-Hafiz. In 1999, Abdel-Hafiz was asked to wear a recording device as part of an ongoing investigation of a charity with alleged ties to terrorist groups. During the internal debate on the tactic, Abdel-Hafiz said that "a Muslim does not record another Muslim." While he would have done it had life been at stake, Abdel-Hafiz says (and he had in fact investigated Muslims this way before), there was already a considerable amount of other evidence available. Since the taping seemed unnecessary for law enforcement objectives, Abdel-Hafiz said, he wanted the other agents to understand that if he were found to be wearing a wire, it would compromise his ability to undertake investigations among Muslims in the future.[116]

Abdel-Hafiz's FBI supervisor, Danny Defenbaugh, head of the FBI office in Dallas where Abdel-Hafiz was posted, backed the decision not to have him wear the recording device.[117] But one of the other agents involved did not, accusing Abdel-Hafiz of putting loyalty to his religion over loyalty to the FBI. Robert Wright, an agent at the bureau's Chicago office, took the unheard-of step of calling a Washington, D.C., news conference, at which he accused an unnamed Muslim FBI agent who worked at the Dallas office of undermining an investigation into Hamas, the Palestinian terrorist group. Wright accused the agent of refusing to tape a subject of the investigation because he was a Muslim, describing it as an instance of the FBI's incompetence in antiterrorism investigations before September 11.[118] Given the few Muslim agents in the FBI, both ABC News and the *Wall Street Journal* were able to confirm quickly that Abdel-Hafiz was the agent Wright referred to in the news conference.[119] (Danny Defenbaugh, Abdel-Hafiz's supervisor, urged Abdel-Hafiz to file a religious discrimination complaint against Wright. He filed the complaint in May 1999, but it remained pending as of this writing.[120]) Less than two years later, FBI director Louis Freeh assigned Abdel-Hafiz to the deputy legal attaché post in Saudi Arabia, where he got the confessions in the *Cole* and Lackawanna cases.[121]

When Abdel-Hafiz and his supervisor in Saudi Arabia, himself a converted Muslim, made a religious pilgrimage to Mecca, a top FBI official complained.[122] The supervisor was transferred back to New York, and Abdel-Hafiz soon found himself under investigation.[123] The bureau, it seems, had received information alleging Abdel-Hafiz's involvement in an insurance fraud in 1991 before he joined the FBI. The source for these accusations was, of all people, Abdel-Hafiz's ex-wife. According to her, Abdel-Hafiz had faked a burglary at his residence in order to collect insurance money. She had not reported the alleged fraud before, but said she was reporting it now because "she was upset about her former husband's life with his new wife and three children."[124]

Despite this rather obvious motive for Hafiz's ex-wife to lie, the FBI pursued the investigation. It eventually fired Abdel-Hafiz, ending the career of one of its few Muslim Arabic speakers. The FBI confirmed the firing, but would not give a reason for it. Comments by an FBI spokesman clearly point to the conclusion that the bureau fired Abdel-Hafiz because he had not disclosed the existence of a lawsuit over the insurance claim in his FBI background investigation.[125] The application, Abdel-Hafiz later explained, asked about involvement in court actions; he thought that he had only filed a claim with his insurance carrier and was unaware of anything filed in a court, so he had not listed the matter. The suit was settled in 1994, before he became an agent.[126] Nevertheless, this meant he was fired. The FBI spokesman said that, generally speaking, failing to give fully truthful answers on an application showed "a lack of candor"[127] and that that was the cause of his firing; Abdel-Hafiz says that this oversight would have been excused or punished less severely if he were not a Muslim.[128] Even after the FBI reinstated Abdel-Hafiz in early 2004, one of the FBI's most potentially valuable assets in the struggle against terror has been compromised, since he is now useless as an undercover agent because of his very public firing.[128a]

Unfortunately, Gamel Abdel-Hafiz is not the only FBI agent to be affected by the FBI's culture. In mid-2003, Bassem Youssef, the FBI's highest-ranking Arab American agent, filed a lawsuit alleging discrimination in the way the FBI used him in the time since September 11, 2001.[129] Youssef alleged that he had been excluded from key assignments since that date, and especially those involving counterterrorism.[130] Fluent in Arabic and possessed of an intimate understanding of Arab culture, politics, and diplomacy that is exceedingly rare among FBI agents, Youssef is also the bureau's only agent qualified to give polygraph examinations in Arabic.[131] Yet the FBI allegedly held him back from senior positions and assignments in which he could be most useful—those involving possible terrorist acts at the hands of Middle Eastern Arabic-speaking terrorists.

This has had concrete consequences, according to Youssef. In one instance, a man allegedly walked into the FBI's field office in Miami claiming to have information about Osama bin Laden and Al Qaeda terrorists. Agents in the Miami office requested that Youssef, who was fluent in Arabic, interview the man, but the FBI's counterterrorism section objected to Youssef's involvement in the interview, and Youssef was barred from it.[132] The informant could not disclose what he knew since there was no one to interview him in Arabic, and he stopped cooperating with the FBI. Whatever information he might have had was lost.[133] The harmful effect of this treatment, Youssef alleges, only begins with its impact on him. Cutting him out of this work and losing intelligence opportunities amounts to a profound loss in the war against terrorists. "The FBI permitted racism to interfere with national security," Youssef said in a filing with the FBI's equal-opportunity office.[134]

Are these cases a matter of prejudice, racism, or discrimination against Arab American or Muslim agents, or just the unfortunate difficulties faced by a couple of agents who happen to be Muslims? Are there, perhaps, extenuating circumstances in both cases that the FBI has not disclosed? Are these cases, in other words, part of a pattern that tells us something about the culture of the FBI and whether it welcomes, or has even begun to welcome, Middle Easterners and Muslims whose help it so desperately needs? Anyone looking not just at the cases of Abdel-Hafiz and Youssef but for telltale signs of the cultural atmosphere of the FBI will know the answer, and it is not a happy one.

When Gamel Abdel-Haifz says that he was the subject of suspicion, prejudice, and unfair treatment by "old timers" within the FBI,[135] chances are he means people like John Vincent, a former FBI agent who questions the loyalty of any Muslim agent to the bureau. "The most important thing in a Muslim's life is his religion, the second most important thing is his religion, and the third most important thing is his religion," Vincent told CBS News.[136] "We don't need Muslim agents in the FBI."[137]

Another FBI agent has a softer spin on Vincent's attitudes. "There is a predisposition among many agents at the FBI to believe that in some parts of the world blood is thicker than a citizenship certificate. There's a general perception that family relationships and tribal loyalties mean more to an Arab American than an American whose ties to the Old World are many generations removed."[138] This belief that Arab Americans will be loyal to Islam or to their ethnic groups or families first and to the FBI second, if at all, allegedly infects FBI workplaces; in his lawsuit, Bassem Youssef actually had to ask that Director Robert Mueller issue an explicit order banning FBI employees from calling Arabs "rag heads," "camel jockeys," and "sand monkeys."[139]

In a large room at the very hub of the bureau's translation nerve center in its Washington field office sit the 150 members of CI-19, an FBI counterintelligence office that has the vital task of translating the Arabic conversations captured by wiretaps and bugs in the effort to find the clue that will prevent the next terrorist attack. The room is literally divided by a partition; on one side are cubicles of foreign-born Muslims, and on the other is everyone else. According to Daniel Klaidman and Michael Isikoff of *Newsweek* magazine:

> Some of the U.S.-born translators have accused their Middle Eastern-born counterparts of making disparaging or unpatriotic remarks, or of making "mistranslations"—failing to translate comments that might reflect poorly on their fellow Muslims, such as references to sexual deviancy. The tensions erupt in argu-

ments and angry finger-pointing from time to time. "It's a good
thing the translators are not allowed to carry guns," says Sibel
Edmonds, a Farsi translator who formerly worked in the unit.[140]

Unfortunately, the FBI's culture has an impact beyond what it
does internally to relationships between its own agents. These
internal tensions would be harmful enough, since they can
interfere with the public's safety from terrorism. (Witness
Bassem Youssef's exclusion from the debriefing of the Miami
"walk in" who offered information on bin Laden and Al Qaeda.)
But these FBI cultural attitudes affect the relationship of trust
between the FBI and those it serves when, inevitably, they
escape from the inside of the agency to the outside. In the fall
of 2003, the FBI announced that it would honor an Arab American activist from the Detroit area, the home of the country's
largest Arab and Middle Eastern population. Imad Hamad,
director of the Arab American Anti-Discrimination Committee
and a tireless community activist, had done special service by
helping the Detroit-area FBI and U.S. Attorney's Office build
relations with the Arab American community after September
11, 2001. He had been a leader of ALPACT, the Detroit-area
council set up to build trust between police and communities
(see chapter 3), and had emerged as ALPACT's key person from
the Arab community. Along with U.S. Attorney Jeffrey Collins,
Hamad had also served as co-chair of BRIDGES (Building
Respect in Diverse Groups to Enhance Sensitivity), an organization of law enforcement and Arab community leaders. For
these and other activities, the FBI called Hamad in September
and told him that he would be honored with the Bureau's
Exceptional Public Service Award from FBI director Robert
Mueller. Collins called the award "well deserved" and lavished
praise on Hamad as an effective leader and partner of law
enforcement. "Imad has just been a terrific leader in building
bridges of trust," said Collins. Hamad's role in BRIDGES had
been critical. "Having that dialogue builds confidence and

faith in law enforcement. The absence of that dialogue builds mistrust."[141] Hamad expressed deep feelings of gratitude. "It's like a blessing that gives you the strength and energy to believe that, despite racism and bigotry, America will not fail to recognize those who are of service to their community."

But a couple of weeks later, just before Hamad was to travel to Washington, D.C., to receive the award, everything changed. At Director Mueller's order, the FBI suddenly rescinded the award, casting doubts on Hamad's character and implying possible connections with terrorism.[142] Mueller refused to give a reason for the abrupt change; the FBI later released a statement that "evidence referencing Mr. Hamad has been filed in connection with an upcoming deportation proceeding against associates of his. Accordingly, this award has been withdrawn."[143] Even though Mueller praised Hamad as a great help to the community in a Detroit-area speech, he adamantly refused to change his mind about the award or to offer more reasons for his decision.[144]

Both the FBI's special agent in charge in Detroit, Willie Hulon, who had nominated Hamad for the award, and U.S. Attorney Jeffrey Collins took the highly unusual step of making public statements clearing Hamad of any involvement in terrorism or other wrongdoing, in an effort to remove the stain from Hamad's reputation that the revocation of the award inevitably produced.[145] Both were no doubt acutely sensitive to the damage that Mueller's actions would create to the absolutely crucial relationship between the FBI and the U.S. Attorney's Office and the Detroit area's large Middle Eastern community. And they were right. Mo Abdrabboh, attorney and activist in the Arab American community who has worked with ALPACT, BRIDGES, and many other community organizations, spoke for many. "I'm absolutely furious," he said. "It's a blatant insult without any regard to Hamad or the community."[146] Abdrabboh said that he and other Arab American leaders were giving serious consideration to withdrawing from BRIDGES, the group co-chaired by U.S. Attorney Collins and Hamad. "It's not about the award," Abdrabboh said. "It's about the disre-spect."[147] Noel Saleh, vice president of the Arab Community Center for Economic and Social Services, called the withdraw-al of the award a potentially "fatal blow" to the government's efforts to build relationships with the community. Saleh said that the incident sent a message "that the Arab American com-munity is perhaps expendable, not particularly important, and certainly suspect."[148] Even after a meeting with FBI director Mueller, Saleh and other leaders remained dubious. While they would attempt to "move forward" in their relationship with fed-eral law enforcement, they could do so only with "a considerable amount of skepticism."[149] Despite Imad Hamad's own plea to his fellow members of the community that it was "time to move on and get past this,"[150] the partnership between federal law enforcement and the Arab and Muslim community that had paid real dividends, including generating the highest rate of response in the nation to Attorney General Ashcroft's five thou-sand voluntary "interviews," had been damaged.

As often as the top echelon of the FBI and the Department of Justice had appealed to the Arab and Middle Eastern com-munities for help, for translators and for information, and as much as the people on the ground, like FBI special agent in charge Willie Hulon and U.S. Attorney Jeffrey Collins in Detroit, seemed to "get it," the FBI leadership's culture hadn't changed, or at least had not changed enough. If the FBI, as the nation's top antiterrorism agency, truly wants a real partner-ship with Middle Eastern communities, it cannot treat both its own Muslim agents and its partners in the community like sus-pects. Only an insular culture that believes these things do not count would think that it is possible to do the difficult task of stopping Middle Eastern terrorists before they act without the assistance of those communities.

Instead of building partnerships based on relationships of trust, the efforts of the Department of Justice have instilled fear, and will have the effect of driving immigrants underground and away from cooperative work with law enforcement. Instead of pursuing a problem-solving approach, the Department of Justice has used ethnic profiling as a convenient way to focus on the "obvious" suspects, despite the proven failure of this policy. And instead of moving toward cultural change, elements in the FBI, Ashcroft's prime weapon in the fight against terror, cling to their "nativist" culture,[151] which remains suspicious of anyone in the organization who is not white even as the bureau's new circumstances cry out for the help of agents, translators, and others from Middle Eastern countries.

USING PREVENTIVE POLICING
AGAINST TERRORISM

The use of Ashcroft policing in the war on terror is all the more regrettable because it comes at a time when law enforcement is poised to cross into what can be described, without exaggeration, as a new era, centered on the practices that constitute preventive policing. As the many stories in this book show, preventive policing has proven that we need not be forced into a bargain with the devil in which the civil rights of some or all of our citizens are sacrificed in the name of safety and security. Yet the attorney general's campaign against terrorist activity is destroying the best set of weapons we have to fight terrorists. Preventive policing offers the best tools and the greatest number of opportunities to fight terrorists in our own country. It is geared toward prevention instead of reaction, as antiterrorist tactics must be. It is grounded in practice and in proven methods, not in Department of Justice ideology. It is focused on addressing the twin pillars of real law enforcement: the observation of suspicious conduct and the gathering and use of intelligence. It makes the Middle Easterners who live in our country our allies and partners in this struggle, not our enemies or our cowering quarry.

For example, problem solving, one of the core strategies of preventive policing, offers a promising approach to terrorism.

A problem-solving approach would begin by forcing an immediate change in focus. The problem is not, as some believe, certain kinds of people, or people from countries that, now or in the past, have supported terrorism. *The problem is not terrorism, but terrorist behavior.* Focusing totally on terrorist behavior is the key to beating terrorism.

One can think of Rafi Ron as a terrorism problem solver par excellence. Ron offers an alternative to racial and ethnic profiling: Behavioral Pattern Recognition, a proprietary method that is both more effective against terrorism and more respectful of civil rights.

Ron,[152] the chief proponent of Behavioral Pattern Recognition in the United States, helped to establish Israel's air marshal program, the world's first, and served as an Israeli air marshal himself.[153] Ron headed security at Ben Gurion Airport in Tel Aviv, Israel—an airport that has surely been in the crosshairs of international terrorist organizations longer and more intensely than any other.[154] Despite sitting in the "epicenter of terrorist activities," Ben Gurion, where Ron pioneered his techniques, has never had a hijacking.[155] Little wonder, then, that in the aftermath of the September 11 disasters, Boston's Logan International Airport, the airport from which two of the hijacked planes took off, turned to Ron to make comprehensive security improvements.[156]

Behavioral observation has formed the centerpiece of his work there. Ron's Behavioral Pattern Recognition system is "based on the field-proven experiences of major national security systems."[157] It is not a hypothesis but a usable set of strategies and tactics. "This method has been and continues to be used to successfully identify people with hostile intentions."[158] Ron's company describes Behavioral Pattern Recognition as a training program that "provides law enforcement officers with the most practical tools available to identify and confront terrorist activity in a wide variety of public venues."[159]

The basics of Behavioral Pattern Recognition are straightforward; more to the point, it could not be more different from racial profiling.[160] In fact, Ron says, unless law enforcement uses a method like Behavioral Pattern Recognition, which focuses security personnel on useful behavioral indicators, racial, ethnic, and other prejudices are likely to creep into security work, distracting personnel from what is really important.[161] Ron begins by pointing out that the missing link, the piece of the security puzzle too long neglected in antiterrorism work, is the study of the human behavior of terrorists.[162] Terrorists behave differently from others in subtle but observable ways. "When a person intends to terminate his life on a plane in a few minutes' time, he will not be acting normally," Ron says. "You have to observe someone's body language, whether they make eye contact with security officials, whether they make or do not make contact with other people in the airport, the way they are dressed, and what kinds of bags they are carrying."[163] By zeroing in on observable human behaviors as the key clues for spotting potential terrorists, users of Ron's methodology are able to make the optimal use of law enforcement resources. More and more, security authorities agree with Ron's central principle: subtle but observable differences in terrorist behavior make terrorists detectable, and these patterns can indeed become visible to those trained to look for them. "We've come a long way" in the accuracy of our knowledge and assessment of body language and behavior, says Joe Navarro, an FBI special agent who trains others in the intricacies of the subject. "We believe the study of nonverbal behavior has progressed to such a degree that in capable hands, it is now more accurate than lie-detector tests."[164]

The Behavior Pattern Recognition process, Ron says, has several steps. The student of preventive policing will recognize a problem-solving process at work in Ron's recognition that the problem is terrorist behavior, not terrorism, and in his description of the steps. First, one must study the environment—the airport terminal, the train station, the city square or market—in an effort to figure out ways in which the setting might lend itself to terrorist activity, or to concealment.[165] From the terrorist point of view, what in the environment would be a potential target? What actions would potential terrorists take, given the environment, and what behaviors would this lead to?[166] Second, one must look for relevant behavior patterns, typically of three types.[167] These patterns may be (1) physiological behaviors that show that the person under observation is under unusual stress, or fears being discovered;[168] (2) tactical, aimed at avoiding detection, at getting around the measures designed to protect against them, or at furthering their plans;[169] or (3) indicative of the presence of weapons.[170] For example, Ron says, many suicide bombers wear their explosives in "belts" under their clothing. These belts are large and bulky, and that fact shows up in behavior: a change in the body's silhouette as it moves, wearing inappropriately large or heavy clothing, or how the person wearing the belt uses his or her hands.[171] Once the officer spots these suspicious behavioral patterns, he or she focuses closely on the subject exhibiting these patterns.[172] If the surveillance does nothing to dispel, or even seems to confirm, the suspicions raised by the behavior patterns, officers approach the suspect for "targeted conversation," asking questions designed to elicit particular pieces of information and to ferret out further clues to possible terrorist intentions. With all of this information, the officer is now well positioned to make a decision: Is further investigation, such as extended questioning or an intrusive search of the person and his or her belongings, necessary? Or has the initial suspicion, based on the behavior patterns observed, been dispelled?

Ron's method may come as something of a surprise to those who have assumed for years that Israel's successful efforts at keeping their airplanes out of the hands of hijackers and other terrorists depended upon using a profile that picked out Arabs, particularly Palestinians, for extra security and surveillance. Ron states unequivocally that race and ethnicity are not effective criteria for antiterrorism work. He calls

the use of racial and ethnic profiles "a typical mistake of a simplistic approach to the problem" that presents not just legal
problems, but operational ones.[173] He points out that terrorist
groups have, in the past, worked in coalitions, across racial or
ethnic lines. As an example, he points to an attack launched
against Tel Aviv's Ben Gurion Airport in 1972. The attack was
carried out on behalf of Arabs or Palestinians, but not by
Arabs or Palestinians. Rather, the attack came from members
of the Japanese Red Army, an organization that had not
affiliated itself with Arab or Palestinian causes before this, as
far as anyone knew.[174] According to Ron, this was surely no
accident but a deliberate strategic decision to use a group who
would not "look like" the group perceived to be a threat, to
defeat security.

Ron is quick to point out that the underlying issue is not
race or ethnicity but radicalism: extremism that turns fringe
opinions into deadly deeds. The kind of radicalism that fuels Al
Qaeda is global, existing all over the world, from India, to
China, to Indonesia, to Europe, and even the U.S. itself.[175] Radicalism has no race or ethnicity.[176] The perfect example, of
course, was Timothy McVeigh: the blue-eyed, blond, all-Ameri-
can U.S. Army veteran who achieved infamy as the bomber of
the Murrah Federal Building in Oklahoma City in 1996. After
the bomb went off, authorities quickly began searching for a
Middle Eastern male suspect, even detaining a Jordanian air-
line passenger. The real killer of the more than 163 people who
died that day, of course, did not "fit the profile." He looked just
like "us," and he was in fact nearly overlooked as a possible suspect even when he was in custody for an unrelated crime.
Moreover, cautions Ron, an organization that has shown itself
to be as adaptable, as willing to do whatever it takes to find the
weaknesses in its opponents, as dedicated to achieving its
goals, and as patient as Al Qaeda will simply adapt its recruiting strategies to beat a profile that features race or ethnicity.[177]
A racial or ethnic profile is thus not only a weak defense, Ron

says; it is something our enemies are very much aware of, and they can and will use this weakness against us.

The no-nonsense, practical, field-tested orientation of Ron's Behavior Pattern Recognition system has great appeal to law enforcement and aviation security officials. Once they understand the system, science, and experience behind it, they often become strong converts. The unblemished track record of Behavior Pattern Recognition at Ben Gurion Airport speaks volumes to law enforcement and security professionals. Little wonder that real law enforcement officials in charge of securing our airports and other critical infrastructure—not Department of Justice leaders, but the FBI agents, state and local police officers, and other first responders charged with the responsibility for security on the ground—find in Ron's method an answer they have long sought. Behavioral Pattern Recognition gives officers and agents a systematic way to apply this idea—and, in the bargain, a reason to avoid failed tactics like racial profiling. Major Tom Robbins, head of the Massachusetts State Police unit that uses Behavior Pattern Recognition to secure Boston's Logan International Airport, says that "if you're looking at race or ethnicity," as others have done, "you're missing the boat. And you're going to miss the terrorists."[178] Jose Juves, a spokesman for the Massachusetts Port Authority, which runs Logan, says the important thing to remember is that "terrorists behave in similar ways, no matter what their race or religion." Perhaps Todd McGhee, a member of the state police at Logan, puts it best: "I'm looking for everybody, from Tim McVeigh to Osama bin Laden, and anyone in between who wants to do us harm."[179]

If observation of suspicious behavior is one of the pillars of truly effective policing, particularly in counterterrorism, the other pillar is the comprehensive collection, careful analysis, and consistent use of intelligence. The events of September 11, 2001, represented a massive failure of the intelligence community to pick up the signals of the impending terrorist attack and to prevent it. And this was especially true of domestic intelligence operations. Both Attorney General Ashcroft and FBI director Mueller have made clear that, in the new post–9/11 world, prevention of terrorism will be the FBI's top priority. If so, this new mission must be accomplished by improving the FBI's domestic intelligence gathering and analytic capabilities.

As they make this transition, officials should consider the opinions of Harry "Skip" Brandon and Vincent Cannistraro. Brandon was with the FBI for twenty-three years, during which time he served as the FBI's deputy assistant director for counterterrorism and counterintelligence, with worldwide responsibility for the bureau's terrorism and national security efforts. He worked with intelligence agencies of the government at the highest levels. Cannistraro is the former chief of operations and analysis in the CIA's Counterterrorism Center. He was special assistant for intelligence in the Office of the Secretary of Defense, and served for a number of years as a clandestine CIA officer in the Middle East, Africa, and Europe.

According to Brandon, the only way in which the attacks of September 11 might have been prevented is if we had had a much greater, more finely tuned capacity for intelligence gathering and analysis—not just abroad, but in the United States.[180] Cannistraro is, if anything, even more adamant than Brandon on the importance of intelligence gathering and analysis to the prevention of terrorism. "I've always said that the problem of terrorism is one of getting intelligence, having the information that is necessary to preempt" terrorist acts before they occur, he says. "If you don't have good intelligence, you don't have good antiterror," Cannistraro says, and that will mean that the authorities simply will not be able to prevent attacks. "If you're investigating [the results of] an act of terrorism, then you've already failed.[181]

In Cannistraro's view, the Department of Justice's approach to the problem is dangerously misguided. It may actually interfere with or even destroy the best, and only, opportunities for successful domestic intelligence gathering on suspected Al Qaeda "sleeper cells" on our own soil. He explains that there is only one possible source of information that we can tap into for intelligence on suspicious Arabs or other Middle Easterners in our country: Middle Eastern and Arab communities themselves, and particularly the recent immigrants among them. They are the ones who speak the language, understand the cultural cues, and notice when someone new in the community is behaving strangely, espouses radical opinions, or encourages others to act dangerously. "The FBI needs to be able to collect intelligence on imminent threats in the United States," he says. "To do that, it needs to work with immigrant communities."[182]

To accomplish this, the FBI will need to work with immigrants who come from countries whose police agencies and security services may have inspired great fear and engaged in violent repression. This makes it hard for law enforcement and intelligence agencies to form the trust with these communities necessary to make them comfortable bringing information forward, and the agencies must therefore work hard to create the conditions for that trust. The problem with the immigration policies and actions of the Department of Justice, Cannistraro says, is that these policies and actions destroy trust. The department has made the mistake of "using immigration policy as a proxy for law enforcement,"[183] a potentially disastrous move. The major problem has been "our immigration policy and the act of the U.S. government toward immigrants because, in many respects, what we're doing with immigrants and visa holders is counter-productive."[184] It actually undermines the intelligence collection mission. Says Cannistraro, "When we attach the blunt instrument of immigration policy and enforcement to those [immigrant] communities, we undercut the basis of any cooperation with the FBI and local law enforcement."[185]

Cannistraro explains that there is an inevitable and unbreakable connection between how the authorities treat the people with whom they deal, and the willingness of those same people and their friends, neighbors, and family members to cooperate with law enforcement and intelligence authorities. Treating whole communities as suspicious, incarcerating some of them on petty immigration violations, and questioning them on the chance that they might know something useful alienates and terrifies them. This is something that law enforcement and intelligence-gathering agencies simply cannot afford, Cannistraro says, "because we need to have the trust and cooperation of people in those communities. If someone . . . who is a stranger comes into that community, the people who are long established in that community know it or are in a position to know it, and therefore [they can] provide early warning information," exactly the object of counterterrorist intelligence gathering. But if members of that community "have been rounded up by the INS, forced to report, and if everyone who reports knows that if they're illegal . . . they can and will be deported, you've really kind of eliminated the ability to get information that you really need." [186]

Cannistraro's words should awaken anyone concerned with homeland security, and should serve to shake the Department of Justice out of its slumbering reliance on the failed methods that it has adopted. Nothing is more critical right now, experts like Vincent Cannistraro and Harry Brandon tell us, than building relationships with Arabs and Muslims in our country. We need these partnerships not as a matter of good public relations, or as a way to boost the FBI's image, but to stay ahead of the deadly terrorists in our midst. The Department of Justice's leadership has steered our enforcement and intelligence-gathering efforts in precisely the wrong direction. They neglect the lessons that preventive policing offers and cut us off from the most important resources that we have to make our country safe.

9

Securing the Blessings of Preventive Policing

But our fathers were not absurd enough to put unlimited power
in the hands of the ruler and take away the protection
of law from the rights of individuals. It was not thus that they meant
to "secure the blessings of liberty to themselves and their posterity"

—EX PARTE MILLIGAN, U.S. Supreme Court, 1866

This book begins with a message of hope for America's police forces and for the public they serve. The last ten to twenty years have seen the advent of a new form of police work in America: preventive policing—a constellation of practices that has the potential to remake the way police enforce the law. Police are moving toward making partnership the central pillar of their relationship with the communities they serve, in an effort to build trust with their citizens, according to the community policing model. They have adopted new problem-solving strategies and moved beyond the respond-and-arrest mode of the past. The new policing paradigm addresses not symptoms but underlying issues and causes of crime. An increasing number of departments have adopted one or more accountability strategies, such as early-warning systems, citizen complaint review mechanisms, police auditors, and "customer" feedback devices, striving to conform their practices to the aspirations of their communities.

Leaders have emerged in police departments who can bring their institutions into the new era of prevention. Just as important, a number of law enforcement agencies have begun to transform their own cultures, attempting to inculcate the new values inherent in preventive policing. From New York to Los Angeles, from Pittsburgh to Chicago, from Wichita to Lowell, we see that this cultural shift is not confined to any one region, nor only to police departments urban or rural, large or small. Preventive policing has begun to flourish everywhere—not in every police department, to be sure, and not even in the whole of some departments where it has taken root, but in enough places that we can clearly see its promise.

The advent of a new American policing culture comes at an opportune time. During the mid to late 1990s, crime fell dramatically across the country. Leading the way, of course, was New York, with its tough-on-crime mayor, Rudolph Giuliani, and its innovative police commissioner, Bill Bratton. To borrow the title of Bratton's book, *Turnaround: How America's Top Cop Reversed the Crime Epidemic*,[1] New York's dramatic "turnaround" on crime entailed deep changes in attitude, beginning with the conviction that police could, indeed, make a difference in the fight against crime and had no reason to resign themselves to self-defeating complacency. The creation of the Compstat system (see chapter 5), and the NYPD's adoption of the "broken windows" theory and its "zero tolerance" policies on public disorder of all kinds get most of the credit for the dramatic drop in crime in the minds of Americans everywhere.[2] This is not surprising. Giuliani could never be accused of shrinking from the spotlight or hesitating to claim credit, and as one of the centers of the media universe, New York often becomes a kind of national metaphor. But as the many stories in this book show, New York's is not, by any means, the only story.

When we look beyond New York, we see that there are many ways to control crime. Almost every city in America experienced a dramatic drop in crime through the 1990s, and other cities have often taken very different approaches to crime control from New York's. Furthermore, the preventive tactics adopted in other cities were often able to do something that New York's did not: they controlled crime about as effectively as—and sometimes more effectively than—New York without compromising civil rights, as the NYPD's tactics often did. The "New York–centric" view of crime control in the 1990s convinced many people that in order to have dramatic crime reduction, the police had to use tough tactics, and some aspects of civil rights had to be sacrificed. But the examples of police work in other cities in this book prove that there is no necessary trade-off between public safety and the dignity due us as citizens of a free and democratic society. As the new century began, American policing stood poised to launch into a new era, with prevention as its guiding star.

After September 11, 2001, the detection and prevention of terrorism began to dominate all discussion of domestic law enforcement. Understandably, we feared our newly revealed enemies, realized that they were different from enemies we have faced in the past, and demanded that government protect us from them. Al Qaeda, a loosely organized worldwide terrorist network devoted to an extreme Islamist and reflexively anti-Western ideology, poses an unprecedented threat. Al Qaeda operatives are not only terrorists but suicidal and therefore potentially undeterrable: they want to harm and kill us more than they want to live. As we struggled to grasp the implications of September 11, it inevitably became the responsibility of the federal government, particularly the U.S. Department of Justice, to take up the task of making us safe, of apprehending the terrorists in our midst, and of preventing another catastrophe.

Perhaps we should not judge the actions of Attorney General Ashcroft and the Department of Justice too harshly; after all, the need was dire, the danger great, and quick action necessary. But Ashcroft erred in overlooking the possibilities for antiterrorism security presented by preventive policing. Instead he adopted one measure after another that, while ostensibly intended to increase our safety and security against terrorists, did only the opposite, by endangering the carefully cultivated police partnerships that could facilitate intelligence gathering among Middle Eastern immigrants, by abandoning proven problem-solving strategies in favor of failed approaches like enforcement based on racial and ethnic stereotypes, and by wielding immigration law like a blunt instrument to bludgeon Arab and Muslim American communities into yielding up the terrorists they might unwittingly harbor.

At the same time, the federal government has tried to force state and local law enforcement agencies to adopt Ashcroft's crude, sweeping methods. These local departments often knew better, and the Department of Justice should have deferred to their expertise. Yet the Justice Department has shown little concern with feedback of any kind on the effectiveness of its initiatives. The U.S. General Accounting Office found that, shockingly, a year and a half after the department's "voluntary" mass interrogation of 8,000 young Arab men began, the Department of Justice "has not conducted an assessment of the interview project and as of January of 2003, had no specific plans to do so, although [Justice] officials told [GAO] that they thought such an assessment would be valuable."[3] Instead, Ashcroft and his team forge ahead, deaf to the chorus of protest from state and local law enforcement professionals, ignoring even those who have spent years in the trenches of federal intelligence and counterterrorism work. Besides being ineffective against terrorists, Ashcroft's tactics may have unintended but grave and long-lasting negative consequences for law enforcement across the country: preventive policing may be crushed under the heavy and heedless federal boot, even though the new policing strategies hold the greatest promise of any for fighting terrorism.

Still, there are at least two reasons for hope. One involves the foot soldiers in the struggle to prevent terrorism: the FBI agents and police officers on the ground, not their theory and ideology-bound leaders in Washington. The other lies in the capacity of the American people to get what they want and what they need.

ARE THEY LEARNING?

The stories in this book, particularly those in chapter 2 concerning metropolitan Detroit; Chicago; Seattle; Lowell, Massachusetts; and Wichita, Kansas; and the connections of police in these places to their local Arab American communities, make a strong case that many state and local police departments clearly "get it." They understand how important it is to have strong partnerships built on trust with all the communities they serve, particularly among recent immigrants. In order to protect these advances, state and local law enforcement agencies are resisting federal efforts to compel them to enforce immigration law. Not only is it highly unusual for members of the law enforcement brotherhood to break ranks publicly with each other in this way, but their sharp and substantive critique makes it obvious that state and local agencies understand that they have much to lose by adopting Ashcroft's approach.

Just as heartening, perhaps, is evidence from within the FBI itself. As the nation passed the second anniversary of September 11, 2001, one could see signs that many FBI agents—perhaps not its director, Robert Mueller, and certainly not its ultimate boss, Attorney General Ashcroft, but a growing number of the 11,500 agents in field offices around the country—understand what is at stake in the post–9/11 world. They see that the success of their counterterrorism measures and actions will ultimately hang not on the latest action plan from Washington, but on the effort to build relationships with partners in America's Middle Eastern communities, and on the agents' own ability to understand the people who comprise them.

Linda Schmidt works in the FBI's Cleveland field office, where she has been a community outreach specialist since 1997,[4] dealing with such issues as street gangs, school violence, hate crimes, and outreach and education. After September 11, Cleveland, like most American cities, saw an increase in hate crimes directed at people perceived to be Muslims or Arabs. Schmidt was one of the linchpins of the Northern Ohio Hate Crimes Working Group, which saw the number of Muslim, Arab, and Asian attendees at its meetings from these groups suddenly surge, as people from Arab, Asian, and Sikh communities in Cleveland found themselves at the center of public concern about terrorism. The Working Group designed a poster featuring the Statue of Liberty and the message that the group wanted to help communities under fire; the poster ran as a full-page advertisement in the Cleveland *Plain-Dealer*. The Working Group meetings soon became a well-known forum on cross-cultural issues for the community and members of Cleveland law enforcement agencies, "a safe environment for everyone to learn about other cultures,"[5] says Schmidt. "If I'm curious—'Why do you wear that turban on your head?'—I can ask you and you can ask me the same type of things."[6] Citizens have a chance to talk to the FBI or local police on an ongoing basis, which opens lines of communication that will help citizens when they have problems. Seeing the importance of these meetings, Schmidt and her colleagues have expanded their efforts, hosting workshops lasting as long as three days. All have proved immensely popular.

Schmidt knows that some will see the Cleveland FBI field office's community outreach efforts as fluff, as a waste of valuable time and resources that would be better spent on "real police work." But, she says, these critics could not be more wrong. First, the FBI desperately needs new agents from Middle Eastern and Asian cultures, as well as translators. Recruiting in these communities, especially among immigrants, will always be difficult, but building the multicultural organization that the FBI simply must become in the new post–9/11 world depends on the kinds of connections that outreach efforts forge. The meetings, workshops, and speaking engagements in the community that Schmidt and others in the FBI conduct provide the best possible opportunity to recruit.[7] Second, such initiatives offer law enforcement professionals unparalleled opportunities for cultural education. Neither police officers nor students of policing will find it surprising when Schmidt notes that law enforcement "has always been a very cloistered world. You spend so much time working at the job, ten, twelve hours a day, that you don't have an opportunity to see anything other than your own culture, which is the culture of law enforcement." Consequently, officers and agents may have "skewed opinions" of particular communities, who they stereotype as standing united in their hatred of police and law enforcement. The cultural knowledge police officers gain enables them to do a better job, and realizing how much support there is for their work makes them more comfortable and confident in what they do.[8] Third, the wisdom gained from interacting with the community improves officer and agent safety on the street.[9] For example, in some Asian cultures, the customary way of putting a handcuffed person into a squad car (by putting a hand on the top of the person's head and pushing them downward) would be terribly insulting, because the officer would be touching what is considered the receptacle of the soul; this, Schmidt says, could result in the officer being attacked. Understanding these cultural ideas is important to keeping the temperature of cross-cultural police-citizen encounters low, or at least helping to avoid an escalation of tensions to the point of violence.[10]

Happily, Schmidt is not alone at the FBI. There are signs that many agents in field offices around the country have begun to understand, despite occasional gaffes that seem to originate from FBI headquarters (such as awarding the FBI's prestigious community service award to Detroit's prominent Arab American activist Imad Hamad and then revoking it without explanation just before the ceremony).[11] Despite the sense of crisis that Ashcroft's rash strongarm tactics have provoked, it is possible to see signs of better efforts in the future:

- In 2003, the FBI's Washington, D.C., field office established an Arab American Advisory Committee, with the goal of building relationships between the Bureau and the Arab community.[12] The committee meets monthly with field office personnel.
- In Detroit, FBI officials and members of the Arab American community continue to meet monthly in the BRIDGES group (see chapter 8), along with officials from the U.S. Attorney's office. The regular meetings have given the participants a forum in which to tackle "hot issues" and to head them off before they mushroom into public battles.
- In the Baltimore-Washington area, outreach efforts have resulted in the growth of a partnership between the FBI and the Arab and Middle Eastern communities.

One can only hope that some of Linda Schmidt's optimism and obvious good sense will rub off on those who run the Department of Justice. For now, that remains a hope, not a reality. But perhaps time is on the side of those like her. The professional staff of the Justice Department and the FBI stay with their organizations, often throughout their careers, while political leadership comes and goes as administrations change.[13] Perhaps that is the best reason for hope.

THE ROLE OF THE PUBLIC
How Do We Get Preventive Policing?

If citizens want to see the tactics, strategies, and methods of preventive policing employed in their communities, or if they want to support those efforts that may already be under way, what can they do? Are these kinds of reforms beyond the ability of the ordinary person to affect? Must we simply wait for police institutions themselves to come around in their own good time, when those who run them finally see that doing things this way is ultimately in their own best interest?

If the citizens of a city, county, or town want change in the way that their police force works, they must use every tool in the democratic arsenal to demand that their public officials serve them. Where there are models of this kind of police action and strategy already in place, citizens must be equally energetic in supporting, lauding, and honoring them, and demanding that such efforts continue.

Easier said than done? To be sure. Certain to succeed in creating change? Far from it. But only by making these demands and supporting the good policing efforts that already exist will progressive and reform-minded police be empowered and emboldened to pursue these goals. There are good officers in every police department; they are not the ones we are accustomed to hearing about in news reports that typically cover nothing but police misconduct and corruption. But they are there. They want their departments to become better, and, with the tools of preventive policing, they can make it happen. It is up to us to support them. For those who think citizen involvement in these matters can make no difference, the following examples tell a different story.

- In Pittsburgh, after a series of incidents involving dubious searches and seizures and questionable uses of force, citizens established a civilian body to review complaints against police. At the time citizen complaints *were* reviewed and adjudicated, but only by a body inside the police department, creating at least the appearance of a conflict of interest. In a move that clearly stunned the power structure of both the Police Bureau and the city government, a referendum establishing an independent citizen complaint review authority passed overwhelmingly with support from all segments of the city's population.
- In San Francisco, voters have passed laws through California's initiative process to help insure police accountability. One

provision of these initiatives established a civilian review board, and guaranteed that it would have an acceptable level of staffing to do an adequate and defensible job. Another required that damages resulting from police misconduct be paid directly from the police department's operating budget instead of from the city's general funds. Having the monetary costs of police misconduct show up in the department's own budget helps insure that misconduct gets the attention of the leadership of the department itself, as well as the city government, which ultimately holds the department's purse strings.

Police reform is not always a suitable subject for ballot measures, and noisy public demands are not always necessary to effect reform. But we must never forget that the institutions we have created are all subject to inertia. They are always most likely to continue operating as they have rather than to change—unless citizens insist on change as persistently and as vocally as is necessary to make sure it happens. We will not always get the policing that we *deserve*, but, if we exercise our rights as Americans, we may get the policing that we *demand*.

Preventive policing is now a reality. Our task as citizens is to make its successes the standard by which we judge our police services and expect of them to be measured. Police chiefs, police officers, and police departments cannot accomplish this without citizens to encourage it. We cannot afford to ignore the potential of preventive policing. With the threat of international terrorism at our doorstep, the stakes are simply too high.

Notes

CHAPTER 1: The Struggle for the Soul of Policing

1. For example, Missouri's current attorney general, Jay Nixon, says that he was elected "on a platform of fighting crime, cleaning up government corruption, and protecting consumers and the environment . . ." and describes his job as "working with law enforcement daily to fight crime and prosecute criminals," even though those roles are very small in comparison to the many others that his office has. See "Missouri Attorney General's Office, Missouri Attorney General Jay Nixon," accessed at http://www.ago.state. mo.us/nixonbio.htm, May 3, 2004.

2. Eric Lichtblau, "Justice Officials Introduce Tighter Immigrant Policy," *Los Angeles Times*, Nov. 1, 2001, at A3 (announces Dept. of Justice plans to crack down on foreigners with suspected terrorist ties); David Firestone, "U.S. Makes It Easier to Detain Foreigners," *New York Times*, Nov. 28, 2001, at B7 (Justice Dept. "has quietly expanded its power to detain foreigners"); Susan Sachs, "U.S. Begins Crackdown on Muslims Who Defy Orders to Leave Country," *New York Times*, April 2, 2002, at A13 (detailing federal law enforcement actions in which Dept. of Justice agents "have started to hunt down and arrest Muslim immigrants who failed to comply with pre-Sept. 11 depor-

tation orders"); Senator Dianne Feinstein and Jon Kyl, "We Can't Afford to Be Cavalier About Our Borders," *Los Angeles Times*, Nov. 12, 2001, at 11 (discussing proposed legislation to tighten border control and immigration enforcement); Richard Lamm, "The Immigration Deliberation: Lax Borders Leave Us At Risk," *Denver Post*, Feb. 10, 2002, at E1 (proposing greater immigration enforcement and quoting Pew Research polling finding that "72 percent of Americans favor reducing immigration"); Reeda Peel, "Our Porous Borders," *Dallas Morning News*, Sept. 16, 2001, at 4J ("We must expel those with known terrorist ties and make the necessary changes in our immigration laws and in our control of our borders so that we have a choice who we let in to our country"); Rick Neumann, "The Color of Terror," *Washington Post*, March 18, 2002, at A16 ("If we don't change our immigration policy—meaning expelling from the United States and refusing entry to the United States of the obvious suspects from the obvious countries—we eventually will be hit harder than we were on Sept. 11."); Lamar Smith, "Tighten Up the Borders," *Washington Post*, Oct. 13, 2001, at A27 (advocating stricter immigration enforcement); Bob Allan, "Illegal Immigrants: There's a Law," *New York Times*, May 11, 2002, at A16 ("Legal law-abiding citizens have nothing to fear concerning their civil rights. The rest should be kicked out of our country, as our lives may depend on it.").

3. Eric Schmitt, "Ruling Clears Way to Use State Police in Immigration Duty," *New York Times*, April 4, 2002, at A19 (ruling by Dept. of Justice's Office of Legal Counsel declares that state and local police have the power to enforce immigration law); Cheryl W. Thompson, "INS Role for Police Considered," *Washington Post*, April 4, 2002, at A15 (new Dept. of Justice opinion declares that state and local police have "inherent authority" to enforce immigration law); "Local Police Help on Immigration Weighed," *Los Angeles Times*, April 4, 2002, at A18 (discussing Dept. of Justice's new opinion allowing state and local police to enforce immigration law); Michelle Mittelstadt and Alfred Corchado, "Local Groups Could Enforce Immigration," *Dallas Morning News*, April 4, 2002, at 1A (calling new opinion of Dept. of Justice "a major shift from current practice.").

4. Section 274 of the Immigration and Nationality Act, 8 U.S.C. sec. 1324 (c).

5. Memorandum of law on local police agencies' authority to enforce immigration law prepared for Attorney General John Ashcroft, 2003, by the Migration Policy Institute, New York; copy on file with the author.

6. Note, Local Police Involvement in the Enforcement of Immigration Law, 1 Tex. Hisp. J.L. & Policy 9, 36 (1994) (quoting Atty. Gen. Griffin Bell, U.S. Dept. of Justice press release, June 23, 1978).

7. The 1996 opinion stated that "state [and local] police lack legal authority to arrest or detain aliens solely for purposes of civil immigration proceedings, as opposed to criminal prosecution." Theresa Wynn Roseborough, deputy assistant attorney general, Office of Legal Counsel, "Assistance by State and Local Police in Apprehending Illegal Aliens," memorandum for U.S. Atty., S.D. Cal., Feb. 5, 1996. In 1996, Congress created new but very limited authority for state and local police to enforce immigration law. The new law confined state and local authority over immigration to very particular circumstances, and required close federal supervision of the effort. See sec. 287 (g) of the Immigration and Nationality Act (INA), added to the INA by the Illegal Immigration Reform and Immigrant Responsibility Act or 1996, Pub. L. No. 104–248.

8. To be cautious, one must say that the department *apparently* reversed its policy, since up to the date of this writing the Department of Justice has refused to release the opinion. It has not, however, denied the opinion's existence or disavowed its contents.

9. Letter to President George W. Bush, signed by leaders of the American Immigration Lawyers Association, Arab American Institute, Leadership Conference on Civil Rights, League of United Latin American Citizens, Lutheran Immigration and Refugee Service, Mexican American Legal Defense and Education Fund, National Association of Latino Elected and Appointed Officials Educational Fund, National Council of La Raza, National Immigration Forum, and Southeast Asian Resource Center, April 24, 2002.

10. Letter to President George W. Bush from Raul Yzaguirre,

president and chief executive officer, National Council of La Raza, April 22, 2002.

11. The national Fraternal Order of Police (FOP) organization was one of the few notable exceptions to comment positively about the Justice Department's initiative. Eric Schmitt, "Administration Split on Local Role in Terror Fight," *New York Times*, April 29, 2002 (Jim Pasco, executive director of the National Fraternal Order of Police, quoted as saying that "if these people are in violation of the law, then state, local, and federal police have an obligation to move against violators of the immigration law"); Julia Malone, INS-Police Alliance Stirs Concerns," *Atlanta Journal-Constitution*, April 5, 2002 (quoting FOP spokesman Pasco as equating federal request for immigration law enforcement help from local police to participation of local police on task forces on federal violations of all kinds); "Day Laborers in U.S. Illegally," *Oakland Tribune*, May 23, 2002 (quoting FOP spokesman Pasco as urging local police involvement in immigration law enforcement because "by definition, if you are an illegal alien, you're not supposed to be here"). The FOP's legislative office confirmed that Pasco's statements represent the organization's position. "Generally, we do believe that state and local law enforcement already have the full authority to enforce immigration laws." Statement of Chris Granberg, senior legislative liaison, Fraternal Order of Police, Washington, D.C., telephone conversation with the author, May 17, 2004.

12. Michael Riley, "Immigration Bill Has Police Uneasy," *Denver Post*, April 22, 2002, at A-01.

13. Karen Brandon, "U.S. Weighs Local Role on Immigration," *Chicago Tribune*, April 14, 2002, at 10.

14. Eric Westervelt, "How Closely Local Police and Immigration Officials Should Work Together," *Morning Edition*, National Public Radio, Feb. 1, 2002.

15. Letter from Chief Bob McDonnell, president, California Police Chiefs Association, April 10, 2002 (copy on file with the author).

16 Jim Brunner and Ian Ith, "Immigration Status: 'Don't Ask,' City Says," *Seattle Times*, Dec. 15, 2002, at B1.

17. Patricia Zapor, "Counterterrorism Experts Say New Immigration Controls Not Much Help," *National Catholic Reporter*, April 25, 2003, at 12.

18. Ibid.

19. Ibid.

20. Deputy Attorney General of the U.S., Memorandum for All United States Attorneys, All Members of the Anti-Terrorism Task Forces, 9 November 2001 (copy on file with author).

21. Fox Butterfield, "Police Are Split on Interviewing Mideast Men," *New York Times*, Nov. 22, 2001, at A1.

22. Ibid.

23. Jim McGee, "Ex-FBI Officials Criticize Tactics on Terrorism; Detention of Suspects Not Effective, They Say," *Washington Post*, Nov. 28, 2001, at A1.

24. Ibid.

25. Ibid.

26. Ibid.

27. Ibid.

28. Philip Shenon, "Justice Dept. Wants to Query More Foreigners," *New York Times*, March 21, 2002, at A19. Incredibly, the Department of Justice seems not to have abandoned this technique, and was still using some of the same approaches as late as mid-2004. Mary Beth Sheridan, "Interviews with Muslims to Broaden," *Washington Post*, July 17, 2004, A1.

CHAPTER 2: The History Behind Preventive Policing

1. Samuel Walker, *The Police in America* (New York: McGraw-Hill, 1983), 7.

2. National Commission on Law Observance and Enforcement, *The Police* (U.S. Govt. Printing Office., 1931), 90–98.

3. Geoffrey P. Alpert and Roger G. Dunham, *Policing in America* (3d ed., Waveland Press, 1997), 33.

4. Ibid.

5. George Kelling and Mark Moore, *The Evolving Strategy of Policing* (Washington, D.C.: National Institute of Justice, 1989), 1–15.

6. David H. Bayley, *Policing for the Future* (New York: Oxford University Press, 1994), 7–9.

7. Ibid.

8. Ibid., 59.

9. Report of the U.S. Advisory Commission on Civil Disorders (Kerner Commission), March 1, 1968, at 70 (routine police actions "were also identified as the final incident preceding 12 of the 24 disturbances" that the commission examined.

10. David H. Bayley, *Policing*, 26.

11. George, Kelling et al., The Kansas City Preventive Patrol Experiment: A Summary Report (Police Foundation, 1974), v.

12. Kansas City, Mo., Police Dept., Response Time Analysis: Executive Summary (Kansas City, Mo., Board of Police Commissioners, 1977), 23.

13. William Spelman and Dale Brown, *Calling the Police: Citizen Reporting of Serious Crime* (Washington, D.C.: National Institute of Justice, 1984), xi.

14. Ibid., vii.

15. One can even see this contrast in documents produced for police departments themselves—that is, in writings designed to introduce police and communities to the concepts of community policing. For example, the Community Policing Consortium, a national organization that promotes community policing sponsored by the U.S. Department of Justice's Office of Community Oriented Policing Services, says on its Web site that "at the center of community policing are three essential and complementary core components: community partnership, problem solving, and change management." Community Policing Consortium, "About Community Policing," at http://www.communitypolicing. org/about2.html, accessed April 15, 2004. But a monograph prepared by the consortium, called "Understanding Community Policing: A Framework for Action," Aug. 1994, NCJ 148457, at http://www.communitypolicing.org/chap3fw.html, accessed

April 15, 2004, states that community policing consists of just "two complementary core components, *community partnership* and *problem solving*" (emphasis in original). What, one wonders, of change management?

16. For example, Robert Trojanowicz and Bonnie Bucqueroux, *Community Policing: A Contemporary Perspective* (Cincinnati: Anderson Publishing, 1990).

CHAPTER 3: Building Bridges

1. Interview with Deadre McGhee, March 23, 2003 (copy on file with the author).

2. The new chief was Benny Napoleon, who was appointed chief in July 1998. See City of Detroit, Mayor's Office, "Mayor Archer Appoints Benny Napoleon as Chief of Police," July 14, 1998. Napoleon served as chief for three years.

3. Interview with Dan Krichbaum, executive director, NCCJ Detroit, March 13, 2003 (copy on file with the author).

4. U.S. Dept. of Commerce, Bureau of the Census, *1970 Census of Population*, vol. 1, "Characteristics of the Population," Part 24, Michigan (March 1973), 24–59 (listing Detroit's population "percent Negro or other races" at 44.5 percent).

5. Black majority population in Detroit came sometime between the census of 1970, which listed Detroit's population "percent Negro or other races" at 44.5 percent; U.S. Dept. of Commerce, Bureau of Census, *1970 Census of Population*, vol. 1, "Characteristics of the Population," part 24, Michigan (March 1973), 24–59, and the census of 1980, which described Detroit's population of approximately 1.2 million as consisting of 759,000 blacks and 414,000 whites, with a considerably smaller number of other races and ethnicities; U.S. Dept. of Commerce, Bureau of Census, *1980 Census of Population*, vol. 1, "Characteristics of the Population," part 24, Michigan (Aug. 1982), 24–26. By 1990, the census showed an even smaller city population— 1.027 million—with 778,000 blacks and 222,000 whites. U.S. Dept. of

Commerce, Bureau of Census, *1990 Census of Population*, "General Population Statistics," Michigan, 1990 CP–1–24 (July 1992), 81.

6. "Detroit and Its Police: A 60-Year Saga," *Detroit Free Press*, June 13, 2003, at 7A.

7. Ibid.

8. Ibid.

9. Ibid.

10. For example, "Racism Charges Return to Dearborn," *New York Times*, Jan. 5, 1997, at 13 (city ruled by Mayor Orville Hubbard, "openly a segregationist," from 1942 to 1978, and city police slogan, "Keep Dearborn Clean," was widely understood to mean "keep Dearborn white"); Mark Johnson, "Black U.S. Attorneys Describe Warning Sons About Racial Profiling," *Tampa Tribune*, May 31, 1999, at 1 (describing how Detroit's U.S. Attorney warned driving-age son that he would be stopped by police as he drove "from Detroit and into the suburbs"); "Oakland Targets Discrimination," *Detroit News*, Aug. 12, 1999, at 4D (county in suburban Detroit devises plan to stop racial profiling after police stop of Detroit Mayor's son); "Black Drivers Say They're Targets of Suburban Cops," *Detroit News*, April 15, 1999, at 1A (widespread impression in black community that suburban police officers target them for traffic enforcement as a way of sending the message that blacks are not welcome); Amber Arellano, "When Race Adds Up: In Traffic, Blacks Are Cited More in Detroit Suburb," *Detroit Free Press*, June 1, 2000.

11. Reynolds Farley, et al., "Continued Racial Residential Segregation in Detroit: 'Chocolate City, Vanilla Suburbs' Revisited," *Journal of Housing Research*, v. 4, 2 (1993); see also "History's Lesson: Segregation Persists in Metro Area," *Detroit News*, Feb. 7, 1999, at 12A (confirming Detroit area's reputation as one of nation's most segregated); "Segregation Has Detroit in Iron Grip," *Detroit News*, Nov. 5, 1999, at 1A ("Detroit ranks only behind Atlanta and Cleveland as one of the most racially segregated cities in the nation . . ."); Geordie Greig, "From Motown to No Town," *New York Times*, March 20, 1994 (calling metropolitan Detroit "the worst case of racial segregation in America").

12. Robyn Meredith, "Near Detroit, A Familiar Sting in Being a Black Driver," *New York Times*, July 16, 1999, at A10 (son of Mayor Dennis Archer pulled over and he and female companion removed from vehicle at gunpoint by police officers, who said he matched the description of robber in the vicinity); "Son of Detroit Mayor Files Complaint After Police Stop," *Chicago Tribune*, July 20, 1999, at 2.

13. "Security Guard Charged in Choke Hold Fatality," *Washington Post*, July 7, 2000, at A12 (private guard at mall charged with voluntary manslaughter in the death of black shopper suspected of shoplifting); "As 1,000 Protest, Some See Fairlane Shoppers on Edge," *Detroit News*, July 18, 2000, at 1A (discussing boycott of mall where black shopper was killed by security guards after suspected shoplifting).

14. Interview with Saul Green, former U.S. Attorney, Eastern District of Michigan, March 25, 2003 (copy on file with the author).

15. Mark Johnson, "Black U.S. Attorneys Describe Warning Sons About Racial Profiling," *Tampa Tribune*, May 31, 1999, at 1 (describing how Detroit's U.S. Attorney described to a U.S. Department of Justice meeting of law enforcement officials from around the country that, although he was the U.S. Attorney and a full-fledged member of law enforcement himself, he warned his driving-age son that he would be stopped by police as he drove throughout the Detroit area).

16. Interview with Heaster Wheeler, executive director, NAACP, Detroit Branch, March 18, 2003 (copy on file with the author).

17. Interview with Kary Moss, executive director, ACLU-Michigan, March 13, 2003 (copy on file with the author).

18. Interview with Imad Hamad, executive director, Arab American Anti-Discrimination League, Michigan, April 2, 2003 (copy on file with the author).

19. Interview with attorney Mohammed Abdrabboh, March 12, 2003 (copy on file with the author).

20. Deputy Attorney General of the U.S., Memorandum for All United States Attorneys, All Members of Antiterrorism Task Forces, Nov. 9, 2001 (copy on file with the author); Philip Shenon, "Justice

Dept. Wants to Query More Foreigners," *New York Times*, March 21, 2002 (announcing expansion of program of interviewing thousands of young Arab and Muslim men who were not suspects but might have knowledge of foreign terrorists).

21. There is some disagreement over exactly who conceived of the letters, but no one disagrees that it would likely have never come about without the months of groundwork laid by ALPACT. Interview with U.S. Attorney Jeffrey Collins, Eastern District of Michigan, March 20, 2003 (copy on file with the author); interview with Daedre McGhee, March 23, 2003; interview with Imad Hamad, April 2, 2003; interview with Kary Moss, March 13, 2003.

22. Robert Trojanowicz and Bonnie Bucqueroux, *Community Policing: A Contemporary Perspective* (Cincinnati: Anderson Publishing, 1990), xiii–xv.

23. Ibid., xiii.

24. Ibid, 11.

25. Ibid., 12.

26. Ibid., xiv.

27. U.S. Dept. of Commerce, Bureau of Census, *1990 Census of Population, Race and Hispanic Origin*, Table 6, Washington (June 1992), 40.

28. For example, Rob Carson, "Black, African: As Different as Black & White," *News-Tribune* (Tacoma, Washington), Jan. 5, 2003 (according to detailed census data, the entire Puget Sound area "experienced an unprecedented wave of immigration from Africa during the 1990s.").

29. Interview with Brad Hoover, Seattle Police Department, March 19, 2003, and Officer Kim Bogucki, Seattle Police Department (copies on file with the author).

30. Interviews with Detective Clem Bentson, Seattle Police Department, March 27, 2003 (copy on file with the author).

31. Interview with Detective Clem Bentson, March 27, 2003.

32. Interview with Officer Kim Bogucki, Seattle Police Department, April 8, 2003 (copy on file with the author).

33. For example, Mehmud Ahmed, "Hate Crimes Against Muslims and Arabs Escalating," *Business Recorder*, Oct. 1, 2001 (detailing attack by

man who doused cars at mosque with gasoline, hoped to burn the mosque, and fired shots at several people who intervened); Samantha Chanse, "Hate Free in Washington," *Colorlines*, Dec. 1, 2001 (discussing attack on Idris Mosque).

34. Lewis Kamb, "Community Answers Targeting of Mosque," *Seattle Post-Intelligencer*, September 15, 2001, at A2 (mayor and police chief pledged to protect religious freedom by increasing patrols and assigning officers to mosques to reassure Muslims); interview with Chief Gil Kerlikowske, Seattle Police Department, June 20, 2003 (copy on file with the author).

35. Mike Barber, "Supporters of Mosque Thanked with Neighborhood Barbeque," *Seattle Post-Intelligencer*, Aug. 12, 2002, at B1 (mosque supported in aftermath of attack by people of all faiths "standing guard in round-the-clock vigils to protect the house of worship"); John Zebrowski, "Muslims Stress: We're Americans, Too," *Seattle Times*, Oct. 2, 2001, at A5 (quoting man who formerly lived near mosque who, along with many living near the mosque, stood guard to help protect it).

36. Interview with Chief Gil Kerlikowske.

37. Ibid.; Vanessa Ho, "Prayer and a Message of Peace," *Seattle Post-Intelligencer*, Dec. 17, 2001, at A1 (Chief Kerlikowske among several public officials at service).

38. Many of Lowell's textile mills, the basis of its founding and early prosperity, closed in the years after World War I, and during the Great Depression. By the mid-1930s, only three of the original mills were left. Two of these closed in the 1950s, and mill employment "all but disappeared." But the last twenty years have brought a revitalization through a combination of a renewal plan based on making the town a living historical park, and the booming Massachusetts economy of the 1980s and 1990s. See "Decline and Recovery," Lowell National Historical Park, accessed at http://www.nps.gov/lowe/loweweb/Lowell_History/decline.htm, July 6, 2003.

39. U.S. Dept. of Commerce, Bureau of Census, *1980 Census of Population*, vol. 1, "Characteristics of the Population," part 23, Michigan (Aug. 1982), 23–16, U.S. Dept. of Commerce, Bureau of Census,

2000 Census of Population, American FactFinder Quick Tables, Geographic Area: Lowell city, Massachusetts., accessed at http:// factfinder.census.gov/bf/_lang_en_vt_name=DEC_2000_SF1_U_Q TP3_geo_id+16000US..., July 6, 2003.

40. Interview with Cynthia Callahan, Lowell Police Department, June 26, 2003 (copy on file with the author).

41. Ibid. Changes in census categories between the 1990 census, which listed Cambodians as a separate group, and the 2000 census, which grouped them under "Other Asian," make tracing this exact numbers more difficult than it used to be. However, few dispute the extraordinary growth of Cambodians, due to both immigration and internal migration—much of it from Long Beach, California, the location of the only Cambodian community in the United States bigger than that in Lowell. See, e.g., Cindy Rodriguez, "Jobs, Community Lure Cambodians to Lowell," *Boston Globe*, July 21, 2001, at A1 (noting growth in Lowell's Cambodian population of over 50 percent from 1990 to 2000, the bulk of which has come from migration of Cambodians already in the United States, giving Lowell the third largest Cambodian population among the world's cities, after the Cambodian capital city of Phnom Penh and Long Beach, California).

42. Interview with Captain William Taylor, Lowell Police Department, June 12, 2003 (copy on file with the author).

43. Ibid.

44. Interview with Cynthia Callahan.

45. Ibid. According to Callahan, the discussions began after the Police Executives Research Forum held a focus group on racial profiling in Lowell. The group consisted of both police officers and community members. The upshot, according to Callahan, was that while not everyone from the community believed that racial profiling was a problem in Lowell, they were often puzzled about why police did what they did at traffic stops, and this would sometimes cause people to think that they were treated differently than others because of who they were. Chief Davis, receiving this information, pulled the core of this focus group together to become the Race Relations Forum, which took as its mission addressing these concerns.

46. Lowell Police Department, "The Lowell Police Department Race Relations Council" (copy on file with the author).

47. Interview with Cynthia Callahan.

48. Lowell Police Department, "The Lowell Police Department Race Relations Council" (copy on file with the author).

49. Ibid.

50. Lowell Police Department, "Law Enforcement Traffic Stops & Safety Guide" (undated copy on file with the author). The police department prepared a parallel publication, "Motorists Traffic Stops & Safety Guide," for members of the public.

51. Interview with Cynthia Callahan.

52. Lowell Police Department, "The Lowell Police Department Race Relations Council" (copy on file with the author).

53. Interview with Cynthia Callahan.

54. Wichita Police Department Web site, "Wichita Police Department Demographics," accessed June 27, 2003, at http://www.wichitapolice.com/demographics.htm.

55. U.S. Dept. of Commerce, Bureau of Census, *2000 Census of Population*, American FactFinder Quick Tables, Geographic Area: Wichita city, Kansas, accessed at http://factfinder.census.gov/bf/_lang_en_vt_name=DEC_2000_SF1_U_PP1_geo_id=16000US2079000.html, July 6, 2003.

56. Interview with Deputy Chief Terri Moses, Wichita Police Department, April 3, 2003 (copy on file with the author).

57. Ibid.

58. Howard Swindle, "Eight Bloody Days Send a Racial Tremor Through Mainstream Wichita," *Dallas Morning News*, April 4, 2001.

59. Ibid.

60. Interview with Deputy Chief Terri Moses, April 3, 2003.

61. Interview with Sue Castille, executive director, National Conference on Community and Justice, Wichita, Kansas, April 28, 2003 (copy on file with the author). NCCJ had helped Mayor Knight form, direct, and facilitate the Building Bridges initiative, so they were a natural choice for this role.

62. Interview with Deputy Chief Terri Moses, April 3, 2003.

63. Interview with Professor Brian Withrow, Wichita State University, March 13, 2003 (copy on file with the author).

64. Interview with Professor Brian Withrow, March 13, 2003.

65. Ibid.

66. Ibid.

67. Interview with Terri Moses, April 13, 2003.

68. For example, "Segregation in U.S.," *Chicago Sun-Times,* November 28, 2002, at 1 (showing Chicago as ninth "most segregated metropolitan area for blacks"); Dennis Byrne, "Words to Live By in 'Our' Neighborhoods," *Chicago Tribune,* June 25, 2001, at 13 (census figures show that Chicago is one of the ten most segregated cities in the nation); "Diversity Rising, But Walls Remain; Color Persists for Blacks, Whites," *Atlanta Constitution,* Dec. 3, 2001, at 8A (blacks most segregated from whites in Chicago, with Atlanta second).

69. For example, Stephanie Banchero and Flynn McRoberts, "Forces Collided to Highlight Cop-Abuse Charges," *Chicago Tribune,* Oct. 13, 1997, at 1 (incident in which police allegedly broke man's jaw "have severely strained an already tenuous relationship between black citizens and police officers" in which blacks see police "as the enemy"); William Claiborne, "Chicago Police in Shakedown Scandal," *Washington Post,* Sept. 24, 2000, at A5 (Chicago police officers videotaped demanding cash from immigrants on threat of deportation); Matt O'Connor, "Suit Charges Cops With Illegal Stops; ACLU says African-Americans, Hispanics Targeted," *Chicago Tribune,* March 25, 2003 (Chicago police alleged to be making indiscriminate stops of young black and Latino men and subjecting them to illegal searches).

70. Interview with former Deputy Superintendent Barbara McDonald, June 20, 2003 (copy on file with the author); Chicago Police Department, Special Report, "Strengthening Relations Between Police and Minority Communities," (2000).

71. Ibid.

72. Interview with Chuck Wexler, Executive Director, Police Executives Research Forum, April 25, 2003 (copy on file with the author).

73. Chicago Police Department, Special Report, "Strengthening Relations Between Police and Minority Communities," (2000).

74. Interview with former Deputy Superintendent Barbara McDonald, June 20, 2003.

75. Chicago Police Department, Special Report, "Strengthening Relations Between Police and Minority Communities," (2000).

76. Ibid., 5.

77. Ibid.

78. Ibid.

79. Ibid., 6.

80. Ibid.

81. Interview with former Deputy Superintendent Barbara McDonald, June 20, 2003.

82. Ibid.

83. Jim Hughes, "Ignorance Fuels Anger Against Sikhs in U.S.," *Denver Post*, Nov. 18, 2001, at A1 (because of their appearance—beards, turbans, often dark skin—Sikhs, who are neither Arabs nor Muslims, have become targets of post–9/11 backlash, with hundreds of such incidents nationwide); Frances Grady, "An Identity Threatened: Mistaken for Muslim, American Sikhs Face Intolerance, Tension," *Hartford Courant*, Oct. 12, 2001, at D1 (over 200 cases of violence directed at Sikhs after September 11, including a murder of a Sikh man in Mesa, AZ); Karima A. Haynes, "Sikhs Address Hate Crimes," *Los Angeles Times*, Dec. 8, 2001 (discussing attack on Sikh store owner, whose assailants asked if he knew Osama bin Laden); Maki Becker, "Sikhs Facing Anti-Muslim Harassment Due to Beards, Turbans," *New York Daily News*, Sept. 29, 2001, p. 20 (detailing attacks on Sikhs in New York).

84. Interview with Sergeant Anthony Scalise, June 11, 2003 (copy on file with the author).

85. Ibid.

86. Bill Dedman, "Midwest Gunman Had Engaged in Racist Acts at 2 Universities," *New York Times*, July 6, 1999, at A1.

87. Ibid.

88. Interview with Anthony Scalise, June 11, 2003.

89. Ibid.

90. Ibid.; Bill Dedman, July 6, 1999.

91. According to Commander Dave Boggs of Chicago's Twenty-Fourth police district, where the shootings took place, Wolf was clearly "the main player" in the whole scenario, both as to helping the police get things under control at the scene and as to encouraging the crucial witness to speak to police even though it was the Jewish Sabbath. Interview with Commander Dave Boggs, Chicago Police Department, Twenty-Fourth District, May 19, 2004.

92. Interview with Moshe Wolf, Aug. 1, 2003 (notes on file with the author).

93. Interview with Anthony Scalise, June 11, 2003.

94. Ibid.

CHAPTER 4: Solving Problems

1. See, e.g., Susan Popkin, et al., *The Hidden War: Crime and the Tragedy of Public Housing in Chicago* (New Brunswick, N.J.: Rutgers University Press, 2000), 1–9 (detailing depth and seriousness of violent crime problems in public housing in Chicago); U.S. Department of Justice, National Institute of Justice, "Drug and Crime in Public Housing: A Three-City Analysis," (March 1994), vi–xiv., (rates of violent offenses and drug offenses often very high in public housing relative to other areas, with particular developments often much higher than others).

2. These problems are at once so pervasive and so crippling that it can seem impossible for any individual or family to cope with them, except by attempting to escape by moving out of the developments. See Susan Popkin, et al., *The Hidden War*, 2 ("Hidden inside these forbidding developments lies a humanitarian disaster" beyond the considerable crime problems—poisoning of young children by lead-based paints, much higher than normal rates of asthma, dangers to young children presented by unprotected window openings, serious injuries caused by broken elevator equipment and poorly maintained stairwells and walkways, or abuse by neglectful or drug-addicted parents); William

Julius Wilson, *When Work Disappears* (New York: Knopf, 1996), 47–48, 155. (public housing policies have ended up concentrating poor, predominantly minority residents in isolated areas of inner cities, cut off from employment opportunities and networks of people who might help one get a jobs). There is a considerable amount of writing on life in public housing. For readers who want to sample it, begin with Alex Kotlowitz, *There Are No Children Here: The Story of Two Boys Growing Up in the Other America* (New York: Doubleday, 1991), which describes the lives of two young boys in one of Chicago's worst public housing projects, and LeAlan Jones and Lloyd Newman, *Our America* (New York: Pocket Books, 1998), an account of life, and a tragic death, in the Ida B. Wells Homes housing project in Chicago.

3. Interview with Betsy Lindsay, June 26, 2003 (copy on file with author).

4. Ibid., 2.

5. Personal correspondence via email from Betsy Lindsay to David Harris, July 1, 2003 (copy on file with the author).

6. See, for example, U.S. Dept. of Justice, Federal Bureau of Investigation, "2002 Preliminary Uniform Crime Report," June 16, 2003, accessed on July 2, 2003, at http://www.fbi.gov/ucr/cius_02/02prelimannual.pdf.

7. Betsy Lindsay, "Housing Authority of the County of Los Angeles, Problem-Solving Through Partnerships," presented at U.S. Department of Justice, Second Annual Conference on Community Oriented Policing, June 17, 2003, Washington, D.C. (hereinafter "Problem-Solving Through Partnerships") (copy of powerpoint slides on file with the author).

8. The idea of the crime triangle comes from routine activity theory; it assumes that all crimes require victims, offenders, and locations. See M. Felson and R. Clarke, "Opportunity Makes the Thief: Practical Theory for Crime Prevention," Police Research Series, Paper No. 98, Home Office Policing and Reducing Crime Unit (1998).

9. Ibid., 8.

10. Ibid., 9.

11. The U.S. Supreme Court recently upheld such a trespass policy at a public housing development against a First Amendment challenge. Virginia vs. Hicks, 593 U.S. 113 (2003) (policy of barring nonresidents from public housing properties who have no legitimate business on the property upheld because policy does not impinge on any First Amendment activity).

12. Interview with Betsy Lindsay, June 26, 2003 (copy on file with the author).

13. Ibid.

14. Ibid.

15. Ibid.

16. Ibid.

17. George Kelling, et al., *The Kansas City Preventive Patrol Experiment: A Summary Report* (Washington, D.C.: Police Foundation, 1974), v.

18. Herman Goldstein, *Problem-Oriented Policing* (New York: McGraw-Hill, 1987), 13.

19. Herman Goldstein, "Improving Policing: A Problem-Oriented Approach," *J. Crime & Delinquency* 236, 242 (1979), 25.

20. Goldstein, *Problem-Oriented Policing*, 19.

21. Ibid., 14–15.

22. Ibid., 32.

23. Note that Goldstein presents systematic inquiry and analysis as two separate basic principles. Ibid., 32–33, 34–35, 35–36, 36–38, 40–41, 43–45, and 49. For purposes of this discussion, I have left out disaggregating and accurately labeling problems, ibid., 38–40, capturing and critiquing the current response, ibid., 42–43, adopting a proactive stance, ibid., 45–47, and strengthening the decisison making process and increasing accountability, ibid., 47–49, either because they are less relevant than others to our discussion or because I believe they are fairly covered or implied in other of these principles.

24. By stressing some of the aspects of Goldstein's problem-oriented policing idea over others, I do not mean to imply that other aspects of his theory are unimportant. Nor do I wish to urge the use of some truncated, bastardized version of Goldstein's system—

"problem-oriented policing for dummies." On the contrary, these five elements of Goldstein's theory represent the core of his outlook—the aspects of his system that no real problem-solving effort can do without. For example, Betsy Lindsay of the Housing Authority of the County of Los Angeles stresses that police often make the mistake of failing to conduct deep and searching enough analyses of the problems they face, and risk ending up with superficial, ineffective responses. (Interview with Betsy Lindsay, June 26, 2003). Similarly, she warns, skipping the assessment stage means that one simply cannot tell whether the effort at problem solving was highly successful, or all for naught. Michael Scott, an independent police research and management consultant who has both served in police management and helped design and implement problem-oriented policing strategies for agencies around the country, cautions that there is an important distinction between problem-oriented policing and mere problem solving—the former representing a "comprehensive framework for improving the police's capacity to perform their mission," and the latter a much more limited idea that simply describes "the mental process that is at the core of problem-oriented policing." Michael S. Scott, "Problem-Oriented Policing: Reflections on the First 20 Years," Washington, D.C., U.S. Dept. of Justice, Office of Community Oriented Policing Services, Oct. 2000, at 3. To say one engages in the latter, Scott says, does not mean that one has fully engaged in the former, and may sow both confusion and unreasonably high expectations in the public mind. Ibid., 45–46. Further, though frontline police officers often attempt to engage in the entire process of problem-oriented policing, they usually have no training or experience as objective analysts. Ibid., 59-60. It would be much better, Scott says, for police to have an experienced researcher as part of their team, who would collect and analyze data and draw conclusions, and also would actively participate in the process by proposing strategies and interventions as the process continues in an effort to effectively address the problem. (Ibid., 62–63.) Surely all of this is correct, and following the steps and process now well described in a host of materials available to practitioners would be the best possible route. Any thoughtful person would advocate nothing less, at least where resources and commitment allow. The overall point here is simply this: police must get away from thinking of the entire job as simply responding and reacting to problems that have occurred, and must instead view themselves as (with apologies to Michael Scott) problem solvers with the job of figuring out how to get ahead of crime and disorder. Problem-oriented policing, in its fullest, most expansive sense, surely supplies the best template for doing this. But even if police officers did not get, or did not bring into practice, every one of Goldstein's eleven basic concepts, thinking and acting as problem-oriented officers, grouping incidents together, focusing on problems, and measuring their efforts by their effectiveness would still go a long way.

25. Jenny Berrien and Christopher Winship, "An Umbrella of Legitimacy: Boston's Police Department—Ten-Point Coalition Collaboration," in *Securing Our Children's Future: New Approaches to Juvenile Justice and Youth Violence*, Gary S. Katzman, ed., 2002, (Washington, D.C.: Brookings Inst. Press), 204.

26. "The Boston Strategy to Prevent Youth Violence: Police: Sgt. Robert Merner," downloaded from http://www.bostonstrategy.com/players/01_police/05_merner.html, March 12, 2003.

27. Peter S. Canellos and Irene Sage, "Couple Shot After Leaving Hospital; Baby Delivered," *Boston Globe*, Oct. 24, 1989, at 1.

28. Sally Jacobs and Diego Ribadeneira, "No Wallet, So Killer Opened Fire," *Boston Globe*, Oct. 26, 1989, at 1.

29. Ibid.

30. Ibid.

31. Sean Murphy and Thomas Palmer, "Bennett Case Built on a story Reportedly Later Denied," *Boston Globe*, Jan. 12, 1990, at 1. Those who had allegedly told the police that Mr. Bennett had confessed said after Stuart killed himself that the police had pressured and threatened them with long prison sentences if they did not lie and say that Bennett had admitted that he shot Carol Stuart.

Jerry Thomas and Thomas Palmer, "New Charges of Coercion in Bennett Investigation," *Boston Globe*, Jan. 20, 1990, at 1.

32. Constance L. Hays, "Husband of Slain Boston Woman Becomes a Suspect, Then a Suicide," *New York Times*, Jan. 5, 1990, at A1.

33. Ibid.

34. Ibid. (quoting, inter alia, a community leader who said that "black people in particular have to look at it and wonder what hope we have for justice in a country that took this man's lie and made him and his family a symbol of national mourning"); Peter J. Howe, "From Nightmare to Reality, A City Is Reeling," *Boston Globe*, Jan. 7, 1990, at 1 (Boston's black leadership "has erupted in outrage at how the Mission Hill neighborhood and black Boston as a whole were maligned by a false story—a story black leaders charge the mayor, police and general public were all too quick and willing to believe."); Diane Lewis, "Black Residents Remain Outraged," *Boston Globe*, Jan. 9, 1990, at 19 (quoting community resident as saying "he was a white man and his word was like gold . . . . He set up black people. He set up Mission Hill and any-one who says that racism wasn't involved is fooling himself."); Karen Tumulty, "Wife Killing Puts Boston in Worst Racial Crisis in Years," *Los Angeles Times*, Jan. 10, 1990, at A1 ("the case has sent Boston into what [Boston] Mayor [Raymond] Flynn calls its worst racial crisis since court-ordered school desegregation sparked riots in the mid-1970s"); Peter J. Howe, "Legacy of the Stuart Mur-der; Poll: Case Hurt Race Relations," *Boston Globe*, Jan. 21, 1990, at 1 (poll finds 9 out of 10 blacks believe Boston police overreacted in Stuart investigation, but whites, by 5–4, don't believe police overreacted).

35. Victoria Benning, "Violence Erupts at Drive-by Victim's Rites," *Boston Globe*, May 15, 1992, at 1.

36. Ibid.

37. Ibid. (minister of church calling the attack "a desecration of a reli-gious service" that has to be "a turning point for this community"); Efrain Hernandez, Jr., "I've Never Seen Anything Like It; Four Men Arraigned at Melee at Funeral," *Boston Globe*, May 16, 1992, at 1

(quoting minister as say that "through God's grace and Mercy, that we are going to see a lot of good come from this experience"); Efrain Hernandez, Jr., "Four City Ministers Propose a 10-Point Plan to Curb Gang Violence," *Boston Globe*, May 20, 1992, at 54 (ministers propose what later becomes the Ten Point Coalition); Robert A. Jordan, "Outreach Sparks a Ray of Hope," *Boston Globe*, May 23, 1992, at 21 (describing ten-point agreement emerging from meeting of 300 ministers and its encapsulation in an open letter to be read to congregations).

38. Interview with David Kennedy, Harvard University, March 13, 2003 (copy on file with the author).

39. Brown recalls that, on one visit to a gang in a troubled park, one of the gang's soldiers took one of Brown's colleagues aside. The gang member had told Brown's colleague that he'd done some bad things in his life, and wanted help. Brown recalls that his colleague said, "The kid says, 'Out of all the things that I've done in my life, I seemed to have lost my conscience. Can you help me get my conscience back?'" Interview with Reverend Jeffrey Brown, March 7, 2003 (copy on file with the author).

40. "The Boston Strategy to Prevent Youth Violence: Police: Sgt. Robert Merner."

41. David M. Kennedy, "A Tale of One City: Reflections on the Boston Gun Project," in *Securing Our Children's Future: New Approaches to Juvenile Justice and Youth Violence*, Gary S. Katzman, ed. (Washington, D.C.: Brookings Inst. Press, 2002), 239; interview with David Kennedy, March 13, 2003.

42. Ibid.; David M. Kennedy, "A Tale of One City," 238–239.

43. Ibid., 239.

44. Ibid.

45. Interview with Assistant Supt. Paul Joyce. Boston Police Department, April 19, 2003 (copy on file with the author).

46. Ibid.

47. David M. Kennedy, "A Tale of One City," 245.

48. Ibid., 233.

49. Ibid.

50. Ibid.

51. Ibid.

52. Ibid.

53. Fox Butterfield, "Killing of Girl, 10, and Increase in Homicides Challenge Boston's Crime-Fighting Model," *New York Times*, Jan. 14, 2002, at 14 ("For two and a half years in the late 90s, not a single juvenile was killed with a handgun."); Peter Hermann, "Police Plan Clampdown on Baltimore Youth Gangs," *Baltimore Sun*, Jan 23, 1998, at 1A (describing Boston's "29-month run without a youth being slain").

54. Christopher Winship and Jenny Berrien, "An Umbrella of Legitimacy," 216.

55. Laurel J. Sweet, "Police Report Violent Crime Hits 31-Year Low in Hub," *Boston Herald*, Jan. 31, 2003.

56. The description of the efforts of San Diego police to address crime at the "Blue Roofs" apartment complex comes from Rana Sampson and Michael S. Scott, "Tackling Crime and Other Public Safety Problems: Case Studies in Problem-Solving," Washington, D.C., U.S. Dept. of Justice, Office of Community Oriented Policing Services (1999), at 9–12. This work is an excellent collection of examples of the use of problem-oriented policing in communities around the country. It can serve both as an introduction to what problem-oriented policing is and how it works, and as a resource guide for experienced problem-oriented officers eager to find out how police officers elsewhere have successfully tackled problems similar to those they face.

57. For more information about the Section 8 program, see U.S. Dept. of Housing and Urban Development, "Housing Choice Vouchers Fact Sheet," accessed at http://www.hud.gov:80/offices/pih/programs/hcv/about/fact_sheet.cfm, July 14, 2003; National Association of Housing and Redevelopment Officials, "Section 8 Housing Choice Voucher Program," Washington D.C., 3–5.

58. Much of the information in this section is based on author's interview with Assistant Chief Jon Jeter, Stamford Police Department, March 14, 2003.

59. Much of the information in this section is based on author's interview with Officer Scott Baldwin, Stamford Police Department, March 14, 2003.

60. William R. Blount and Associates, "An Assessment of The Domus-SRO Community Camp, a Partnership Between the Stamford Police Department, Domus Foundation, and Stamford Board of Education," prepared for the Office of Community Policing Services, U.S. Department of Justice, June 19, 2002.

61. Ibid.

62. Interview with Officer Tim Howard, Stamford Police Department, Stamford, Connecticut, July 17, 2003.

63. Personal electronic communication with Sergeant William Hnatuk, Stamford Police Dept., to David Harris, Jan. 2, 2004 (copy on file with the author).

64. Ibid. According to Sergeant Hnatuk, "the State of Connecticut classifies a juvenile as anyone under the age of sixteen." (Ibid.) Therefore, some of those arrested included in the statistics may be older than the average camper. However, those older than middle school age, including those up to age sixteen, can participate as counselors in training. Therefore, the camp cutbacks affect this group, too.

65. Ibid.

66. Ibid.

CHAPTER 5: Being Accountable

1. The description here of a quarterly CompSTAR meeting comes from the author's observation of one of those meetings in June 2003. In keeping with an agreement that personnel matters of particular individuals would not be disclosed, the identities of particular officers and of the commanders commenting on them have been removed, and details of individual cases have been changed.

2. In keeping with the agreement with the Pittsburgh Police Bureau, the name and identifying information of this commander at the CompSTAR meeting and all officers reviewed have been changed.

3.   Samuel Walker, *Police Accountability: The Role of Citizen Oversight* (Belmont, CA: Wadsworth, 2001), 4–5.

4.   For a comprehensive look at these arguments and why failing to counter perceived unfairness with accountability mechanisms can undermine the integrity of police and the law, see generally David Harris, *Profiles In Injustice: Why Racial Profiling Cannot Work* (New York: The New Press, 2002).

5.   Ibid., citing IACP Resolution, "Police Review Boards," Oct. 6, 1960, in *Police Chief* magazine, 34 (Feb. 1964).

6.   Samuel Walker, *Police Accountability*, 25, citing Paul Jacobs, *Prelude to Riot* (New York: Vantage, 1968), 13–60.

7.   Samuel Walker, *Police Accountability*, 27–28.

8.   Ibid., 28.

9.   New York City, Commission to Investigate Allegations of Police Corruption and the Anti-Corruption Procedures of the Police Department [the Mollen Commission], Commission Report (New York: Mollen Commission, 1994).

10. Christopher Commission, Report of the Independent Commission on the Los Angeles Police Department (Los Angeles: Christopher Commission, 1991).

11. Walker, *Police Accountability*, 57.

12. Los Angeles Police Dept., Board of Inquiry, "Rampart Area Corruption Incident" (Los Angeles Police Department, March 2000).

13. Ibid.

14. Ibid.

15. Interview with Sergeant Jim Malloy, Pittsburgh Police Bureau, June 12, 2003 (copy on file with the author.)

16. Interview with Robert McNeilly, chief, Pittsburgh Police Bureau, December 5, 2000.

17. Telephone communication with information office, City of Pittsburgh, May 19, 2004.

18. Personal communication by e-mail with Carol A. Archbold, Marquette University, August 5, 2003 (copy on file with the author). In an unpublished study from May 2002, Archbold found that, of police departments with 200 or more officers, approximately half

have an in-house legal advisor, risk manager, or both; in the other half, such staff are often shared with other city departments. See Carol A. Archbold, "Police Accountability, Risk Management, and Legal Advising" (New York: L B F Scholarly Publishing, 2004).

19. James Kolts, *The Los Angeles County Sheriff's Department* (Los Angeles: Los Angeles County, 1992), 26.

20. New York City Public Advocate, *Disciplining the Police: Solving the Problem of Police Misconduct* (New York: Public Advocate, 2000), 2.

21. U.S. Commission on Civil Rights, "Who Is Guarding the Guardians?" (Washington, D.C., 1981).

22. Ibid., 81.

23. Samuel Walker, et al., "Early Warning Systems: Responding to the Problem Police Officer," U.S. Department of Justice, National Institute of Justice, Research in Brief, (July 2001), 1.

24. "Kansas City Police Go After Their 'Bad Boys,'" *New York Times*, Sept. 10, 1991.

25. "Waves of Abuse Laid to a Few Officers," *Boston Globe,* Oct. 4, 1992.

26. Christopher Commission, *Report of the Independent Commission*, 32–47.

27. Goldstein, *Policing in a Free Society*, 171.

28. Walker, et al., "Early Warning Systems," 2.

29. Ibid., 3.

30. Ibid.

31. Interview with Patrick Sullivan, June 4, 2003 (copy on file with the author).

32. Walker, et al., "Early Warning Systems," 4.

33. Interview with Commander Linda Barone, Pittsburgh, June 3, 2003 (copy on file with the author).

34. Ibid.

35. Walker, et al., "Early Warning Systems," 7.

36. Interview with Commander Linda Barone, June 3, 2003.

37. Even an early-warning system as advanced and well-thought-out as the one in Pittsburgh has problems and blind spots. For example, sergeants and lieutenants complain that they are overburdened with in-office work related to PARS which cuts into their

opportunities to observe officers in the field. Robert C. Davis, et al., "Turning Necessity into Virtue: Pittsburgh's Experience with a Federal Consent Decree," Vera Institute of Justice (September 2002), 50. If true, this indicates that some adjustments of the system and front-line supervisory responsibilities are needed. Perhaps more important is the problem of the invisible or do-nothing officer: an officer can simply lie low and decrease his or her activity in all aspects of police work, especially in the areas that might result in being selected for intervention. The invisible-officer problem is especially important in light of "depolicing" or "N/C, N/C" (no contact, no complaints) practices that some police officers have allegedly adopted in the wake of strong efforts at police reform, including implementation of early-warning systems. Most notably in Cincinnati and Los Angeles (Kevin Johnson, "Crime Keeps Cincinnati Reeling," USA Today, July 8, 2002; Peter Bronson, "Are Cops Being Too Careful?" Cincinnati Enquirer, Dec. 20, 2002; Alex Tizon and Reid Forgrave, "Wary of Complaints, Police Look the Other Way in Black Neighborhoods," Seattle Times, June 26, 2001), officers have supposedly "disengaged" from their assignments; they answer radio calls but take no proactive or preemptive action. The implications are dangerous indeed. In effect, officers are saying to civilian and even departmental authorities who attempt to reform their organizations and change their behavior, "No way—it's our way or the highway, and you can't make us do anything we don't want to do." This attitude represents a challenge to the principles of police accountability and civilian leadership of police departments, and to the rule of law. Despite all of the talk about depolicing, however, there appears to be less to it than meets the eye. For example, the Vera Institute of Justice's study of policing in Pittsburgh found no evidence to support assertions that officers there had disengaged from their jobs to avoid PARS. On the contrary, relevant officer activity levels had not changed in response to PARS. Robert C. Davis, et al., "Turning Necessity into Virtue," 53–58, 63. Nevertheless, the possibility of "flying under the radar" by disengaging from the job shows that as we design new early-warning systems, they ought to focus not only on conduct that might indicate problems, but also on indicators of insufficient activity.

38. Jodi M. Brown and Patrick Langan, U.S. Dept. of Justice, Bureau of Justice Statistics, *Policing and Homicide, 1976–98: Justifiable Homicide by Police, Police Officers Murdered by Felons* (March 2001), 3.

39. Ibid.

40. Geoffrey P. Alpert, "Police Pursuit: Policies and Training," U.S. Department of Justice, National Institute of Justice, Research in Brief, May 1997.

41. Andrew Blankstein, "Car Chases Way Down, Police Say" *Los Angeles Times*, Aug. 20, 2003.

42. Ibid.

43. Ibid.

44. Ibid.

45. Information on the origin of Compstat comes in part from William Bratton with Peter Knobler, *Turnaround: How America's Top Cop Reversed the Crime Epidemic* (New York: Random House, 1998).

46. See Jack Maple with Chris Mitchell, *The Crime Fighter, How You Can Make Your Community Crime-Free* (New York: Broadway Books, 1999), 33.

47. Interview with William Bratton, December 14, 2000 (copy on file with the author).

48. Interview with anonymous New York Police Department commander, name and assignment withheld by request, May 20, 2003.

49. The author was permitted to attend a Compstat meeting in 2003. To preserve confidentiality, the identities of the borough command officer and the various senior staff members quoted here are not disclosed. The author wishes to thank Commissioner Raymond Kelly for granting permission to observe the meeting.

50. Overland Park Police Department, Overland Park, Kansas, "2003 Strategic Operations Plan" (copy on file with author).

51. "Public Solidly Favors Mixed Police/Civilian Review Boards," *Law Enforcement News*, Oct. 31, 1992, 1.

52. Walker, *Police Accountability*, 43.

53. Ibid., 71.

54. Ibid., 72, citing Dibb v. City of San Diego, Dec. 12, 1994, and the Michigan Court of Appeals decision on the Flint, Michigan, ombudsman.

55. Interview with Sergeant Jim Malloy, June 11, 2003 (copy on file with the author); interview with Elizabeth Pittinger, executive director, Citizen Police Review Board of Pittsburgh, June 4, 2003, Pittsburgh.

56. Walker, *Police Accountability*, 77.

57. Ibid., citing New York Civil Liberties Union, *Police Abuse: The Need for Civilian Investigation and Oversight* (New York: NYCLU, 1990).

58. Walker, *Police Accountability*, 77–78, note 92.

59. Ibid., 77, citing Oakland Citizens' Police Review Board, "1997 Annual Report," January 20, 1998, 8.

60. Ibid., 78.

61. The requirements passed in Proposition G are now found in the San Francisco Charter, Article IV, Sec. 4.127 (2002), accessed at http:///amlegal.com/sanfrancharterlpext.dll/Infobase/8c/13a?fn=document-frame.htm&f=templates, Sept. 28, 2002.

62. Ibid.

63. Ibid.

64. Michael Fuoco and Jim McKinnon, "The Victims of 1995," *Pittsburgh Post-Gazette*, January 1, 1996.

65. Interview with John Burkoff, professor of law, University of Pittsburgh, and first chair of CPRB, Aug. 5, 2003 (copy on file with the author).

66. Ibid.

67. Citizen Police Review Board, "2001 Final Report," Pittsburgh, issued May 9, 2002, 6.

68. Interview with John Burkoff, Aug. 5, 2003.

69. Citizen Police Review Board, "2001 Final Report," 6.

70. Ibid., 7, 9, 10.

71. Ibid., 9.

72. According to one source close to the events, much of this has been passive resistance—foot dragging, stalling, and even outright

dishonesty by other city departments that CPRB has to work through to obtaining budgeting authority, staffing, and equipment. Interview with source in Pittsburgh, August 2003, who spoke to author on condition of anonymity. Some of the resistance has been active and quite overt. For example, the Fraternal Order of Police has stated that its members will not speak to the board, despite the board's authority to obtain sworn testimony with subpoenas. The union contends that the officers' statements might be used against them in other proceedings; the board strongly disagrees. An appeal of a lawsuit dealing with the issue is pending at this writing.

73. Interview with John Burkoff, Aug. 5, 2003.

74. Interview with Bill Valenta, Pittsburgh Police Bureau, and head of OMI, March 16, 2003 (copy on file with the author).

75. Interview with Elizabeth Pittinger, June 4, 2003.

76. According to Pittinger, the Office of Municipal Investigations is part of the Department of Law, which also defends the Police Bureau in all lawsuits against it. Its investigations must be done in accordance with the FOP union contract between the city and the union. OMI is not independent of the Police Bureau, Pittinger says, but made up of police officers, with one sitting at OMI's helm. Interview with Elizabeth Pittinger, June 4, 2003.

77. The board's annual report for 2001, the latest currently available, was issued May 9, 2002. In 1999, 2000, and 2001, the board received 80, 76, and 77 sworn complaints respectively, for a total of 233. The board took action on these cases, ordering investigations, holding hearings, and so on, 420 times; 186 of these actions, or 42 percent, were dismissals of complaints. Of the 233 sworn complaints, the board issued findings of any kind, for or against police officers, in just 21 cases—less than 10 percent. In those cases, the board sustained the complaint and made a recommendation for action (usually some form of discipline and some additional training) against the officer in 18 cases. In one case, the board sustained the complaint but recommended no action, and in another found the complaint not sustained. One case was still pending as of the end of 2001.

78. Personal communication from Elizabeth Pittinger to the author, Aug. 13, 2003.

79. There is at least one hybrid version of oversight that lies between the complaint review model and the auditor, what one might call monitor systems, that give the agency a role in the handling of individual complaints but only in a limited way. In these systems, the focus is on complaints, but the investigations and recommendation for discipline still come from the department's internal affairs unit. The agency does no investigation of its own; it simply goes over what the police have already done, and may then either agree or disagree, or perhaps ask for further investigation. While the monitoring agency is independent of the police department, this is largely independence in form only; it is completely dependent on the police department for all of its information and investigation. For purposes of our discussion, we will limit ourselves here to the complaint review model and auditor models, which represent the true forms of the types of oversight.

80. See, for example, John Crew, "A Campaign of Deception—San Jose's Case Against Civilian Review," ACLU of Northern California (1992). However, these arguments against auditors implicitly depend on the assumption that independent investigation of individual complaints will stop police misconduct—an assumption that the collective records of these agencies do not support. Rather, complaint review bodies, police departments, and especially their unions fight and frustrate at every turn. Their independence is often compromised, their investigative reach is limited, and their resources range from meager to nonexistent. Little evidence suggests that cities with complaint review systems have less police misconduct than cities using auditors.

81. Walker, *Police Accountability*, 86.

82. All of these materials are available at the City of San Jose Office of the Independent Police Auditor, accessed at http://www.ci.san-jose.ca.us/ipa/home.html#, Aug. 13, 2003.

83. Walker, *Police Accountability*, 90.

84. James G. Kolts, *The Los Angeles County Sheriff's Department* (Los Angeles County, 1992), 25.

85. All of the Special Counsel's semiannual reports are available on the Web site of the Police Assessment Resource Center (PARC), at http://www.parc.info/pubs/index.html, accessed Aug. 14, 2003. PARC is a Los Angeles–based organization directed by Merrick Bobb to provide careful evaluation of police departments.

86. Special Counsel to the Los Angeles County Sheriff's Department, "Ninth Semiannual Report" (Los Angeles, June 1998), 9–10, 17–18, 18–20, 18–19, 21–22, and 22–23.

87. Walker, *Police Accountability*, 99.

88. Ibid., 1–2.

89. Ibid., 25–26.

90 Ibid.

91. Ibid., 12.

92. Ibid.

93. Ibid., 26-27.

94. Ibid., 27-35.

95. The first such survey was conducted in 1996 and involved more than 6,000 people; the second survey surveyed more than 90,000 respondents.

96. Patrick A. Langan, et al., "Contacts Between Police and the Public: Findings from the 1999 National Survey," U.S. Department of Justice, Bureau of Justice Statistics, survey form; "Police Public Contact Survey, Supplement of the National Crime Victimization Study," February 2001, NCJ 184957, accessed at http://www.ojp.usdoj.gov/bjs/pub/pdf/cpp99.pdf, Dec. 11, 2003. The data from the 1999 study were released in 2001. Given the prominence of racial profiling in that period, the bureau added an extra section to the survey on profiling.

97. Ibid.

98. For an excellent discussion of transparency in policing, see generally Erik Luna, "Transparent Policing," *Iowa Law Review* 1107 (2000), 85.

99. Robert L. Jackson, "Push Against Bias in Traffic Stops Arrested," *Los Angeles Times*, June 1, 1998.

100. Paul Van Slambrouck, "Two Cities Tackle Racial Profiling," *Christian Science Monitor*, March 29, 1999. The other—and actually the first—chief to do this was Chief Jerry Sanders of San Diego.

101. Bill Lansdowne, "A Chief's View: Why Police Should Embrace Tracking of Racial Data," *San Jose Mercury News*, June 16, 1999.

102. Ibid.

103. Brian Hazle, "Police Chief Arrives in S.D. with Raves from Public, Cops," *San Diego Union Tribune*, Aug. 24, 2003.

104. Julie N. Lynem, "San Jose Study on Police Stops Sparks Debate," *San Francisco Chronicle*, Dec. 18, 1999.

105. Ibid.

106. New York Public Advocate, *Disciplining the Police*, 2.

107. Telephone communication with information office, City of Pittsburgh, May 19, 2004.

108. For example., William J. Stuntz, "Race, Class, and Drugs," 93 *Columbia Law Rev.*, 1795, 1799, 1821 (1998).

109. San Francisco City Charter, Art. IV, Sec. 4.127.

110. Even almost eight years after the passage of Proposition G, it remains difficult to ascertain whether it has made a real difference. Even assuming a downward trend in damages for police conduct since the Proposition's enactment, one could not say authoritatively that the latter caused the former, given the number of other plausible variables that might be at work: changes in the behavior of juries, greater or lesser public hostility to police, or other accountability mechanisms put in place during the same time, just to hypothesize a few examples. Without better data and some probing research on the subject, all one can say is that it *should* work.

111. Act of September 13, 1994, P.L. 103-322 108 Stat. 1796.

112. 42 U.S.C. sec. 14141 (a) (1994).

113. In only one case, involving the Columbus, Ohio, police department, has the case moved beyond the threat of litigation. In Columbus, the city and the police department were willing to sign the consent decree, but the police union would not. Since elements of the proposed consent decree would have involved changing certain aspects of department procedure governed by the

department's contract with the police union, the union's refusal to go along killed any prospect of settlement, and the case moved into actual litigation. The government dropped the case unilaterally in the fall of 2002, saying that the police department had in fact done everything the government wanted in terms of changes; the police union, on the other hand, proclaimed itself victorious.

114. Consent Decree, U.S. v. New Jersey et al., Civ. No. 99-5970 (MLC) (D. N.J. 1999).

115. U.S. v. Pittsburgh and Pittsburgh Police Bureau, C.A. 97-354 (1997).

116. Torsten Ove, "Judge Lifts U.S. Oversight of City Police," *Pittsburgh Post-Gazette*, September 14, 2002.

117. Consent Decree, U.S. v. City of Los Angeles and the Lost Angeles Police Department et al., Civ. No. 00-11769 GAF (N.D. Cal. 2001).

118. Consent Judgment, U.S. v. City of Detroit and Detroit Police Dept., No 03-72258, U.S. District Court, E.D. Michigan.

119. Consent Decree, U.S. v. City of Steubenville et al., 2:97 CU 966 (E.D. Ohio 1997).

120. Memorandum of Agreement Between U.S. Department of Justice, Montgomery County, Maryland, Montgomery County Department of Police, and Fraternal Order of Police, Montgomery County Lodge 35 (Jan. 14, 2000).

121. "Special Litigation Section FAQ."

122. Remarks of Joseph Brann, former director of the U.S. Department of Justice Office of Community Oriented Policing Services, at event sponsored by Police Executives Research Forum at the annual meeting of the International Association of Chiefs of Police, San Diego, California, Nov. 13, 2000.

123. Calif. Code Ann., Civil Code, Div. 1, Section 52.3, "Action to obtain equitable and declaratory relief to eliminate pattern or practice by law enforcement officers depriving persons of legal rights" (2000).

124. Scott Gold, "State Steps into Police Reform in Riverside," *Los Angeles Times*, Feb. 18, 2001.

125. The End Racial Profiling Act of 2004, S. 2132, H.R. 3847 (108th Congress).

CHAPTER 6: Leading the Way

1. Interview with Deputy Inspector Thomas King, April 28, 2003 (copy on file with the author). I was able to contact Tom King with the help of Robert Davis at the Vera Institute of Justice, who gave me enough information that I was able to locate him with the help of the NYPD personnel office. Davis and his colleagues had spotlighted King's successful work in their report, cited in note 3, following. I also attempted to contact another commander who was also a subject of the Vera report, but he had retired and did not respond to my attempts to communicate.

2. James Q. Wilson and George Kelling, "Broken Windows," *Atlantic Monthly,* Feb. 1982.

3. Robert C. Davis, Pedro Mateu-Gelabert, and Joel Miller, "Can Effective Policing Also Be Respectful? Two Examples in the South Bronx," unpublished manuscript on file with the author. An earlier version of the study (March 1999) under the same title is available from the Vera Institute of Justice at http://www.vera.org/publication_pdf/respectful_policing.pdf.

4. Ibid., 16.

5. Interview with Deputy Inspector Thomas King.

6. Davis, et al., "Can Effective Policing Also Be Respectful?", 17.

7. Interview with Deputy Inspector Thomas King.

8. Ibid.

9. Ibid.

10. Ibid.

11. Ibid., 18.

12. Interview with Jerry Barker, chief of police, Indianapolis, Indiana, May 20, 2003 (copy on file with the author).

13. Tyrone Chandler, "Reducing Gun-Related Crimes Through a Comprehensive Multi-Pronged Program," in U.S. Dept. of Justice, *Weed and Seed Best Practices*, issue 3, Spring 2000, 9.

14. Interview with Jerry Barker, May 20, 2003.

15. Ibid.

16. Ibid.

17. See, e.g., U.S. Dept. of Justice, *Weed and Seed Best Practices*, issue 3, Spring 2000; interview with Liz Allison, Indianapolis Police Department, March 24, 2003 (copy on file with the author).

18. Interview with Liz Allison, March 24, 2003.

19. Interview with Jerry Barker, May 20, 2003.

20. Chandler, "Reducing Gun-Related Crimes," 10–11.

21. Interview with Jerry Barker, May 20, 2003.

22. Chandler, "Reducing Gun-Related Crimes," 10–11

23. Ibid.

24. Interview with Chief Dean Esserman, March 18, 2003 (copy on file with the author).

25. Ibid.

26. For example, Amanda Milkovits, "Dean's List," *Providence Journal Bulletin*, Jan. 15, 2003 (recounting testimony of former chief that he helped officers cheat on exams).

27. Amanda Milkovits, "Cicilline, Esserman Defend Revised Academy Ranks," *Providence Journal-Bulletin*, April 29, 2003.

28. Interview with Chief Dean Esserman, March 18, 2003.

29. Amanda Milkovits, "This Is the Best City to Be a Cop—The New Blue Line," *Providence Journal-Bulletin*, Nov. 11, 2003 (explaining that fourteen of the members of the city's newest graduating class from the police academy had had to file a lawsuit because they had perhaps wrongfully been excluded from the class through a prior administration's favoritism).

30. Amanda Milkovits, "Secret Phone-Tap System Found at Police Complex," *Providence Journal-Bulletin*, Feb. 14, 2003; Tom Farmer, "Call Taping System Found in Providence Police Offices," *Providence Journal-Bulletin*, Feb. 21, 2003.

31. Interview with Dean Esserman, March 18, 2003.

32. Ibid.

33. Ibid.

34. Richard C. DuJardin, "Mayor, Chief Announce Commanders in New Districts," *Providence Journal-Bulletin*, May 6, 2003.

35. Ibid.

36. Amanda Milkovits, "A New Place in the Community—A Satellite

Police Office Opens on Providence's South Side," *Providence Journal-Bulletin*, Aug. 26, 2003.

37. Amanda Milkovits, "The Best Police Chief in America," *Providence Journal-Bulletin*, Feb. 8, 2004.

38. Adrian Walker, "Minister's Widow Seeks $18M for Botched Drug Raid," *Boston Globe*, June 16, 1994.

39. Kevin Cullen, "Legal Fight Upstages Police Remorse for Raid," *Boston Globe*, April 22, 1996.

40. To Evans's considerable dismay, the state civil service commission overturned the suspension because the Boston Police Department failed to show just cause that the lieutenant should be suspended for failing to supervise the raid properly. Brian MacQuarrie, "Botched Raid Suspension Overturned," *Boston Globe*, Dec. 30, 1996.

41. Kevin Cullen, April 22, 1996.

42. Michael Cooper, "Mayor's Response to a Fatal Police Shooting a Departure From His Predecessors'," *New York Times*, January 26, 2004 (detailing how Giuliani reacted to Dorismond's killing by "authorizing the release of the victim's police record which had been sealed because he was a juvenile at the time. . . .").

43. Interview with Reverend Jeffrey Brown, Boston, Massachusetts, March 7, 2003 (copy on file with the author).

44. Ric Kahn, "Crimes of the Century: McLaughlin Murder—A Killing that Shattered Boundaries," *Boston Globe*, December 10, 1999.

45. Ibid.

46. Ibid.

47. John Ellement, "McLaughlin 'Assassinated,' Prosecutor Says," *Boston Globe*, Feb. 21, 1998.

48. Ibid.

49. Ibid.

50. Ibid.

51. Francie Latour and Douglas Belkin, "Man Held as Driver at Fatal Shooting," *Boston Globe*, Sept. 10, 2002.

52. Michael S. Rosenwald, "Deadly Violence Hits Boston," *Boston Globe*, July 3, 2002.

53. Ibid.
54. Latour and Belkin, "Man Held as Driver."
55. Raphael Lewis, "Police Fatally Shoot Woman in Fleeing Car, Officer Injured," *Boston Globe*, Sept. 9, 2002.
56. Ibid.
57. David Abel, "Shooting Puts Focus on Deadly-Force Policy," *Boston Globe*, Sept. 9, 2002.
58. Latour and Belkin, "Man Held as Driver."
59. Ibid.
60. Derrick Z. Jackson, "Clergy's Backing Saves Evans on No-Shoot Policy," *Boston Globe*, Sept. 25, 2003.
61. Latour and Belkin, "Man Held as Driver."
62. Ibid.
63. Peter Gelzinis, "Old Bitterness Boils Up," *Boston Herald*, Sept. 22, 2002.
64. Megan Tench, "2d Group Offers Support for Evans, Points to Progress in Curbing Violence," *Boston Globe*, Sept. 21, 2002.
65. Michael S. Rosenwald and Douglas Belkin, "Evans Takes Heat from a 2d Union But Clergy Backs Commissioner," *Boston Globe*, Sept. 20, 2002.
66. Ibid.
67. Ibid.
68. Marie Szaniszlo, "Black Leaders Back Police Commissioner," *Boston Herald*, Sept. 21, 2002.
69. Ibid.
70. Ibid.
71. Ibid.
72. Ibid.
73. Interview with Reverend Jeffrey Brown, March 7, 2003.
74. Ibid.
75. Marie Szaniszlo, "Street Tensions: Menino, AG Back Top Cop," *Boston Herald*, September 22, 2002.
76. Ibid.

CHAPTER 7: Bending Granite or Curving Wood?

1. Dorothy Guyot, "Bending Granite: Attempts to Change the Rank Structure of Police Departments," in *Police Administrative Issues: Techniques and Functions,* Mark R. Pogrebin and Robert M. Regoli, eds., (Millwood, NY: Associated Faculty Press, 1986), 43.
2. 15 *J. Police Science and Administration* (1987), 196 .
3. Ibid., 201.
4. Ibid., 202–203.
5. Samuel Walker, "Police Accountability: The Role of Citizen Oversight" (Belmont, CA: Wadsworth, 2001), 5.
6. Interview with Assistant Chief Steve Creighton, San Diego Police Department, San Diego, California, November 14, 2000 (copy on file with the author).
7. Presentation by Captain Ron Davis of the Oakland Police Department at the Performance Institute, Washington, D.C., July 2001. The author was one of the other speakers that day and witnessed the exchange quoted here, which is reconstructed from notes and verified by Captain Davis.
8. Ibid.
9. Captain Ronald Davis, "Police Accountability: Looking Beyond the Videotape" December 2002, 13 (unpublished manuscript on file with the author).
10. Ibid.
11. Interview with Captain Ron Davis, Oakland Police Department, September 2003 (copy on file with the author).
12. Peter M. Sheingold, "National COPS Evaluation Organization Change Case Study: Colorado Springs, Colorado," prepared for the Urban Institute, accessed September 20, 2002, at http://www. ncjrs.org/nij/cops_casestudy/colorado.html.
13. Ibid.
14. Ibid.
15. See interview with Deputy Chief Pat McElderry, Colorado Springs Police Department, July 11, 2003 (copy on file with the author).
16. See interview with Mora Fiedler, civilian administrator and social

scientist, Colorado Springs Police Department, March 18, 2003 (copy on file with author).

17. Presentation by Thomas Paine, Colorado Springs Police Department, "The PASS Model in Colorado Springs (Police Accountability and Service Standards)," presented at the Second Annual National Community Policing Conference, sponsored by the U.S. Department of Justice, Office of Community-Oriented Policing Services, June 16, 2003 (copy of presentation slides on file with the author); interview with Mora Fiedler, March 18, 2003.

18. Presentation by Thomas Paine, "The PASS Model."

19. Ibid.

20. Ibid.

21. Ibid.

22. Ibid.

23. Ibid.

24. Ibid.

25. Interview with Deputy Chief Pat McElderry, July 11, 2003.

26. Ibid.

27. Ibid.

28. Ibid.

29. Interview with Thomas Paine, Colorado Springs Police Department, June 20, 2003 (copy on file with the author).

30. Ibid.

31. Interview with Deputy Chief Pat McElderry, July 11, 2003.

32. Interview with Captain Ron Davis, September, 2003.

33. Interview with Dennis Conroy, March 27, 2003 (copy on file with the author).

34. Ibid.

35. Ibid.

36. Ibid.

37. Ibid.

38. Ibid.

39. Ibid.

40. Ibid.

41. Ibid.

42. Ibid.

43. Ibid.

44. Ibid.

45. See, for example, U.S. Dept. of Justice, *Weed & Seed Best Practices*, issue 3, Spring 2000; interview with Liz Allison, Indianapolis Police Department, March 24, 2003 (copy on file with the author).

46. Ibid.

47. Ibid.

48. Ibid.

49. Ibid.

50. Ibid.

51. Interview with Kenneth Howard, U.S. Department of Justice, October 16, 2003 (copy on file with the author).

52. Ibid.

53. Ibid.

CHAPTER 8: Ashcroft Policing

1. Deputy Attorney General, U.S. Department of Justice, "Memorandum for All United States Attorneys, All Members of the Anti-Terrorism Task Forces," U.S. Department of Justice, Nov. 9, 2001, Part 2. L.

2. Deborah Barfield Berry, "Arabs Question FBI's Questions; Issues of Rights Surface Amid Terrorist Probe," *Newsday*, Dec. 23, 2001.

3. The tapes were provided to the author on the condition that the attorney(s) and client(s) involved not be identified in any way. Issues of client confidentiality were address and cleared.

4. U.S. General Accounting Office, "Homeland Security: Justice Department's Project to Interview Aliens After September 11, 2001," GAO-03-459, April 11, 2003.

5. Interview with Robert Olson, Chief of Police, Minneapolis, Minn., June 19, 2003 (copy on file with the author).

6. Ibid.

7. Ibid.

8. Ibid.

9. There were others, of course, including the federal "material witness" statute, 18 U.S. C. sec. 3144 (2004), which the government has used to hold in custody those against whom it does not have sufficient evidence for charges, and the "material support for terrorism" statute, 18 U.S.C. sec. 2339A (2004), under which an almost infinite variety of behavior can lead to criminal charges.

10. Office of the Inspector General, U.S. Department of Justice, "The September 11 Detainees: A Review of the Treatment of Aliens Held on Immigration Charges in Connection with the Investigation of the September 11 Attacks," issued June 2, 2003, 15–16.

11. Ibid., 51–52.

12. Susan Sachs, "U.S. Defends the Withholding of Jailed Immigrants' Names," *New York Times*, May 21, 2002.

13. Office of the Inspector General, "The September 11 Detainees," 38–40.

14. Ibid., 38 (quoting a Department of Justice memorandum suggesting "Potential AG Explanation" for the hold until cleared policy).

15. Office of the Inspector General, "The September 11 Detainees," especially chapter 6. See also Stuart Taylor, Jr., "Stop Locking Up Muslims: Justice Is on Shaky Ground When Immigrants Are Being Punished Without Due Cause," *Legal Times*, June 3, 2002.

16. Federal News Service, U.S. Senate Judiciary Committee, Oversight on Counterterrorism, June 6, 2002 (Senator Kennedy: "Is it true that none of the 1,200 or more Arab and Muslim detainees, that after September 11th were held, were charged with any terrorist crimes or even certified under the Patriot Act as persons suspected of involvement in terrorist activity?" FBI Director Robert Mueller: "Well, specific terrorist charge of somebody who was going to or had committed a terrorist act, no. But there are a number of persons who have been charged with facilitating either the hijackers or lying about their association with the hijackers or other terrorists."). Director Mueller's attempt to salvage some degree of integrity for the department's action by asserting that there were at least some unspecified number of detainees charged with crimes

because of their association with terrorists or "facilitating" terrorists was directly contradicted by other Justice Department officials. Eric Boehlert, "The Dragnet Comes Up Empty," *Salon*, June 19, 2002 (quoting a Justice Department official as stating that "among the 128 criminal charges that have been filed against the 1,000-plus detainees, none . . . have been for terrorist activity.").

17. Nina Bernstein, "Crime Database Misused for Civil Issues," *New York Times*, December 17, 2003.

18. Ibid.

19. Interview with professor Michael Wishnie, New York University School of Law, June 12, 2003 (copy on file with the author).

20. Ibid. Wishnie is one of the attorneys for plaintiffs who have filed a lawsuit challenging the practice in federal court. Nina Bernstein, "Crime Database Misused" (quoting Professor Wishnie regarding the lawsuit).

21. Eric Schmitt, "Ruling Clears Way to Use State Police in Immigration Duty," *New York Times*, April 4, 2002, at A 19 (ruling by Dept. of Justice's Office of Legal Counsel declares that state and local police have the power to enforce immigration law); Cheryl W. Thompson, "INS Role for Police Considered," *Washington Post*, April 4, 2002, at A15 (new Dept. of Justice opinion declares that state and local police have "inherent authority" to enforce immigration law); "Local Police Help on Immigration Weighed," *Los Angeles Times*, April 4, 2002, at A18 (discussing Dept. of Justice's new opinion allowing state and local police to enforce immigration law); Michelle Mittelstadt and Alfred Corchado, "Local Groups Could Enforce Immigration," *Dallas Morning News*, April 4, 2002, at 1A (calling new opinion of Dept. of Justice "a major shift from current practice").

22. To be totally accurate, one should call it an "apparent" policy change, since up to the date of this writing the Department of Justice has refused to release the legal opinion upon which it is based. It has not, however, denied the opinion's existence or disavowed its contents. According to Wishnie and others, no one— not members of the public or members of Congress—has received a copy of the policy itself, despite numerous requests. Wishnie

has filed a lawsuit for production of the new policy under the Freedom of Information Act, on behalf of the American Civil Liberties Union. Interview with Michael Wishnie, June 12, 2003. As of this writing, neither that lawsuit nor any other effort has resulted in the release of the policy.

23. Clear Law Enforcement for Criminal Alien Removal Act of 2003, H.R. 2671 (108th Congress).

24. Homeland Security Enhancement Act of 2003, S. 1906 (108th Congress). The author testified against the bill at hearings held by the Senate Subcommittee on Immigration. David A. Harris, "The Homeland Security Enhancement Act: The Wrong Way to Public Safety" (testimony), April 22, 2004. A copy of the author's written testimony and the hearing transcript had not yet been posted in the *Congressional Record* as of the date of this writing. A copy of the written testimony is on file with the author.

25. Eric Schmitt, "Two Conservatives Tell Bush They Oppose Plan for Police," *New York Times*, June 2, 2002.

26. Office of the Attorney General of Arizona, "Results of the Chandler Survey" (1997), 1.

27. Ibid.

28. Ibid.

29. Gary Grado, "Hispanic Residents Voice Concerns After Roundup of Illegal Immigrants," *East Valley Tribune*, August 1, 1997.

30. Gary Grado, "Hispanics Ask that Students Be Protected," *East Valley Tribune*, Aug. 2, 1997.

31. Office of the Attorney General of Arizona, "Results of the Chandler Survey" (1997), 30–32.

32. Ibid., 29–30.

33. Ibid., 30–31.

34. Ibid., 29.

35. Ibid.

36. Ibid., 31.

37. Ibid., 31–32.

38. Ibid., 31.

39. Ibid., 32.

40. Ibid., 2.

41. Ibid.

42. Ibid.

43. Jim Walsh, "Attorney General's Office Probes Roundup of Illegals," *Arizona Republic*, Aug. 9, 1997.

44. Ibid.

45. Ibid.

46. For example, Max Bixler, "Illegal, Uninsured . . . But Alive," *Atlanta Journal-Constitution*, April 25, 2004 (quoting U.S. Census estimates at between 7.7 and 8.8 million in 2000, with almost 70 percent from Mexico and almost 10 percent from other Latin American countries in Central America).

47. Eric Schlosser, *Reefer Madness: Sex, Drugs, and Cheap Labor in the American Black Market* (Boston: Houghton Mifflin, 2003).

48. Interview with Rudy Landeros, assistant chief of police, Austin, Texas, June 12, 2003 (copy on file with the author).

49. Ibid.

50. Ibid.

51. Ibid. According to Landeros, the campaign's slogan, "Help us help you" (in Spanish, of course), printed on bumper stickers and posters, was plastered everywhere in Hispanic neighborhoods. The posters and other appeals urged immigrants to call the police when they were victimized, because "Austin's different." Members of the working group attended community fairs, town meetings—any gathering at which they could communicate with Hispanic immigrants. All of the outreach efforts featured a consistent theme: the police set up a hotline that immigrants could use anonymously to ask any question about law enforcement. Perhaps most impressive, the Texas Association Against Sexual Assault helped the working group develop five brief skits on different crimes—(one on robbery, one on sexual assault, one on domestic violence, and two others)—each of which demonstrated the importance of reporting crimes, and explained that those who did so would not suffer immigration consequences. A company that owned five radio stations that cater to the Hispanic population turned the skits into professional-quality

public service announcements that ran frequently on all of the company's stations and four other Hispanic-oriented radio stations in the region for six months. The campaign did wonders to raise awareness and change perceptions, Landeros says; increased reporting resulted because immigrants were in fact beginning to trust the police, and word-of-mouth reports of police actions were reinforcing the advertising and outreach efforts.

52. Ibid.

53. Ibid.

54. Briefing by the Nixon Center and the Center for Immigration Studies, "Mexico's Illegal Alien Card: Should It Be Valid in the United States?" June 12, 2003 (transcript on file with the author).

55. Briefing by the Nixon Center and the Center for Immigration Studies.

56. Ibid.

57. Ibid.

58. Ibid.

59. Ibid.

60. Ibid.

61. Nora Boustany, "Political Tensions Grow in Aftermath of Algerian Earthquake," *Washington Post*, May 28, 2003.

62. Ricardo Alonso-Zaldivar, "Mexican Migrants Win an ID Victory," *Los Angeles Times*, Sept. 19, 2003.

63. Associated Press, "Treasury O.k.s Use of Mexican ID Cards," *Chicago Tribune*, September 19, 2003; Yolanda Rodriguez, "Mexican-Issued ID Up to Banks," *Atlanta Journal-Constitution*, Sept. 19, 2003.

64. Rob Blackwell, "Treasury Opts to Leave ID Rule in Patriot Act As Is," *American Banker*, September 19, 2003.

65. Ricardo Alonso-Zaldivar, "Mexican Migrants Win an ID Victory" (spokesman for Sensenbrenner says that Treasury's decision "will not deter lawmakers from seeking curbs on the widening acceptance of the cards").

66. Jennifer Ludden, "Consular ID Cards for Aliens Draw Fire," National Public Radio, *Morning Edition*, Nov. 25, 2003.

67. Associated Press, "Treasury OKs Use of Mexican ID Cards."

68. Frank Newport, "Racial Profiling Seen as Widespread, Particular-ly Among Young Black Men," *Gallup Poll Monthly*, Dec. 9, 1999.

69. Jeffrey M. Jones, "Americans Felt Uneasy Toward Arabs Even Before September 11," *Gallup Poll Monthly*, Sept. 28, 2001 ("Nearly six in ten Americans interviewed in a September 14–15 Gallup poll favored requiring people of Arab descent to undergo special, more intensive security checks when flying on American airplanes").

70. Richard Zoglin and Sally B. Donnelly, "Welcome to America's Best-Run Airport, and Why It's Still Not Good Enough," *Time*, July 15, 2002, 22.

71. Ibid.

72 This research is discussed in depth in David A. Harris, *Profiles in Injustice: Why Racial Profiling Cannot Work* (New York: The New Press, 2002), especially chapter 4.

73. Ibid.

74. Ibid.

75. Eliot Spitzer, attorney general of the state of New York, "The New York City Police Department's 'Stop & Frisk' Practices: A Report to the People of the State of New York," Dec. 1, 1999.

76. Ibid.

77. Ibid.

78. Ibid.

79. See David A. Harris, *Profiles in Injustice*, chapter 8.

80. Ibid.

81. Ibid.

82. Ibid.

83. Bill Dedman, "Memo Warns Against Use of Profiling as Defense," *Boston Globe*, Oct. 12, 2001.

84. Ibid.

85. Ibid.

86. Ibid.

87. President George W. Bush's Address to Congress, Feb. 27, 2001.

88. Confirmation Hearing on the Nomination of John Ashcroft to Be Attorney General of the United States: Hearings Before the Senate Committee on the Judiciary, 107th Cong. 492 (Jan. 22, 2001).

89. Ibid.

90. Dana Milbank and Emily Wax, "Bush Visits Mosque to Forestall Hate Crimes; President Condemns an Increase in Violence Aimed at Arab Americans," *Washington Post*, Sept. 18, 2001.

91. Thomas B. Edsall, "Anti-Muslim Violence Assailed; Justice Dept. Probing Incidents Across the Nation," *Washington Post*, September 15, 2001.

92. Michael Chertoff, "Testimony Before the Senate Judiciary Committee Hearing on Preserving Freedoms While Defending Against Terrorism," *Federal News Service*, Nov. 28, 2001.

93. See notes 10 through 15 to chapter 8, and accompanying text.

94. See note 16 to chapter 8 and accompanying text.

95. U.S. Department of Justice, "Guidelines for Absconder Apprehension Initiative," Jan. 25, 2002, at http://news.findlaw.com/hdocs/docs/doj/anscndr012502mem.pdf.

96. The INS no longer exists as a separate agency within the Justice Department. With the creation of the Department of Homeland Security, INS became part of the that new agency. Combined with the former U.S. Customs Service, it is now part of the Bureau of Immigration and Customs Enforcement of the Department of Homeland Security.

97. U.S. Department of Justice, "Guidelines for Absconder Apprehension Initiative"; Susan Sachs, "U.S. Begins Crackdown on Muslims Who Defy Orders to Leave Country," *New York Times*, April 2, 2002; Dan Eggen and Cheryl W. Thompson, "U.S. Seeks Thousands of Fugitive Deportees; Middle Eastern Men Are Focus of Search," *Washington Post*, Jan. 8, 2002.

98. For example, Ana Radelat, "INS Chief Defends New Plan to Round Up Muslim Immigrants, Gannett News Service, Jan. 8, 2002 (explaining that the "Justice Department decided to place the names of some 6,000 Arab and Muslim absconders in the database first, even though immigrants from Latin America constitute the vast majority of those who ignore deportation orders"); "On the Fence: Former INS Commissioner Doris Meissner on the Contradictions of Migration Policy in a Globalizing World," *Foreign*

Policy, March 1, 2002 (question to former INS Commissioner Doris Meissner from interviewer, indicating that even though most of the 300,000 absconders "are of Latin American descent, the Justice Department will go after the 6,000 or so from the Middle East"); "Immigration: INS Seeks Illegal Arab and Muslim Men," *Facts on File World News Digest*, Jan. 8 2002 ("Although the vast majority of the 314,000 so-called absconders in the U.S. were from Latin America, the U.S. had decided to prioritize finding men from countries considered havens" for Al Qaeda terrorists).

99. Julie Quiroz-Martinez, "Let Freedom Roll: Immigrants Hit the Road for Civil Rights," *The Nation*, October 27, 2003.

100. Michael Isikoff, "The FBI Says, Count the Mosques," *Newsweek*, Feb. 3, 2003.

101. Eric Lichtblau, "FBI Tells Officers to Count Local Muslims, and Mosques," *New York Times.*, Jan. 28, 2003.

102. Kevin Johnson, "In the Heartland, A Call to Mobilize," *USA Today*, 25 March 2002.

103. U.S. Department of Justice, "Justice Department Issues Policy Guidance to Ban Racial Profiling," June 17, 2003, accessed at http://www.usdoj.gov/opa.pr/2003/June/03/_crt_355.htm, Nov. 7, 2003.

104. U.S. Department of Justice, "Fact Sheet, Racial Profiling," June 17, 2003, accessed through link to http://www.usdoj.gov/opa.pr/2003/June/03/_crt_355.htm, Nov. 7, 2003 (italics in original).

105. Ibid.

106. The End Racial Profiling Act of 2004, S. 2132 (2004). The companion bill in the House of Representatives, which has the same name, is H.R. 3847.

107. U.S. Department of Justice, "Fact Sheet, Racial Profiling."

108. For example, Jacki Lyden and Mandelit Del Barco, "Harassment and Prejudice Against American Muslims," National Public Radio, *Weekend All Things Considered*, Sept. 23, 2001 (numerous stories of Muslims and Middle Easterners removed from airliners); Jonathan Osborne, "Passenger Ejections Seen as Profiling," *Austin American-Statesman*, Sept. 29, 2001.

109. One need go no further than Attorney General Ashcroft's invoca-

tion of Robert Kennedy's "spitting on the sidewalk" challenge to organized crime. Robert Kennedy's Department of Justice, Ashcroft said, had made clear to members of organized crime that he would arrest them for spitting on the sidewalk if this would help advance the department's efforts to rid the nation of them. Ashcroft said he would do the same thing—use every possible state, local, or federal charge, every prosecutorial advantage, take any legal measure— because "our single objective is to prevent terrorist attacks by taking suspected terrorists off the street." Speech by U.S. Attorney General John Ashcroft to the U.S. Conference of Mayors, Oct. 25, 2001, accessed at http://www.usdoj.gov/ag/speeches/2001/agcrisisremarks10_25.htm, May 21, 2004.

110. Toni Locy, "For Linguists, Job Is Patriotic Duty," *USA Today*, Nov. 11, 2003.

111. Daniel Klaidman and Michael Isikoff, "Lost in Translation," *Newsweek*, October 27, 2003.

112. Ibid.

113. Michael Isikoff, "Tensions in the FBI: Why Was This Agent Fired?" *Newsweek*, Oct. 20, 2003.

114. Steve McGonigle, "Ex-FBI Agent Says Bias Led to His Firing," *Dallas Morning News*, Oct. 19, 2003.

115. Ibid.

116. Isikoff, "Tensions in the FBI"; McGonigle, "Ex-FBI Agent."

117. Isikoff, "Tensions in the FBI"; McGonigle, "Ex-FBI Agent."

118. McGonigle, "Ex-FBI Agent."

119. Ibid.

120. Ibid.

121. Ibid.

122. Isikoff, "Tensions in the FBI."

123. Ibid.

124. McGonigle, "Ex-FBI Agent."

125. Ibid.

126. Ibid.

127. Ibid.

128. Ibid.

128a. Steve McGonigle, "Agent Re-Hired by FBI," *Dallas Morning News*, Feb. 26, 2004, p. 1B (Abdel-Hafiz was re-installed by the FBI after an internal review of his case; Abdel-Hafiz "said he would prefer to continue to work in counterterrorism but recognized that his effectiveness in working with the Muslim community had been compromised. . . ."); Michael Isikoff and Mark Hosenball, "Re-instated," *Newsweek*, Feb. 25, 2004 (quoting Abdel-Hafiz after re-instatement as saying "I'm a certified undercover agent who is worthless now.")

129. David Johnston, "FBI Is Accused of Bias By Arab American Agent," *New York Times*, July 20, 2003.

130. Ibid.

131. Ibid.

132. Sharon McCaffrey, "Arab-American FBI Agent Files Discrimination Lawsuit," Knight Ridder News Service, July 20, 2003.

133. Ibid.; Johnston, "FBI is Accused of Bias."

134. Johnston, "FBI is Accused of Bias."

135. McGonigle, "Ex-FBI Agent."

136. Susan McGinnis (anchor), Bob McNamara (reporter), "Foreign-born Muslim Man Suing the FBI for Re-instatement," CBS Morning News, Oct. 21, 2003.

137. Klaidman and Isikoff, "Lost in Translation." The authors say that "[w]hen pressed, Vincent said he'd meant the FBI didn't need Muslims like Abdel-Hafiz." Ibid.

138. Ibid.

139. "U.S. Justice Department Probes 14 Abuses of Alleged Terror Suspects," AFX.com News Limited, July 22, 2003.

140. Klaidman and Isikoff, "Lost in Translation." Edmonds, mentioned in this quote, was herself fired by the FBI after she accused Bureau translators of ineptitude. A report by the Department of Justice Inspector General, still classified as of this writing, reportedly said that Edmonds was indeed fired at least in part because of her whistle-blowing activity. Eric Lichtblau, "Whistle-Blowing Said to Be a Factor in an FBI Firing," *New York Times*, July 29, 2004; R. Jeffrey Smith, "Justice IG Supports FBI Whistle-Blower," *Washington Post*, July 20, 2004.

141. Rochelle Riley, "FBI Target Now Honored for Leadership," *Detroit Free Press*, Sept. 23, 2003.

142. Narij Warikoo, "FBI Revokes Its Service Award from Arab Leader," *Detroit Free Press,* Oct. 10, 2003.

143. Ibid., quoting FBI spokesperson Cassandra Chandler.

144. David Shepardson and Joel Kurth, "FBI Director Firm on Activist's Rescinded Award," *Detroit News*, Oct. 17, 2003.

145. John Bebow and David Shepardson, "FBI Award Flap Threatens Ties to Arab Community," *Detroit News*, October 15, 2003.

146. Warikoo, "FBI Revokes Its Service Award."

147. Ibid.

148. Bebow and Shepardson, "FBI Award Flap."

149. Shepardson and Kurth, "FBI Director Firm."

150. Ibid.

151. Klaidman and Isikoff, "Lost in Translation."

152. "Port & Aviation Security: President," accessed at http://www.ais-sim.com/nass_president.htm, Nov. 8, 2003; interview with Rafi Ron, New Age Security Systems, Dec. 1, 2003 (copy on file with the author).

153. Ibid.

154. "Port & Aviation Security: Media," accessed at http://www.ais-sim.com/nass_press_release_boston_globe.htm, Nov. 8, 2003.

155. "Port & Aviation Security: Media."

156. Ibid.

157. "AIS, Inc., Targets Counterterrorism Training," October 23, 2003, accessed at http://www.ais-sim.com/news_press_releases_102303.htm, Nov. 8, 2003.

158. Ibid.

159. Ibid.

160. Nevertheless, media reports concerning Ron's Congressional testimony in February 2002 persistently said that Ron advocated racial or ethnic profiling. For example, Eunice Moscoso, "Racial Profiling Needed at Airports, Expert Tells Congress," Cox News Service, Feb. 27, 2002; David Eggert, "Security Debate Focuses on Profiling By Nationality," *Seattle Post-Intelligencer*, Feb. 28, 2002.

161. Interview with Rafi Ron, Dec. 1, 2003.

162. Rafi Ron, "The Human Factor in Providing Airport Security: The Missing Link," PowerPoint presentation at the Northwestern University Center for Public Safety's Third Annual Symposium on Racial Profiling, Nov. 3, 2003.

163. Randall S. Geller, "Airport to Launch Terrorist ID Plan," *Boston Globe*, Dec. 1, 2001.

164. Ann Davis, Joseph Pereira, and William M. Bulkeley, "FBI, Customs Agents Step Up Body Language Training," *Wall Street Journal*, Aug. 15, 2002.

165. Ron, "The Human Factor in Providing Airport Security:"

166. Interview with Rafi Ron, Dec. 1, 2003.

167. Ron, "The Human Factor in Providing Airport Security."

168. Interview with Rafi Ron, Dec. 1, 2003.

169. Ibid.

170. Ron, "The Human Factor in Providing Airport Security."

171. Interview with Rafi Ron.

172. Ibid.

173. Ibid.

174. According to Rafi Ron, after the attack it was discovered that in fact there had been extensive contacts between the Japanese Red Army and the Popular Front for the Liberation of Palestine, with Japanese Red Army members taking extensive training in Lebanon at PFLP camps. After the Israelis released the surviving member of the Japanese Red Army attack squad from prison in a prisoner exchange, the man went not to Japan, but to Lebanon's Bekaa Valley to live among "friends." Ibid.

175. Ibid.

176. Ann Davis, Joseph Pereira, and William M. Bulkeley, "FBI, Customs Agents."

177. Ibid.

178. Doug Hanchett, "Airport Cops Are Watching," *Boston Herald*, Nov. 15, 2002.

179. Sally B. Donnelly, "A Chastened Airport Watches for Suspects," *Time*, Aug. 11, 2003.

180. Remarks of Harry "Skip" Brandon, 26th National Legal Conference on Immigration & Refugee Policy, Session I: National Security and Immigrant Rights, sponsored by the Center for Migration Studies and the Catholic Legal Immigration Network, Inc., Thursday, April 3, 2003, Washington, D.C.

181. Remarks of Vincent Cannistraro, 26th National Legal Conference on Immigration & Refugee Policy, Session I: National Security and Immigrant Rights, sponsored by the Center for Migration Studies and the Catholic Legal Immigration Network, Inc., Thursday, April 3, 2003, Washington, D.C.

182. Ibid.

183. Ibid.

184. Ibid.

185. Ibid.

186. Ibid.

CHAPTER 9: Securing the Blessings of Preventive Policing

1. William Bratton with Peter Knobler, *Turnaround: How America's Top Cop Reversed the Crime Epidemic* (New York: Random House, 1998).

2. It is important to note that there is considerable disagreement over how much credit, if any, the "broken windows" theory should get for the drop in crime in New York. For example, Bernard E. Harcourt, *Illusions of Order: The False Promise of Broken Windows Policing* (Cambridge, MA: Harvard University Press, 2001) (challenging the widely-accepted validity of the "broken windows" theory by insightfully interpreting critiquing existing data often used to justify the theory and offering alternative explanations for what its proponents have uncritically deemed the successful results of this type of law enforcement); Ralph B. Taylor, *Breaking Away From Broken Windows: Baltimore Neighborhoods and the Nationwide Fight Against Crime, Grime, Fear and Decline* (Boulder, CO: Westview Press, 2000) (using data on crime-reduction work in Baltimore to argue that broken windows policing, while helpful, is

far from a complete solution to urban crime problems or a complete explanation for the drop in crime in the 1990s).

3. U.S. General Accounting Office, "Homeland Security: Justice Department's Project to Interview Aliens After September 11, 2001," Report No. GAO-03-459, April 2003, 6.

4. Interview with Linda Schmidt, Cleveland field office, FBI, Aug.29, 2003 (copy on file with the author).

5. Ibid.

6. Ibid.

7. Ibid.

8. Ibid.

9. Ibid.

10. Ibid.

11. See chapter 7.

12. Allan Lengel and Caryle Murphy, "FBI, Arab Community Join Forces With Panel," *Washington Post*, March 29, 2003.

13. The attorney general and the heads of all of the major divisions of the Department of Justice are appointed by the president and would presumably leave office with the president or earlier, at his pleasure. The director of the FBI has a ten-year term of office, once he is nominated by the president and then confirmed by the Senate.

Index

ABC News, 206
Abdel-Hafiz, Gamel, 205–8, 282n. 128
Abdrabboh, Mo, 33, 174, 211–12
"Absconder Apprehension Initiative" (INS), 200, 280n. 98
Abstrat system, 102–3
accountability, 81–126
    in chain of command, 139–42
    in Chicago, 49
    commitment to, 93
    effects of lack of, 85–86
    external, 103–26
    internal, 90–103
    and litigation, 89
    measures for, 158–61
    opposition to, 86–88
    in Pittsburgh, 81–84
    and police culture, 84–85
    as preventive policing element, 24–26
    proponents of, 88–89
    in San Francisco, 230–31
advisory councils, 38
Advocates and Leaders for Police and Community Trust (ALPACT), 29–36, 210, 241n. 21
African American communities:
    in Boston, 64, 143
    in Detroit, 29–30, 238–39n. 5
    isolation of police from, 21
    in Pittsburgh, 108
    police shootings in, 95
    and traffic stops, 117
agility test, 168
Aiken county (South Carolina), 95
airlines, 203
air marshal program, 214
airports, 52
airport security, 196, 214
Allison, Liz, 167–68
ALPACT. See Advocates and

Leaders for Police and
Community Trust
Alpert, Geoffrey, 95, 96
Al Qaeda, 217, 224
American Immigration Lawyers
Association, 6
anti-immigration groups, 189–95
antiterrorism:
in Detroit, 31–32
and FBI leadership, 203–13
preventive policing used for,
213–21, 224
and problem-oriented
policing, 198
traffic stops used for, 201
apologies, 143
Arab American Advisory
Committee (FBI), 229
Arab American Institute, 6
Arab and Muslim communities:
and Ashcroft policing, 182–95
in Chicago, 50–52
cultural knowlege about, 51–52
in Detroit, 10, 13, 28–36
as intelligence sources, 220
mass questioning of, 9–12
racial profiling of, 195–203
in Seattle, 40–41
Archbold, Carol A., 257n. 18
Archer, Dennis, 30, 240n. 12
Ashcroft, John, 4–5, 34–36, 181,
199, 202, 219, 224–25, 281n. 109
Ashcroft policing, 3–5, 174–221
and the Chandler fiasco, 186–89
and FBI antiterrorism, 203–13

of immigrants, 5–9, 182–95
interview conducted under,
174–80
of nonsuspects, 9–12
in post-9/11 era, 5–6
preventive policing vs., 4
and racial profiling, 195–203
assessment center, recruiting, 163
attitudes:
citizen, 22–23
us-versus-them, 133–34
auditors, 111–16
in Los Angeles County Sheriff's
Department, 113–16
outreach activities of, 112
overall focus of, 111
policy review by, 112
Aufhauser, David, 195
Austin (Texas), 112, 191–93,
276–77n. 51
authority, 139–42
automobile, 19–21
autonomy, officer, 131–32

backlash-related crimes, 28, 32,
40, 41, 50
Baldwin, Scott, 75–77, 139
Baltimore, 106
Baltimore-Washington area, 229
banking, 192–94
Barker, Jerry, 135–39, 166
Barone, Linda, 93, 94
Barros-Cepeda, Eveline, 148–50
Baumgartner, Bruce, 196
Bayley, David H., 20–21

beat cops:
  and community policing, 23
  patrol cars vs., 19–21
behavioral observation, 197–99,
  214–18
Behavioral Pattern Recognition,
  214–18
bekouach nefesh, 55–56
"Bending Granite: Attempts to
  Change the Management
  Perspective of American
  Criminologists and Police
  Reformers" (James F. Gilsinan
  and James R. Valentine), 154
"Bending Granite: Attempts to
  Change the Rank Structure of
  Police Departments" (Dorothy
  Guyot), 154
Ben Gurion Airport, 214, 217, 218
Bennett, William, 64, 252n. 31
Benton Harbor (Michigan), 86
Bentson, Clem, 38, 40
Berrien, Jenny, 70
"beyond a reasonable doubt," 106
Blue Roofs apartment complex
  (San Diego), 71–74
Bly, Jeffrey, 145, 147
Bobb, Merrick, 113–15
Boggs, Dave, 247n. 91
Bogucki, Kim, 40
borders, national, 6
Boston:
  Paul Evan's leadership in,143–52
  gang violence in, 63–71
  police misconduct in, 91
    violent crime in, 71
Boston Chamber of Commerce, 151
Boston Globe, 198
Boston Gun Project, 66–68
"the Boston Miracle," 71
Boston Police Patrolmen's
  Association (BPPA), 149–50
Boston Streetworkers, 66, 67
BPPA. *See* Boston Police
  Patrolmen's Association
Brady, Cindy, 71–74
Brandon, Harry, 9, 219
Brann, Joseph, 125
Bratton, William, 97, 98,
  127–29, 223
bridge building, 28–56
  in Chicago, 47–52
  in Detroit, 29–36
  dividends of, 53–56
  importance of, 36
  in Lowell, 41–44
  in Seattle, 37–41
  in Wichita, 44–47
Bridgeport (Illinois), 53
BRIDGES. *See* Building Respect
  in Diverse Groups to Enhance
  Sensitivity
broken windows theory, 127–28,
  223, 285–86n. 2
Brown, Dale, 23
Brown, Jeffrey, 65–66, 144, 146,
  147, 152, 253n. 39
Bucqueroux, Bonnie, 36
budget process:
  and accountability standards,161

and damage awards, 120–21, 231
Building Bridges program
   (Wichita), 44–45
Building Respect in Diverse
   Groups to Enhance Sensitivity
   (BRIDGES), 210, 211, 229
Bureau of Justice Statistics, 117
Burkoff, John, 109
Bush, George W., 186, 199
buy-in, public, 159

cable television call-in show, 43
California, 119, 125
Callahan, Cynthia, 243n. 45
Cambodian community, 42,
   243n. 41
Cannistraro, Vince, 9, 219–21
cars, radio-equipped, 19–21
Century Station (Los Angeles),
   114–15
chain of command, 131–32, 139–42
Chandler (Arizona), 186–89
changing police culture.
   See cultural change
Chertoff, Michael, 199
Chicago:
   bridge building in, 47–52
   hate crimes in, 53–56, 247n. 91
   preventive policing in, 13
chiefs of police:
   disciplinary authority of, 106,
   134–35
   mini-chiefs, 139, 142
   political oversight of, 132–33
Christamore House, 138

Christopher Commission (LAPD),
   87–88, 91
Churchill, Winston, 3
CI-19, 209
Cianci, Vincent "Buddy," 140
Cincinatti, 86, 106, 138
citizen attitudes, 22–23
citizen encounters with police, 117
citizen oversight, 103–4
   auditor model of, 111–16
   complaint review systems as,
   104–11
   hybrid model of, 262n. 79
citizen police academy, 43, 118
Citizen Police Review Board
   (CPRB), 108–11, 261–62nn.
   72, 77
citizen satisfaction, 160
civilian complaints, 128–30
civilian oversight, 87
civil rights training, 169
CLEAR Act. *See* Clear Law Enforcement for Criminal Alien
   Removal Act
Clear Law Enforcement for Criminal Alien Removal (CLEAR)
   Act (2003), 185–86
Cleveland (Ohio), 227
Cleveland *Plain-Dealer,* 227
collaboration, 14, 24, 143–52
Collins, Jeffrey, 35, 210–12
Colorado Springs, 158–61
Columbus (Ohio), 264–65n. 113
commitment:
   to accountability, 93

to collaboration, 51
to community, 165
communication:
  and community policing, 25
  with immigrant communities,
  7–8, 10, 49
communication skills, 93
"communities of interest," 38
community policing, 23–24
  and preventive policing, 36
  and racial profiling, 37
Community Policing Consortium, 237–38n. 15
"community speak" session, 47–48
complaint review systems, 104–11
  effectiveness of, 104, 262n. 80
  importance of, 104
  in Pittsburgh, 108–11, 230
  powers of, 105–6
  in San Francisco, 231
  staffing of, 106–8
complaints, civilian, 128–30
Compstat system, 97–103
  commander accountability
  under, 100
  Tom King's use of, 129
  layers of, 98
  and NYC crime drop, 223
  rank-and-file accountability
  under, 100–101
Conroy, Dennis, 163–66
consent decrees, 123, 124,
  264–65n. 113
conversation, targeted, 216
Conyers, John, 126

corruption, 18–19, 140
courage, 165
Courtesy, Professionalism, and
  Respect (CPR) (NYPD), 129
CPRB. See Citizen Police Review
  Board
CPR (Courtesy, Professionalism,
  and Respect), 129
credibility, 65, 69
crime triangle, 58, 248n. 8
cultural change, 154–71
  difficulty of, 154–55
  hiring for, 162–68
  leadership's commitment to,
  155
  and measurements, 158–61
  and mission, 156–58
  as preventive policing
  strategy, 26
  successful features of, 155
  with training, 169–71
cultural education, 228
cultural knowledge, 51
cultural misunderstandings, 39,
  43–44
culture:
  of police, 84–85, 133–34
  training videos regarding, 52

damages, financial:
  external accountability for,
  120–22
  payments of, 89
  police budgets used for, 231
Danforth, John, 4–5

Daniels, Rob, 189

database, NCIC, 184–85

data-based police management, 91

data-collection systems, 126

Davis, Ed, 42, 243–44n. 45

Davis, Robert, 128, 266n. 1

Davis, Ron, 156, 157, 162

Dearborn (Michigan), 10, 34, 239n. 10

decentralized leadership, 139–42

Defenbaugh, Danny, 206

democracy, 85

Denver International Airport, 196

depolicing, 258n. 37

Detroit:

   antiterrorism duties in, 31–32

   Arab and Muslim communities in, 31–36

   bridge building in, 28–36, 229

   consent decrees used in, 124

   nonsuspect interviewing in, 9, 10

   population of, 29–30, 238–39n. 5

   preventive policing in, 13

   segregation in, 239n. 11

Dinerstein, Marti, 193

disciplinary action:

   for Boston raid, 268n. 40

   chief's authority for, 106, 134–35

   public perception of, 49–50

   records of, 91

DOJ. See U.S. Department of Justice

Domus Foundation, 76, 78, 79

Dorismond, Patrick, 144

Drescher, Thomas, 149–50

drug activity, 63–64

early warning systems, 90–94, 258–59n. 37

East African community, 38–39

Edmonds, Sibel, 210, 283n. 140

education:

   cultural, 228

   of police and public, 43

effectiveness, 62–63

empowerment, 140

End Racial Profiling Act (2004), 126, 202

Esserman, Dean, 75, 76, 78, 80, 139–42

evaluation of results, 63

Evans, Paul, 70, 268n. 40

"Everyday Heroes' recruiting campaign, 167

exam-taking strategies, 168

expectations, 159

external accountability, 103–26

   with auditors, 111–16

   with citizen oversight, 103–4

   with complaint review systems, 104–11

   and disseminating information, 118–20

   and feedback, 116–18

   and financial damages, 120–22

   and pattern-or-practice law, 122–26

externality, 121

extremism, 217

fair enforcement of standards of conduct, 95

FBI (Federal Bureau of Investigation):
and Gamel Abdel-Hafiz, 205–8
antiterrorism strategy of, 11
Arab linguists in, 204–10
Arab/Muslim-community mistrust of, 210–13
culture of, 204, 208–9
in Detroit, 33, 34
director's term of office in, 286n. 13
immigrant interview conducted by, 174–80
intelligence gathering and analysis by, 219
and mosque census, 201
preventive policing used by, 226–29
and Bassem Youssef, 207–10

fear, freedom from, 49
feedback, community, 25, 116–18, 161
Feingold, Russell, 126
Fiedler, Mora, 158, 159
firearms, 128
Flynn, Raymond, 252n. 34
FOP. See Fraternal Order of Police
force, use of. See use of force
Forty-second Precinct (NYC), 127–30
Fox, Vicente, 192, 194
Fraternal Order of Police (FOP), 235n. 11, 261nn. 72, 77
freedom from fear, 49

Freeh, Louis, 206
funding, data-collection-system, 126

gangs, 63–71, 145, 253n. 39
GAO. See U.S. General Accounting Office
The Gardens apartment complex (San Diego), 72
Germany, 170
Gilsinan, James F., 154
Giuliani, Rudolph, 15, 144, 223
Goldstein, Herman, 24, 61–63, 91, 250–51n. 24
Green, Saul, 30
Greene, Jack, 44
grouping incidents, 62
Guibord, Greg, 10
Gun Project. See Boston Gun Project
guns, 128
Guyot, Dorothy, 154

HACOLA. See Housing Authority of the County of Los Angeles
Hall, Tim, 71–74
Hamad, Imad, 32–33, 210–12, 228
Hammond, Ray, 65, 148–49, 151
Harcourt, Bernard E., 286n. 2
Harris, Bobby Joe, 187, 189
Harris, David A., 15
Harris poll, 103
hate crimes:
in Chicago, 50, 53–56
in Cleveland, 227
in Detroit, 32

in Seattle, 40, 41

high-speed police pursuits, 95–97

Hillard, Terrance, 47–50

hiring for cultural change, 162–68

Hispanic community, 186–89,
    276–77n. 51

Hoch, Jon, 79

the Holocaust, 170

homicide rate, 71

Housing and Urban Development
    (HUD), 72–74

Housing Authority of the County
    of Los Angeles (HACOLA), 57–60

housing management model, 58

Howard, Ken, 170–71

Howard, Tim, 79

HUD. See Housing and Urban
    Development

Hulon, Willie, 211, 212

human rights training, 169

hybrid oversight model, 262n. 79

IACP (International Association
    of Chiefs of Police), 87

Idris Mosque (Seattle), 40

illegal immigrants, 190–94

immigrants/immigration, 4
    and Ashcroft policing, 182–95
    and intelligence collection, 220
    and local police, 5–9, 184–86
    in Lowell, 41–44
    nonsuspect, 9–12

Immigration and Nationality Act
    (INA), 6, 234n. 7

Immigration and Naturalization

Service (INS), 7, 187–89, 200,
    279n. 96

"Improving Policing" (Herman
    Goldstein), 61

INA. See Immigration and
    Nationality Act

incentive structures, 14

Indianapolis:
    community partnership in,
    135–39
    recruiting minority officers in,
    166–68

information:
    from community, 36, 40
    disseminating, 118–20
    and feedback loop, 116–18
    on patterns of misconduct, 91
    sources of, 70

input, community, 36

INS. See Immigration and
    Naturalization Service

intelligence gathering and
    analysis, 218–21

internal accountability, 90–103
    Compstat system used for,
    97–103
    departmental policies for, 94–97
    early warning systems for, 90–94

internal affairs divisions, 104–5

International Association of
    Chiefs of Police (IACP), 87

interviewing. See mass question-
    ing initiative; nonsuspects

invisible-officer problem,
    258–59n. 37

Irfan, Kareem, 50–52
Isikoff, Micahel, 209
Islam, 52
isolation of patrol-car officers, 20–21
Israel, 214

Jackson, John, 102, 103
Japanese Red Army, 217, 284–85n. 174
Jeter, Jon, 75–76, 139
Jews, Orthodox, 52, 54–56
John Hancock Life Insurance Company, 67–68
Joyce, Paul, 67, 68
juvenile crime, 75–80
Juves, Jose, 218

Kansas, 44
Kansas City (Missouri), 21–23, 61, 91
Kansas City Response Time Study, 22–23
Keene, David, 186
Kelling, George, 127
Kelly, Raymond, 98, 197–98
Kennedy, David, 66, 68, 69, 146
Kennedy, Edward, 273–74n. 16
Kennedy, Robert, 281n. 109
Kerlikowske, Gil, 8, 40, 41
King, Tom, 127–30, 266n. 1
Kirkland, Andrew, 9–10
Klaidman, Daniel, 209
Knight, Bob, 44, 244–45n. 61
Krikorian, Mark, 194, 195

Landeros, Rudy, 191, 192, 276–77n. 51
language, 167, 204–5
Lansdowne, Bill, 119–20
LAPD. See Los Angeles Police Department
LASD. See Los Angeles County Sheriff's Department
Latino community, 189–95
lawsuits, 86, 118, 169
leadership, 26, 127–53
    Jerry Baker's example of, 135–39
    and commitment to change, 155
    and community collaboration, 143–52
    decentralized, 139–42
    Dean Esserman's example of, 139–42
    Paul Evans' example of, 143–52
    importance of strong, 131–32
    Tom King's example of, 127–30
    and municipal politics, 132–33
    and organizational politics, 133–35
    and partnership, 135–39
Leadership Conference on Civil Rights, 6
legal advisors, 257n. 18
letters to prospective interviewees, 35
liaison officers, 38, 40
Lindsay, Betsy, 57–60, 250n. 24
litigation, 89, 113, 120–22, 264–65n. 113

local police:
    and antiterrorism, 201, 225
    and immigration law, 5–9,
        184–86
Logan International Airport,
    214, 218
Long Beach (California), 59,
    243n. 41
Los Angeles County public
    housing, 57–60
Los Angeles County Sheriff's
    Department (LASD):
    auditor system in, 113–16
    damages paid for misconduct
        in, 89
    and public housing, 59
Los Angeles Police Department
    (LAPD), 87–88
    consent decrees used in, 124
    financial accountability of, 120
    high-speed chases by, 96–97
Los Angeles Times, 119
Lowell (Massachusetts), 41–44,
    242–44nn. 39, 41, 45
Lowell Race Relations Council,
    42–44

Malloy, Dan, 76
Malloy, Jim, 88
management practices, police,
    114, 126
Maple, Jack, 97, 98
Marion County (Indiana), 167
mass questioning initiative:
    Detroit's handling of the, 33–36

GAO on, 225
    Senate Judiciary Committee
        hearing on, 273–74n. 16
    Kenneth Walton on, 11–12
    "material witness" statute, 273n. 9
matricula consular, 192–95
Mazzullo, Tony, 76
McConnell, Bob, 8
McDevitt, Jack, 44
McDonald, Barbara, 47, 50, 51
McElderry, Pat, 158–61
McGhee, Daedre, 29–31
McGhee, Todd, 218
McLaughlin, Paul, 145–47, 151
McNeilly, Robert, 84, 88–89, 92,
    93, 110
McVeigh, Timothy, 217
measurement of accountability,
    158–61
memoranda of agreement, 124
Mendoza, Frank, 187
Menino, Thomas, 152
Metro-Dade. See Miami-Dade
Mexican American Legal Defense
    and Education Fund, 6
Mexico, 190–94
Miami-Dade, 95–96
    and citizen encounters with
        police, 117–18
    early warning system in, 92
Midway airport, 52
mini-chiefs, 139, 142
Minneapolis, 92, 181
minority communities:
    hiring input from, 164–65

recruiting officers from, 166–68

misconduct. *See* police
    misconduct

mission, 156–58

Mission Hill (Boston), 64, 252n. 34

Missouri, 232n. 1

Mollen Commission (NYC), 87

Montgomery County (Maryland),
    124

Morning Star Baptist Church
    (Boston), 65

Moses, Terri, 44–47

mosques, 40, 51–52, 201

Moss, Kary, 32

Mueller, Robert, 203–5, 209–11,
    219, 274n. 16

"multiple file drawer problem," 91

Murrah Federal Building, 217

Muslim communities. *See* Arab
    and Muslim communities

NAACP (National Association for
    the Advancement of Colored
    People), 31

Napoleon, Benny, 10, 238n. 2

National Association for the
    Advancement of Colored People
    (NAACP), 31

National Association of Police
    Organizations, 119

National Conference for
    Community and Justice (NCCJ),
    29, 45, 244–45n. 61

National Crime Information
    Center (NCIC) database, 184–85

National Immigration Forum, 6

National Security Entry-Exit
    Registration System (N-SEERS),
    184, 200–201

Navarro, Joe, 215

Nazi regime, 170

NCCJ. *See* National Conference
    for Community and Justice

NCIC database. *See* National
    Crime Information Center
    database

Nee, Thomas, 150

Needham,Tom, 8

New Jersey State Police, 124

New Orleans, 92

Newsweek magazine, 201, 204, 209

New York City, 15, 87, 89, 144, 223

New York Police Department
    (NYPD), 15
    Compstat system used by, 97
    financial accountability of, 120
    Tom King's leadership in the,
    127–30
    and racial profiling, 197
    tough-on-crime policy of, 223

911 call systems, 20

Nkimbeng, Fru, 43

nonsuspects. *See also* mass
    questioning initiative
    policing of, 9–12
    questioning of, 4, 181, 184, 200

Norquist, Grover, 186

Northbrook (Chicago), 55, 56

Northern Ohio Hate Crimes
    Working Group, 227

N-SEERS. *See* National Security
Entry-Exit Registration System
nuisance laws, 73
NYPD. *See* New York Police
Department

Oakland (California), 107
oath of office, 156–57
Office of Citizen Complaints
(OCC), 107
Office of Community Oriented
Policing Services (of DOJ), 78,
170, 171
Office of Legal Counsel, 6
Office of Municipal Investiga-
tions (OMI) (Pittsburgh),
109–10, 261n. 76
officer autonomy, 131–32
officer safety, 228
O'Hare airport, 52
Oklahoma City bombing, 217
Olson, Robert, 181
Omaha (Nebraska), 95, 97, 106
OMI. *See* Office of Municipal
Investigations
openness to new ideas, 14
Operation Cease Fire (Boston),
68–71
Operation Scrap Iron (Boston),
67, 68
organizational politics, 133–35
Orthodox Judaism, 52, 54–56
outreach programs, 68
Overland Park (Kansas), 102

Parker, William, 87
PARS. *See* Personnel Assessment
and Review System
Part I crimes, 58, 60
partnership, 37
community-policing element
of, 24
and safety, 53–54
understanding importance of,
135–39
Pasco, Jim, 235n. 11
PASS. *See* Police Accountability
and Service Standards
patrol-car policing, 19–21
pattern-or-practice law, 122–26
patterns:
of behavior, 216
of crime, 61, 62, 97–101
of inappropriate police
behavior, 90, 91, 121
and pattern-or-practice law,
122–26
perceptions, public, 116, 160–61
PERF. *See* Police Executives
Research Forum
Personnel Assessment and
Review System (PARS), 81–84, 88
as early warning system, 90–94
problems with, 258–59n. 37
PFLP. *See* Popular Front for the
Liberation of Palestine
physiological behaviors, 216
Pittinger, Elizabeth, 110–11, 261n. 76
Pittsburgh, 230
accountability in, 81–84, 88–89

Citizen Police Review Board in, 108–11, 261n. 72

consent decrees used in, 124

early warning system in, 258–59n. 37

financial accountability of, 120

PARS in. *See* Personnel Assessment and Review System

preventive policing in, 13

police academy training, 43

Police Accountability and Service Standards (PASS), 159–61

police culture, 84–85, 133–34

police departments, 18

Police Executives Research Forum (PERF), 23, 181, 243n. 45

police misconduct, 86

and complaint review systems, 104–11

damages paid for, 89, 121

and departmental policies, 95

and pattern-or-practice law, 123

perceptions of discipline and, 49–50

and self monitoring, 88

police reform:

and paid professional police, 18

and radio-equipped patrol cars, 19–21

and scientific principles of policing, 20

police review process, 103

police shootings, 95, 147–51

"police speak" session, 48

police unions:

and accountability mechanisms, 87

and complaint review systems, 104, 105, 110

and consent decrees, 264–65n. 113

and internal politics, 134

and shooting-at-moving-vehicles policy, 149–50

policies, departmental:

auditor review of, 112

for civilian complaints, 129

for internal accountability, 94–97

and mission, 156–58

on shooting at motor vehicles, 149

policing, scientific principles of, 20

policy review, 112

political interference, 18–19, 132–33, 140

Popular Front for the Liberation of Palestine (PFLP), 284–85n. 174

Portland (Oregon), 9, 10, 103

"preponderance of evidence," 106

presentations, Compstat, 98–100

Preventive Patrol Experiment (Kansas City), 21–22, 61

preventive policing, 12–17, 222–31

and antiterrorism, 213–21

Ashcroft policing vs., 4

best practices of, 14

and community policing, 36

components of, 23–24

criticisms of, 17

definition of, 4
demanding, 229–31
examples of, 13
in FBI, 226–29
history behind, 18–23
strategies of, 24–26
problem officers, 84, 91, 130
problem-oriented policing, 24,
    25, 57–80
    and antiterrorism, 198, 213–14
    in Boston, 63–71
    elements/functions of, 61–63
    at HACOLA, 57–60
    holistic view of, 58
    in San Diego, 71–74
    in Stamford, 74–80
Problem-Oriented Policing
    (Herman Goldstein), 62
Profiles in Injustice (David A.
    Harris), 15
proof, standard of, 105–6
property management, 60, 72–74
Proposition G, 107, 121–22,
    264n. 110
Providence (Rhode Island),
    139–42, 267–68n. 29
public housing:
    dangers seen in, 247–48nn. 1, 2
    in Los Angeles, 57–60
    trespass policies in, 249n. 11
public perceptions, 116

"qualified immunity," 121
quality of life offenses, 127
questioning of nonsuspects, 4

race relations:
    in Boston, 64–65
    in Lowell, 42–44
    in Wichita, 44
Race Relations Forum (Lowell),
    244n. 45
racial profiling:
    and ALPACT, 29–31
    and Ashcroft policing, 195–203
    behavioral observation vs., 216–17
    in California, 119
    and community policing, 37
    consequences of, 30
    DOJ policy guidance on, 202
    effects of, 85–86
    and hiring policies, 164
    in Lowell, 42
    by New Jersey State Police, 124
    policies against, 50
    Rafi Ron and, 284n. 160
    and traffic stops, 117
    in Wichita, 44, 45
racism, 21
radicalism, 217
radio-equipped patrol cars, 19–21
Ramparts (LAPD) scandal, 88, 124
random patrols, 21–22
rank-and-file officers:
    accountability of, 83, 100–101
    and chain of command, 131–32
    and departmental policies, 94
reactive policing, 20–21, 61
recidivist officers, 130
recruitment/recruits, 162–68
    changing methods of, 14

characteristics desired in, 165
FBI, 227–28
in Indianapolis, 166–68
minority-community input on,
164–65
of minority police officers,
166–68
in St. Paul, 163–66
relationships:
with Arab and Muslim
communities, 10, 12, 33, 46–47
crises defused with prior, 31
with juveniles, 75–77
with Southeast Asian
communities, 42–44
in Wichita, 45–47
Reno, Janet, 5
respect, 49, 70, 129
responses, tailor-made, 63
response times, 22–23, 160
Revell, Oliver "Buck," 11
Richardson, Marlena, 150–51
riots, 21, 86, 88, 138
Rivers, Eugene, 65, 151
Riverside (California), 125
Robbins, Tom, 218
Rodney King riots, 88
Ron, Rafi, 214–18, 284–85nn.
160, 174
Rowan, Karen, 51
Roxbury (Massachusetts), 64
rudeness, 93
rumor control, 33, 138

safety, officer, 40

St. Paul (Minnesota), 163–66
Saleh, Noel, 212
San Diego, 13, 71–74, 103
San Francisco, 103, 107, 108,
121–22, 230–31, 264n. 110
San Jose (California), 112, 119–20
Scalise, Anthony, 53–56
Schmidt, Linda, 227–28
School Resource Officers, 74–80
scientific principles of policing,
20
Scott, Michael, 250–51n. 24
Seattle, 8, 37–41
Section 8 housing, 72
security:
airport, 196, 214
apartment, 73
self monitoring, police, 86–88, 108
Sensenbrenner, F. James, 194
September 11, 2001 terrorist
attacks, 5–6, 31
service standards, 159–61
shooting at moving vehicles,
148–51
Shourbaji, Y. R., 46, 47
Sikh community, 52, 246n. 83
Simmons, Lee, 145
Skokie (Illinois), 54, 56
Smith, Benjamin, 54, 56
SOF (Superior Officers'
Federation), 150
Somali community, 181
Southeast Asian community, 42
Special Litigation Section
(of DOJ), 122–25

Spellman, William, 23

spiritual counseling, 65, 253n. 39

"spitting on the sidewalk,"
    281n. 109

Spreine, Jim, 8

SROS. *See* School Resource Officers

SRO Summer Camp, 74–80, 139

Stamatakos, George, 142

Stamford (Connecticut), 74–80, 139

Stamper, Norm, 37

standard of proof, 105–6

Steubenville (Ohio), 124

Stuart, Carol, 64, 252n. 31

Stuart, Charles, 64, 252n. 31

students, foreign, 185

"subject resistance," 93. *See also*
    use of force

subpoena power, 105

substantive problems, 62

Sullivan, Pat, 92–93

Summer of Opportunity program
    (Boston), 67–68

Superintendent's Multicultural
    Forum (Chicago), 50–52

Superintendent's Race Relations
    Forum (Chicago), 47–50

Superior Officers' Federation
    (SOF), 150

supervisors:
    accountability of, 83
    and Compstat, 100
    impact of system on, 92–94
    and internal politics, 134

systematic inquiry and analysis, 63

tactical behaviors, 216

Tancredo, Tom, 194

"targeted conversation," 216

Taylor, Ralph B., 286n. 2

tenant screening, 59, 73–74

Ten-Point Coalition (Boston), 65,
    69–70, 144, 147, 148, 151,
    253n. 37

terrorist behavior, 214, 215

Texas Association Against Sexual
    Assault, 277n. 51

Thomas, Clarence, 5

Time magazine, 196

traffic stops:
    and antiterrorism, 201
    and citizen encounters with
        police, 117
    and cultural misunder
        standings, 39, 43–44
    in San Jose, 119

training, police, 44
    in civil/human rights, 169–71
    in dealing with the public, 129
    videos used for, 50, 52
    virtual, 167–68

transparency, 14, 118–19

Trojanowicz, Robert, 36

trust:
    benefits of, 40
    of community, 144
    community-policing element
        of, 24–25
    in immigrant communities,
        7, 10
    in minority communities, 49

and outreach programs, 68

and racial profiling, 30

of school children, 77

Turnaround (Bill Bratton), 223

tutoring, 168

two-way radios, 19–20

undocumented workers, 190–94

unions, police. *See* police unions

unofficial community leaders,
  136–38

U.S. Border Patrol, 187

U.S. Civil Rights Commission, 90

U.S. Congress, 185–86, 202

U.S. Customs Service, 197–98

U.S. Department of Homeland
  Security, 279n. 96

U.S. Department of Justice (DOJ), 9

  appointments in, 286n. 13

  and citizen encounters with
  police, 117

  human rights training by,
  170, 171

  and immigration law, 6

  letters to prospective
  interviewees from, 35

  and Lowell Police training, 44

  mass questioning initiative of
  the, 11–12, 32, 34

  and nonsuspect interviews, 181

  and pattern-or-practice law,
  122–26

  and racial profiling, 196–203

  and schoolchildren
  relationships, 78

U.S. General Accounting Office
  (GAO), 181, 225

U.S. Holocaust Museum, 170–71

U.S. Supreme Court, 222, 249n. 11

U.S. Treasury Department, 194, 195

USA Today, 201

use of force, 93, 95, 149

us-versus-them attitude, 133–34

Valenta, Bill, 109

Valentine, James R., 154

Vera Institute of Justice, 90, 128,
  130, 258n. 37, 266n. 1

videos, training, 50, 52

Vincent, John, 209

Violent Crime Control and Law
  Enforcement Act, 122

Virginia vs. Hicks, 249n. 11

"virtual academy," 167–68

Vollmer, August, 19

Walker, Samuel, 84–85, 87,
  90–94, 106, 155

Wall Street Journal, 206

Walton, Kenneth P., 11–12

"war on immigrants" strategy,
  182–95

Washington, D.C., 106–7

weapons, presence of, 216

Webster, William, 10

Weed and Seed program,
  136–37, 167

Wells Fargo Bank, 192

West Rogers Park (Chicago),
  53–54

Wexler, Chuck, 47–48

Wheeler, Heaster, 31

Whitman, Gerry, 7–8

Who Is Guarding the Guardians? (U.S. Civil Rights Commission), 90

Wichita (Kansas), 44–47

Williams, Accelyne, 143, 151

Williams, Norman, 44

Williams, Olgen, 137–38

Wilson, James Q., 127

Winship, Christopher, 70

Wishnie, Michael, 185, 275n. 22

Withrow, Brian, 45–46

Wolf, Moshe, 55–56, 247n. 91

Wood, Grant, 187–89

Wright, Robert, 206

Youssef, Bassem, 207–10

youth violence, 63–71

Youth Violence Strike Force (Boston), 66–68

Yzaguirre, Raul, 6–7

zero tolerance policy, 223